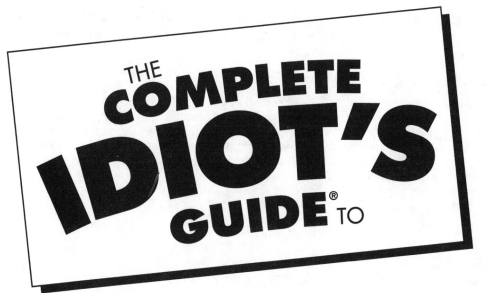

THE COMPLETE IDIOT'S GUIDE® TO

Women's History

by Sonia Weiss with Lorna Biddle Rinear
Produced by BookEnds, LLC

ALPHA

A Pearson Education Company

To our foremothers, whose DNA we carry, but who were written out of history until recently, and to our daughters, who will continue to make history.

Copyright © 2002 by BookEnds, LLC

International Standard Book Number: 0-02-864201-5
Library of Congress Catalog Card Number: 2001092312

04   03   02   8   7   6   5   4   3   2   1

Interpretation of the printing code: The rightmost number of the first series of numbers is the year of the book's printing; the rightmost number of the second series of numbers is the number of the book's printing. For example, a printing code of 02-1 shows that the first printing occurred in 2002.

Printed in the United States of America

Produced by BookEnds, LLC.

Publisher
Marie Butler-Knight

Product Manager
Phil Kitchel

Managing Editor
Jennifer Chisholm

Acquisitions Editor
Randy Ladenheim-Gil

Development Editor
Tom Stevens

Senior Production Editor
Christy Wagner

Copy Editor
Cari Luna

Illustrator
Jody Schaeffer

Cover Designers
Mike Freeland
Kevin Spear

Book Designers
Scott Cook and Amy Adams of DesignLab

Indexer
Lisa Wilson

Layout/Proofreading
Svetlana Dominguez
Susan Geiselman
Nancy Wagner

Contents at a Glance

Appendixes

Contents

Part 2: The Dark and Middle Ages   63

7 A Day in the Life   65

8 Medieval Rights   77

9 Royal Warriors   85

10 The Working Life   95

Foreword

Jumbo shrimp. Bureaucratic efficiency. Women's history. At this point it is common knowledge—if one is not, well, a complete idiot—that for far too long the notion of studying women's lives as a means to understanding the culture at large was considered something of an oxymoron. So the first thought that popped into my head when I was approached to write this foreword was an obvious one: Thank goodness we've come to a point in time when the need for a cogent and comprehensive guide to just such a history is seen as fundamental rather than aberrational. But enough about me, you're thinking; what can I expect to find out for my $18.95 that I don't already know?

The answer is, for better or worse, a lot. Even for someone well-versed and deeply interested in women's studies, there is a shocking amount left to learn. Thankfully, Sonia Weiss and Lorna Biddle Rinear make it, true to the series name, easy. Not easy as in simplistic, but in a way that it is always a pleasure to do something when it interests you. And no matter who you are, you will find something of interest in this volume. Whether it's reading about the trailblazing eleventh-century Byzantine historian Anna Comnena or learning about the origins of the famous (some might argue infamous) "Cosmo girl," the authors intersperse fascinating accounts of individual lives with incisive analyses of larger cultural trends in divisions of labor, leadership, and intellectual life.

As a woman, it is undeniably sobering to learn that patriarchy, as we loosely understand it, took root as early as 3000 B.C.E. But it is equally galvanizing to learn about women who bucked the trend, whether they be world-famous icons like Cleopatra or nearly invisible iconoclasts like Murasaki Shikibu, a member of the noble Fujiwara family who is widely credited for writing the first work of fiction in medieval Japan (see Chapter 11, "Trailblazers").

The point is that for many of us, the notion of women's history runs the gamut, as the old joke goes, from A to B. Oh, we know our seminal figures like the Elizabeth Cady Stantons and Gloria Steinems, and we can tell our Suffragettes from our Blue Stockings, but the great thing about a work like this one is comprehending just how much there is left to learn. And the best and most unexpected bonus is the realization that, in the end, there is really no such thing as women's history, as in a history belonging exclusively to women. Women's history belongs to and reflects the world in all of its complexity and anyone, male or female, can benefit from taking a good, clear look from a fresh perspective.

Adriana Leshko

Adriana Leshko writes frequently on arts and culture for a variety of publications, including *Harper's Bazaar*, *Nylon Magazine*, and *Citysearch.com*. Since graduating from Brown University in 1997, she has worked at Brooklyn Academy of Music, the acclaimed performing arts presenter, and is currently the Arts and Entertainment Editor of *Harper's Bazaar*.

Introduction

Women have done some pretty amazing things throughout history, but you wouldn't know it from reading most history books. There's a lot of truth to the saying that behind all successful men are the women who got them there. But the roles these women played have either been minimized or completely written out of the picture. So, too, were women's unique contributions and achievements apart from their roles as daughters, wives, and mothers.

Until the women's rights movement reorganized in the 1960s, there was little interest in looking at history from the women's perspective. But as women made history by fighting for and winning more rights, it was no longer acceptable to deny them their rightful place in the records of time. While it's often not a pretty picture, we now know more about what life was like for women in the past and what they were able to accomplish even under the severest constraints and the harshest conditions.

History presents the past as a meaningful story. Historians try to make sense of the past by linking events together in a narrative, identifying important events and their results, and by writing about influential thinkers, artists, or politicians.

In the past, issues important to women have been labeled "women's issues"—that is, as issues important *only* to women, not to all human beings. The male experience has been positioned as the generic human experience; women's as "the other." In other words, when men wrote history and only studied the actions of other men, they made the assumption that all people of the past experienced life as they described the experience of important white males. Obviously, this is not true—women, slaves, working-class men lived very different lives from those of upper-class men.

But history is always being retold and reinterpreted. About 30 years ago, the way in which history was constructed began to change. Instead of looking at politics, wars, and male leaders, historians began to wonder about what life was like for the ordinary men and women of the past. They began to research the lives of slaves (not only slave owners), of immigrants (not just white leaders), of common soldiers (not only generals), of women (not just queens).

As part of this new interest in "social history," some historians began to reinterpret the history of men and women by gender rather than sexual roles. Although the two terms are often interchanged, they mean different things. Gender refers to how each sex behaves in a society at a given time. Sex relates to the physiological and biological differences between men and women—how female and male bodies are built differently and have different purposes in the reproduction of the human race.

Unlike the physiological and biological differences between the two sexes, which remain fairly consistent, gender roles vary by culture and over time. There were and are certain assumptions made about the patterns of life for both men and women, acceptable and unacceptable behaviors, and differences between educational and work opportunities. These issues reflect the role gender has played in history.

Like race and class, gender is one of the primary ways of signifying power relationships—that is, how men and women relate, their access to power, and their ability to change the society in which they live. In most societies, the position of a woman, because of her gender, has been a lower position than that of any male of the same class. Gender has also placed woman below man in the hierarchy of most cultures.

Although most women were not able to rewrite the rules that structured their lives, they have been very creative at giving meaning and dignity to their lives by making a space for themselves within the gender boundaries placed on them by society. In some cases, women were victims, but in others, they were able to make choices and chart their own paths.

Historians writing women's history have sought to uncover women's experiences, to meticulously describe and document the lives of women in various times and places. Most women left no records, so historians have had to be creative about filling in the silences. But we can't just "add women and stir" as one historian put it. We need to integrate women's history into mainstream history. But, for the most part, this hasn't happened yet.

By studying how women lived, we learn about power relationships and the dynamics of gender, and thereby gain a realistic understanding of history and how society functions and changes. History is narrative, a story. Without women's history we are missing one character's voice and at least half the puzzle of the past. The study of women's history has provided ancestors for all of us living today.

In writing *The Complete Idiot's Guide to Women's History,* our goal was to tell as much as we could about what it has meant to be a woman throughout the centuries. Obviously, we couldn't be inclusive in a book of this length. So think of what's here as a road map of sorts. If you read something that piques your curiosity and makes you want to learn more, we've accomplished what we set out to do. We've also provided some resources to guide you along your way.

The Complete Idiot's Guide to Women's History is organized into five parts. Each part includes chapters that reflect what life was like for women of a particular era and delves into the history of the women—both famous and not—who lived during that period.

Part 1, "The Ancient World," takes us back to the dawn of civilization and the beginning of gender distinctions between the two sexes.

Part 2, "The Dark and Middle Ages," details how women coped during the darkest period of human history and what life was like when the world began moving forward again during the Middle Ages.

Part 3, "Rebirth and the Beginning of the Modern World," covers the Early Modern period and details the ongoing evolution of women's roles in society during the sixteenth, seventeenth, and eighteenth centuries.

Part 4, "The Nineteenth Century," discusses the strictures placed on women by Victorian ideals and covers the beginning of the women's movement.

Part 5, "The Twentieth Century," charts the growth of the women's movement and its accomplishments, including equal rights and women's suffrage.

In the back of the book are appendixes containing the terms used in this book, lists of women by country and date, and suggestions for further reading.

In addition to the main narrative of *The Complete Idiot's Guide to Women's History,* you'll also find other types of useful information. Here's how to recognize these features:

Hear Me Roar

Quotes by and about famous women.

A Woman's Place

More facts, trivia, and information about the lives of women.

Words for Women

Definitions of terms related to women's history. (Italicized words in the text appear bold in here.)

Going for the Vote

Multicultural perspectives on women's rights and roles in societies around the world.

Acknowledgments

We would like to thank Jacky Sachs and Jessica Faust of BookEnds, LLC, for developing this project and entrusting us with the execution of it.

Trademarks

All terms mentioned in this book that are known to be or are suspected of being trademarks or service marks have been appropriately capitalized. Alpha Books and Pearson Education, Inc., cannot attest to the accuracy of this information. Use of a term in this book should not be regarded as affecting the validity of any trademark or service mark.

Part 1

The Ancient World

The period of time stretching from roughly 2500 B.C.E. to the fall of the western Roman Empire in the fifth century C.E. is generally referred to as the ancient world or antiquity. The civilizations that developed during this period—the Sumerians, Babylonians, Assyrians, Egyptians, Greeks, and Romans shaped the world as we know it today.

These civilizations provide historians with the beginnings of recorded history— although written in hieroglyphics or alphabets that are now obsolete. The records mostly tell us about events that were important to elite men and governments, but interspersed throughout are stories of exceptional women, and by reading the silences, we can recreate the lives of common women.

This book begins with a look at what life was like in general—and particularly, for women—in these ancient civilizations.

Sigh...

Chapter 1

A Woman's Life

> **In This Chapter**
>
> ➤ The first farmers
>
> ➤ Early attempts at birth control
>
> ➤ Goddess worship
>
> ➤ Saying "I do"

By starting our look at women's history at the beginning of civilization—roughly 2500 B.C.E. or so—we're zipping past almost a half-million years of prehistory, dating back to 500000 B.C.E.

That's intentional, as it would probably take another book the size of this one just to recount everything that happened during this time. But it also leaves out some information that's helpful for understanding why things developed as they did once people consciously began leaving records of their existence.

So let's step even a little farther back for a moment and take a quick look at some of the important developments that took place prior to the beginning of antiquity.

Early People

We don't have a great amount of detail about the people of prehistory—the records simply don't exist—but we do know that they were nomads who roamed the earth in search of food. They had no permanent homes or settlements by necessity, as they had to be ready to move on a moment's notice.

Men and women bore equal responsibility for the survival of the group, both in gathering food and fending off attackers. There is some evidence that these earliest groups may have been *matrilineal,* in which descent is traced through the female.

Words for Women

Matrilineal describes descent and kinship that is traced through the mother instead of the father.

Evidence also suggests that work was divided along what most of us would consider traditional gender lines: The men hunted; the women gathered edibles such as nuts, berries, and roots. It would be easy to assume that hunting sustained these prehistoric tribes, but, in reality, it didn't. Men often came back from the hunt empty-handed, and when they did return with a fresh kill, it had to be eaten immediately or it would spoil. The items gathered by the women were a far more reliable food source. The women who gathered them bore the lion's share of responsibility for keeping the tribe fed.

Life as a Nomad

For hundreds of thousands of years, women and men survived by foraging for plants and hunting the animals that they came across wherever they were camped. The process would begin with the hunters leaving their camp at dawn. The women and children began their daily foraging at the same time, staying close to camp for protection. Babies accompanied the foragers, often transported in portable cradles fashioned of hides and short poles cut from trees.

When the nomads exhausted the food sources in one spot, or weather changes brought the growing season to an end, they moved to another spot. Assuring an adequate and steady food supply by cultivating plants and domesticating animals hadn't yet occurred to these early hominids. But it eventually would, and when it did it would transform how they and the people who followed them would live.

Trading Roaming for Farming

We don't know why it happened. Maybe they were just tired of roaming. Maybe it was the result of a simple discovery—that a seed dropped on the ground eventually yielded an edible plant if it received enough light and water.

For whatever reason, people in southwest Europe, southeast Asia, and the Americas began systematically planting seeds and cultivating crops somewhere between 12000 to 7000 B.C.E. Domestication of such animals as sheep and cattle soon followed.

No longer was it necessary to expend precious energy by following wild herds and taking the chance that they'd find adequate vegetation to nibble on when they stopped roaming. Now people could better ensure adequate food supplies by planting and harvesting crops and breeding their livestock. And they could even have the animals do some of the work for them.

The Rise of Civilization

The development of agrarian societies, which is often referred to as the rise of civilization, occurred at different times and places around the world. The nomadic tribes naturally gravitated to areas that were blessed with consistent and plentiful water supplies, such as river valleys and coastal areas, first, in southern Mesopotamia, the Nile Valley in Egypt, India, China, and the Americas, and, later, in Malaysia, Africa, and Northern Europe.

A Woman's Place

Women are believed to have been the first sowers and collectors of seed. They also probably invented many of the first agricultural tools, such as hoes, plows, and digging sticks, to assist their field work.

The extremely fertile area of Mesopotamia, in particular, became what archaeologists and historians often refer to as the "fertile crescent," both for its highly favorable growing conditions and for the many civilizations that it gave birth to. No fewer than seven major civilizations developed in or near this area, including Sumeria, Babylonia, Assyria, Judea, Egypt, Greece, and Rome. Christianity also was born there.

Life in the Fertile Crescent

Compared to what things had been like in the past, life in the Fertile Crescent was about as good as it got for ancient men and women. Life expectancy was still extremely short for both sexes—the average in Egypt, for example, was just 20 years. Many women still died in childbirth, which significantly shortened even that brief life span.

Battles still broke out between fractious tribes and civilizations. Floods, droughts, and insect invasions would often wipe out crops, and the heat and dryness in nearby desert areas wrecked havoc with ancient skin. But all of this was far better than living the life of a nomad and not being entirely sure where their next meal would come from, or whether they'd live long enough to eat it.

Ancient Luxuries

Settling down in one place afforded ancient people a number of luxuries they hadn't had to date. They could build permanent structures for homes and businesses. They now could accumulate private property by storing excess crops in those buildings and by amassing larger herds of livestock. As you'll read more about in Chapter 2, "Ancient Rights," women would also become part of that property, which wasn't necessarily a good thing.

A Woman's Place

Although most women of ancient times generally kept to the home, not all did. In Egypt, some women worked outside of the home as acrobats, musicians, and dancing girls. Greek women were often trained for these occupations as well.

They now had products derived from agriculture, such as flax and wool, that could be spun or woven into cloth, making possible clothing styles far removed from the rough skins that nomadic people fashioned into crude body coverings.

As men quit hunting, they took over the agrarian tasks of planting the fields and tending the livestock. Women, who had shouldered these responsibilities during the transition from nomadic to agrarian society, were now largely relegated to working in the home. They tended to their children and took care of the majority of household chores, including cooking, cleaning, spinning, and weaving.

The houses they cared for were commonly fashioned from local grasses and reeds and had dirt or clay floors. It was desirable to be near a well, river, or stream to make the task of carrying water to the house, another woman's chore, a little less daunting.

Mothers of Invention

As had been the case from prehistoric times, ancient women were adept at inventing the tools and skills they needed in the course of everyday life. While it's hard to tell with any degree of certainty which sex dreamed up which invention, the ones related to typically feminine tasks were most likely the work of women. They include the following:

➤ Needles, scrapers, tanners, and awls, all used to fashion clothing from furs and pelts

➤ Looms and spindles, used to fashion cloth for clothing (The spinning wheel came along much later in the Middle Ages.)

➤ Dyes, used to adorn clothing

➤ Millstones and mortars and pestles, used for grinding grain into flour and herbs into medicine

Across the world in Asia, women were inventing such skills as silk cultivation, calligraphy, and painting.

Early Fashionistas

High temperatures and humidity in the Fertile Crescent made wearing animal skins as clothing virtually impossible. Fortunately, the rise of agriculture provided new products that could be used instead.

Weaving appears to be one of the earliest inventions of the prehistoric period, and it also appears that it was a woman's craft from the start. In Mesopotamia, cloth was woven from flax and made into clothing of simple design—often nothing more than a sleek tunic or sheath that covered the body from breasts to ankles. On cooler days or in the evenings, an overslip or apron could be donned over the tunic. Capes or cloaks were also worn in cool weather.

Some cultures, such as the Babylonians, Greeks, and Romans, preferred more elaborate clothing styles and created draped garments from large squares of fabric, shawls, and scarves. To create a more boyish figure, which Greek men found attractive, Greek women often wore strips of cloth as brassieres under their clothing. They also were fond of adding to their height by wearing sandals with cork heels.

Women of higher status might adorn their clothing—royal Egyptian women, for example, would often wear dresses of purple, red, or blue with white accents. Embroidery and tapestry-darning were also common adornments for the royals, with elaborate designs often crafted by peasants for their rulers. People of the highest distinction often topped off their dress with jeweled collars.

A Woman's Place

Queen Isimkheb of Egypt wore wigs so heavy that she had to have assistants keep her from toppling over under the weight.

Making Up Like an Egyptian

The Egyptians also liked other forms of adornment, especially makeup. Virtually all visible body parts—and some that weren't—were dressed, tressed, and coated with various substances ranging from henna to mashed insect parts. Nipples and breast veins were enhanced with blue and gold accents.

Fingers and feet were dyed red with henna, and faces were elaborately made up with green eye shadow on both upper and lower lids, red rouge, and blue-black lipstick. For variety, eye shadows were sometimes made iridescent with crushed beetle shell.

Good grooming for eyebrows meant creating what often looked like a natural scowl by filling in the

Hear Me Roar

I am the queen of war. I am the queen of the thunderbolt. I stir up the sea and calm it. I am the rays of the Sun.

—The creed of the goddess Isis

space above the nose with kohl if the brows didn't naturally come together there. Kohl was also used to create the characteristic Egyptian eye, with a thick line of black along the rim.

Wigged Out

The Egyptians also were fond of enhancing their beauty with wigs. Elaborate head-dresses became a particular property among the rich, who often shaved their heads to make it easier to wear their finery. The wigs were topped off with cones of perfumed fat, which melted in the desert heat. As they melted, they supposedly gave off pleasant aromas.

Although the Egyptians seemed to be the fondest of this manner of ornamentation, they weren't the only ancient women to change the natural state of their hair. Sumerian women also wore wigs at times or dressed their hair in very elaborate styles. Greek women sometimes died their hair blond.

Going for the Vote

The Chinese, who were also fond of adornment, are believed to have invented nail polish around 3000 B.C.E. Both women and men wore it.

Words for Women

Paleolithic Venuses are prehistoric figurines, usually fashioned of clay, stone, or ivory, that represented the female form.

Ancient Skin Care

Extreme climate conditions led to the development of skin creams, oils, and moisturizers—again, most likely by women. Derived from the materials around them, some of these concoctions were exotic by any measure and included such ingredients as gazelle or crocodile dung. Both were thought to help preserve the skin of older women and lessen wrinkling.

Other substances used for ancient skin care were far more common, including milk, incense, wax, olive oil, and essential oils derived from plants and other substances. Essential oils were also used for perfuming the body, with different scents applied to the arms, legs, and throat.

Gods and Goddesses: Religion

Life for ancient women may have been on the pedestrian side for the most part, but it was anything but that for their divine counterparts. All the funny little statues of women—commonly known as *Paleolithic Venuses*—that were excavated from ruins throughout Europe and the Middle and Near East point to one fact: Woman was worshipped as the giver of life, the Great Mother, the first divinity. She was the Mother-Goddess.

Archaeologists have unearthed numerous goddess shrines throughout this area, again bearing testimony to the important role that divine women played in ancient religion. The Sumerians, one of the oldest and most influential of the Mesopotamian civilizations, worshipped many gods and goddesses, giving each a special function or role. Erishkigal, for example, was the Sumerian queen of the underworld; Nammu was the primeval earth goddess.

The Sumerian's mother goddess, whom they called Innin or Ishtar, was the goddess of war, love, and procreation. So important was she that she was celebrated in the first known poem, "The Exaltation of Inanna" (or Innin), written by the chief priest of Sumeria—also a woman—around 2300 B.C.E.

In Egypt, where religion was central in daily life, a cult developed around Isis, the sister (and wife) of the god Osiris. She was the Egyptian's goddess of fertility and motherhood, a great protector with great supernatural powers. Because she also protected those who traveled by sea, sailors and merchants were instrumental in spreading her cult throughout the Greek empire and into Roman settlements around the Mediterranean. Her cult would become the most widespread and popular in the Roman Empire, surviving until Christianity.

Many women served the temples of the goddesses by working as diviners, magicians, and priestesses. In Babylon and some other cultures, women served as temple prostitutes, whose services glorified the goddess.

Goddess Worship in Greece and Rome

Even in Greece, where the rights of women were severely restricted in many arenas, goddesses played a prominent role in worship. The Greek pantheon, or temple, included Hera, the queen of queens herself; Hestia, the goddess of home and hearth; Artemis, goddess of the moon, hunting and nature; Aphrodite, the goddess of love and beauty; and Athena, the goddess of war and wisdom and the patron goddess of Athens. The nine daughters of Zeus worshipped by the Greeks as the

Hear Me Roar

The goddess alone knew of the all-moving, secret world energy which had helped the gods to victory; it was the power within them, of which they were unaware.

—Heinrich Zimmer, "The Indian World Mother"

A Woman's Place

Babylonian women were required to show respect to the goddess Ishtar by making a one-time sacrifice that involved sex. A woman had to go to Ishtar's temple and remain there until a man offered to have sex with her. After she did, her duty to the goddess was discharged, and she was free.

muses of arts and sciences—Calliope, Clio, Erato, Euterpe, Melpomene, Polyhymnia, Terpsichore, Thalia, and Urania—were originally goddesses who were revered for their ability to inspire.

In Rome, where conditions were often no more favorable for women, two major temples were devoted to goddesses: Minerva, the Roman equivalent of Athena, and Juno, who was the Roman Hera. Vesta, the Roman equivalent of the Greek Hestia, was honored with a round temple that stood in the middle of the Roman Forum.

Vesta's temple, which also housed important relics and a sacred eternal flame, was tended by a group of women called the Vestal Virgins. These young priestesses served the temple for their entire lives, learning their duties for 10 years, serving for 10, and teaching their successors for another 10. As you'll read more about in Chapter 2, this special service gave the Vestal Virgins greater control over many aspects of their lives than the average woman of the time had.

Bearing Babies

Virginity may have ruled in Vesta's temple, but it had no place in ancient society. Most civilizations based a woman's value on her childbearing capabilities, and the expectation was that she would have many.

Ancient people knew little about the mechanics of conception. In some cultures, eating a particular type of food was thought to make a woman pregnant. Others believed that women became pregnant after being invaded by spirits. Such beliefs made attempts at preventing pregnancy, even if desired, iffy at best. Sadly, the most prevalent contraceptive was death, often as a result of childbirth.

Even with the emphasis on having a lot of children, there were some efforts made at contraception, most likely on the sly and almost assuredly with varying results. Contraceptive practices were often based on superstitions and beliefs handed down through generations. Readily available materials that were close at hand were often used, which accounted for some fairly strange substances and concoctions being placed where they perhaps shouldn't have been.

Guided by ancient lore and wives' tales, women tried such measures as …

➤ Contraceptive suppositories fashioned of crocodile dung and honey.

➤ Lint soaked in acacia and honey and placed against the cervix. Wool was also used.

➤ Taking baths in herbal concoctions, such as fenugreek, mallow, and wormwood, mixed together with linseed.

Other substances recommended for contraceptive use included moist alum and ground pomegranate peel. Other practices included heavy exercise, drinking wine and eating spicy food, or squatting and sneezing after sex to expel the semen.

Wedding Rings

Although it wasn't as revered a tradition as it would become in medieval Europe, marriage played an important role in the ancient world. However, the state of matrimony was hardly something most women looked forward to.

As you'll read more about in Chapter 2, men often used their female progeny as barter to secure land holdings and other possessions. Although in some cultures girls had to approve of the unions, in most they had little say in the matter.

The practice of trading women for land and other items was a tradition handed down from nomadic times, when clans would sometimes trade between themselves to augment each other's female population. In the ancient world, it was most prevalent among royalty and the upper classes, who clearly had more to gain from it, but peasant families also subscribed to it.

In ancient Egypt, marriage between brothers and sisters was another fairly common practice, following the example of the god and goddess Osiris and Isis. These unions were often arranged to protect family riches from interlopers. Among Egyptian royals, fathers often married daughters to ensure a pure royal lineage. Many of these liaisons weren't marriages in the true sense of the word, however, as the partners weren't sexually active, at least with each other.

For some women, these arranged marriages were not as desultory as they may seem. With such unions often came power, and it wasn't just the men who got it. As you'll see in the chapters that follow, the tradition of arranged marriages, as odd and awkward as it may seem, gave rise to some of the most formidable rulers and warriors of ancient times.

A Woman's Place

Ancient women often married by age 12, sometimes as late as 13 or 14. In Egypt, girls were often sexually active at 10 years old. This may seem incredibly young, but keep in mind that the average life expectancy of the time was 20.

The Least You Need to Know

➤ The earliest people were nomads who roamed the earth for plants and animals to eat.

➤ Many of humankind's earliest inventions were created by women.

➤ The first deity was a woman.

➤ Ancient marriages were often arranged more for property and power than for true love.

Chapter 2

Ancient Rights

> **In This Chapter**
>
> ➤ How patriarchy began
>
> ➤ The first written laws
>
> ➤ What Egyptian women could and couldn't do
>
> ➤ Rights in Greece and Rome

As you read in Chapter 1, "A Woman's Life," men and women functioned as equals in the earliest hunter-gatherer societies. Unfortunately, equality between the sexes didn't last for long.

How and why men assumed the dominant role has been the focus of much debate and continues to be to a certain extent. What isn't debatable is that by the beginning of recorded history, men, for the most part, had the upper hand.

Some ancient societies gave women more rights than others, but even in these societies those rights often diminished over time. By the end of the ancient era, women in virtually every society had lost both status and rights—a trend that would continue for many centuries.

The Beginning of Male Dominance

The subordination of women seems to have started at about the same time the hunter-gatherers settled down to farm. When men gave up hunting, they took over agriculture and animal domestication, which had been women's jobs. The new division of labor gave men greater authority and responsibility outside the home. It put women inside the home for the first time, where their responsibilities were limited and within a more private sphere.

A Woman's Place

While women were no longer responsible for the overall management of crops and cattle, they still had to work to maintain them both. In fact, they put in the same amount of hours doing such secondary tasks as weeding and carrying water to the fields. These ancillary tasks, while important, provided no direct economic benefit to their families and contributed to the growing subordination of women and the erosion of their status. Where and when women lost control over agriculture and animals, they lost control over the primary economic resources of their families.

In many respects, the division of labor made sense. A woman's role as mate and mother naturally kept her closer to home anyway. But when women lost control over crops and animals, both vitally important in the new agrarian-based societies, they also lost the status they had enjoyed in being responsible for both. Their previous roles had placed them on equal or better footing than men. Tending to children and taking care of the house didn't.

Settling down gave ancient people the chance to amass personal property for the first time. As they accumulated surpluses of crops and livestock, they could sell or barter them for other goods and services. In the past, there had been few distinctions between rich and poor. Now, there were. Successful farmers had large holdings, which gave them greater status than those who had little or nothing. For the first time, what people did or didn't own determined how they were treated and the rights they enjoyed. This was the beginning of social stratification, or the class system, the haves and have-nots.

Now that men had possessions, protecting them became important. Men with great wealth wanted to make sure that their holdings went to children they could verify as their own. It quickly became obvious that the best way to do this was to control women's sexuality, and in turn, the children they bore. This led to the establishment of the monogamous family (at least from the male point of view) and the beginning of *patriarchy*.

Patriarchy placed men at the head of the household and gave them authority over its contents, including women and children. While it became an aspect of virtually all human societies, it, like social stratification, didn't happen overnight or at the same pace in all cultures.

The earliest written records of humankind show that patriarchy was firmly in place as early as 3000 B.C.E. So was the difference between the classes. Both factors shaped women's ability to …

> ➤ Control their own bodies.

> ➤ Earn a living.

> ➤ Own their own businesses.

> ➤ Get a good education.

> ➤ Participate in politics and religion.

> ➤ Inherit property.

Words for Women

Patriarchy recognizes the father or the eldest male as the head of the family or tribe.

While patriarchy affected women's rights in these areas and many others, it didn't impact all women in the same way. Their specific status and the rights they had still varied from culture to culture. As you'll see in the descriptions of the ancient civilizations that follow, women often had fairly equal footing with men in the earliest periods of each society. As each culture developed, however, it generally placed more power and control into the hands of men. As a rule, it also placed more restrictions and regulations on what women were allowed to do.

The Rights of Babylonian Women

The ancient code of laws drafted by Hammurabi, who ruled Babylonia in the late eighteenth century B.C.E., reflected the now common belief that women were the property of men. But Hammurabi's laws also gave women substantial rights in the areas of property ownership, commerce, and inheritance.

The Code of Hammurabi was the world's first set of written laws and gives us the best representation of women's rights in the earliest recorded societies. Carved on clay tablets, it contained 282 laws related to various facets of daily life. Of these, 73 dealt specifically with issues concerning sexual matters, marriage, and property rights. Under Hammurabi's code, women …

> ➤ Shared equal authority with men over their children.

> ➤ Could own property, even after marriage, and could will their property to anyone they pleased.

> ➤ Could inherit property.

➤ Received a dowry when married (in some other cultures, the dowry went to the husband).

➤ Could serve as judges, elders, witnesses, and scribes.

Other regulations gave women the right to divorce cruel spouses. A woman who hated her husband enough to deprive him of sex could be released from her marriage, but only if she was found to be completely blameless and if her husband had talked against her. Women could sell their property, and, in cases of the death of their spouse, received lifetime rights to their husbands' property.

Marriage was a form of purchase for the Babylonians and other ancient societies. Babylonian fathers sold their daughters to their prospective husbands for an agreed-upon price, a practice that was carried on for many centuries to come. But Hammurabi's code also affirmed marriage as a legal contract between man and wife. A husband was required to support his wife in cases of illness, unless she wanted to go back to her father's house. If she did, her dowry went with her.

Men were responsible for their wives' debts, including any that may have been incurred before marriage. A man wishing to divorce could do so, but he also had to return his wife's dowry and provide some form of financial assistance for their children's upbringing.

Others of Hammurabi's dictates were less favorable to women. For example, a man was allowed to take a second wife if his first was chronically ill; however, he still had to support and care for his first wife. He could obtain a divorce merely by saying "Thou are not my wife." If a woman uttered these words against her husband, however, she would be drowned.

A Woman's Place

Thought to be amendments to the Code of Hammurabi, the laws that governed Assyria (900 to 600 B.C.E.) placed extreme limits on the rights of women. They were forbidden to appear unveiled in public and had to adhere to a strict code of fidelity while their spouses had few, if any, restrictions.

Hear Me Roar

In their manners and customs the Egyptian women seem to have reversed the ordinary practices of mankind. For instance, women go to market and engage in trade, while men stay home and do the weaving.

—Herodotus

Equality in Egypt

In the long-lived Egyptian civilization—it lasted from 3000 to 332 B.C.E.—women had far greater privileges and rights than in any other ancient culture.

The favor given to Egyptian women was in large part due to the civilization's tradition of goddess worship. In the earliest days of Egyptian civilization, each village had its own deity, which was often female. These original goddesses hadn't even gained their status through marriage. They had their own power and authority. Even when many goddesses were later linked to gods, their earlier status was never forgotten.

Because of the matriarchal aspect of Egyptian religion, women were given tremendous freedom to participate in its rites and ceremonies. A fair number served as priestesses in early Egypt. Their responsibilities were the same as male priests: They mummified bodies and prepared funeral orations, maintained temple buildings, copied important manuscripts, and provided religious education to the community.

Women in less-exalted positions also enjoyed a full panoply of rights and authority in both law and business. They not only owned their own property, including land, money, servants, and slaves, but they also could administer and dispose of their possessions as they wished. They could enter into contracts on their own behalf, execute wills, and bring lawsuits against others.

All Egyptian women received equal treatment at first. As in other societies, however, the advent of social stratification soon gave elite women more status and rights than women of the lower classes. Status became such a big deal to Egyptians that it even governed how they would spend their afterlives. The Egyptians showed no preference in how women's and men's tombs were decorated. The best stuff, however, was reserved for higher-class members of both sexes.

Status also came to determine the jobs women could hold and the education they received. Upper-class women rarely worked in public unless they were priestesses, but they might own and manage wig-making or weaving operations in their own homes. Women of the upper classes in Egypt, Mesopotamia, and India were often taught by private tutors and attained the same educational levels as the men in their families did.

Women's Rights in Ancient Jewish Society

The Jews, or Hebrews, were unique among ancient societies. Like the others, they had once worshipped many gods and goddesses. But they tossed them all out in favor of monotheism, or the belief in one god—a male god.

The earliest Hebrews were nomads or semi-nomads who raised cattle, sheep, and goats and farmed on a seasonal basis. The tribes were comprised of patriarchal families, but evidence of the opposite exists in the Old Testament, suggesting that earlier tribal formation may have been matrilineal and *matrilocal*.

A Woman's Place

The freedom enjoyed by Egyptian women even allowed them to lend their husbands money and charge them interest.

Words for Women

A couple in **matrilocal** societies lived in the home of the bride's mother following marriage.

Yeah, RIGHT.

A Woman's Place

As part of their daily prayers, Jewish men of antiquity thanked God for not making them women. Women uttered a prayer giving thanks for being made according to God's will.

Even with evidence of earlier matriarchal traditions, the predominant family structure in Hebrew society, as was the case in neighboring cultures, was patriarchal.

There are differences in opinion regarding the status and rights of women during the earliest periods of Jewish society. Some believe that the status of women during this time was high and that they fully participated in their communities. Others see Hebrew women as excessively dominated by men and their status inferior in all aspects.

Even the Old Testament offers conflicting views of women's status and rights. It's full of stories about great and powerful women who were venerated for their actions. Rachel and Leah are called "builders of Israel" in the Book of Ruth. Deborah was an esteemed female judge and led her people into battle. Esther, who didn't let on that she was Jewish when she married the Persian king Ahasueras, put her own life at risk to save the lives of the Jews living in Persia, whom her husband had sentenced to death. Women are clearly venerated in the Book of Proverbs and are worshipped in the Song of Solomon. But a woman takes the blame for the fall of humankind right off the bat, and there are many other passages that paint women in far from favorable light.

Even the stories of respected or heroic women pale when compared to the accounts of many others who were clearly in servile or submissive roles. Specific strictures against women can be found throughout the Old Testament, and especially in the Pentateuch, the first five books of the Old Testament once believed to be the work of Moses. They include the following:

➤ The burning to death of prostitutes (while their customers went free)

➤ Not allowing women to inherit from their husbands, or daughters from their fathers, except in situations where there were no male heirs

➤ Not allowing women to divorce their husbands (although men had this right)

If read chronologically, the Old Testament reveals the same old story. Jewish women started out strong (if you don't count Eve), but their status and rights diminished over time.

The Un-Democratic Greeks

For a civilization noted as the cradle of modern democracy, the Greeks were hardly democratic when it came to their treatment of women. In most parts of Greece—there were some notable exceptions—Greek women had virtually no status and hardly any rights at any time during the course of this civilization. Maybe this had something to do with its short life—it lasted for less than a thousand years—from 800 B.C.E. to 146 C.E.—the shortest life span of any ancient society.

The Greeks took patriarchy to the extreme. Women in Athens, for example, were considered minors for their entire lives and were always under the guardianship of a male. The Greeks also espoused slavery, which made life even worse for women as they, and their children, often were treated as poorly as slaves.

It's hard to find an area in which most Greek women had any rights at all. They couldn't engage in most monetary transactions. They also weren't allowed to own any property beyond their own clothing, jewelry, and slaves. They couldn't buy or sell land, enter into contracts, bring legal actions, or inherit from their husbands.

Contrary to some accounts, most women were allowed to interact with the public. Only women of the highest classes lived in seclusion, and even they accompanied their husbands to some public events. Their main role, however, was to produce male heirs and run their husband's households, which effectively kept them at home.

Women of the lower classes moved about freely in public. So did slaves, former slaves, entertainers, intellectuals, and the hetaerae, or high-class courtesans.

Greek women enjoyed better status and rights away from Athens, which was famously misogynistic. In Sparta, girls were allowed to train for athletic events and study with boys. As you'll read in Chapter 5, "Ground-Breakers," they enjoyed similar privileges on the Greek island of Lesbos. In some later Greek city-states, presumably those located far from Athens, women even ruled in their own right or as regents.

Religion afforded Greek women some freedom. Goddess worship was a component of the Greek civilization and women often participated in

Going for the Vote

The ancient Persians did the Greeks one better when it came to secluding their women. Bound by the tradition of the purdah, married women in Persia weren't even allowed to see their own fathers or brothers.

Hear Me Roar

The male is by nature superior, and the female inferior; and the one rules and the other is ruled; this principle, of necessity, extends to all mankind.

—Aristotle

groups that venerated the mother-goddess. These "cultic clubs" were the only public activity that women could engage in regardless of where they lived.

Women also factored prominently in Greek mythology and drama, where they sometimes were depicted as strong and heroic and at other times as things to be crushed and dominated. But men also dominated the world of comedy and tragedy. Women were banned from appearing on the stage, even in female roles.

Roman Rule

From the earliest times of the Roman Empire, women were expected to be good wives, frugal homemakers, absolutely loyal and absolutely faithful. Such expectations leave little doubt that these women had few rights. In order to maintain their loyalty and fidelity, men ruled them with an iron fist.

Women were under the protection of men at all stages of their lives. Fathers transferred their daughters, along with their dowries, directly into the hands of their husbands' families when they married. They then abdicated all authority. When the dowry was in land, it was added to the husband's holdings. If the husband died, his widow and any children inherited the plot intact, which preserved their livelihood.

Going for the Vote

As bad as women had it in Western Civilization during ancient times, their plight was even worse in China. Confucius said that ancestors were to be worshipped—male ancestors, that is. Although the status of Chinese women varied to a certain extent during different dynasties, for the most part their only value was in producing male heirs. Baby girls were routinely put to death. Those lucky enough to survive infancy were often sold as concubines.

Bound to lifelong obedience to men by Confucianism tradition, Chinese women had no rights or authority. They could own no property and received no education. Their only escape was through suicide, which, sadly, was a fairly common occurrence. Some were able to gain a measure of authority through their adult sons.

Another form of marriage, called *sine manu,* allowed a wife to retain membership in her own family and gave her the right to inherit from it, even though she had married into another. Her family, rather than her husband, retained authority over her. By the first century B.C.E., *sine manu* had become the most popular form of marriage. It also gave women a great deal of control over their affairs. Although they were required to appoint a male family member to watch over them, they had significant freedom to manage their own businesses. They could also carry out cash transactions, accept inheritances, and own property.

Under *sine manu,* women also retained some control over their dowries. Husbands were required to keep them intact and could even be sued by their wives if they put their wive's holdings at risk in any way. Dowries were returned to wives when their husbands died, even if it meant breaking up the estate to extract it. When a woman died, her children inherited her dowry.

By the second century B.C.E., other strictures imposed on Roman women had greatly relaxed. They could move about freely in public and even accompanied their husbands to senate meetings and court proceedings. They participated in commerce and could conduct their other affairs pretty much as they chose. They faced few restrictions when it came to marriage, divorce, and remarriage. They were generally well educated, with all but members of the lowest classes receiving some sort of schooling.

As the Roman Empire grew in size and men were rewarded with gifts of land, their wives also helped manage these estates. Women who were married to politicians showed little hesitation in assuming greater authority in the political arena as well. As you'll read in subsequent chapters, a good number of them plotted and schemed to deliver thrones to their husbands and children. Some even ascended to the throne themselves.

The ancient world came to an end toward the end of the fifth century C.E. with the fall of the Roman Empire. Sadly, as the century drew to a close, the status of women in general significantly diminished and their rights were severely restricted. Even sadder is the fact that it would be many centuries before there would be any significant changes in either arena.

A Woman's Place

The Oppian Law, established in 215 B.C.E. as an austerity measure during wartime, banned women from owning more than half an ounce of gold, wearing multicolored dresses, or driving chariots in town. The law was successfully repealed in 195 B.C.E. when a group of matrons staged a public uprising in the Forum, much to the embarrassment of their husbands.

The Least You Need to Know

➤ Male dominance is believed to have started with the establishment of early agrarian societies.

➤ The Code of Hammurabi, the first set of written laws, dealt very specifically with many aspects of women's rights.

➤ Egyptian women enjoyed some of the broadest rights and privileges of the ancient world.

➤ Roman women eagerly took to public life and enjoyed few restrictions over what they could do while there.

Chapter 3

Queen for a Day: Rulers and Warriors

> ### In This Chapter
>
> ➤ The power of warrior queens
>
> ➤ Beauty and brains: Cleopatra
>
> ➤ Female pharaoh: Hatshepsut
>
> ➤ The Trungs, warrior sisters

As ancient farming societies became more established, they also grew more sophisticated and complex. With this growth came new challenges and opportunities for humankind. Developments such as commerce and trade brought outside influences to formerly isolated empires and kingdoms and new challenges to those who ruled them.

To keep their empires strong, these leaders had to be more than powerful warriors. They also had to possess the political savvy that would tell them when to curry favor with the enemy and when to defend their empires against them.

Men led many of these efforts, but as you'll discover in this chapter, women played an important role in a number of them as well. Their numbers may have been small, but they knew how to kick some serious *gluteus maximus* when they needed to, both on and off the battlefield.

Woman in Pharaoh's Clothing: Hatshepsut

Only men were supposed to rule as pharaohs in ancient Egypt. Obviously, someone forgot to tell Hatshepsut about that.

All told, there were actually five women who ruled as pharaohs over Egypt. But Hatshepsut was one of the most successful Egyptian rulers of either sex. Her brilliance on the throne makes her the best known of the female pharaohs as well.

Hear Me Roar

Almost every culture throughout history has had its Warrior Queen or Queens either in fact or fiction, or in some combination of both.

—Antonia Fraser, *The Warrior Queens*

A Woman's Place

Hatshepsut solidified her power as pharaoh by wearing the traditional trappings of these rulers—the beard, headdress, and kilt—throughout her reign. Her male role was upheld even in death—instead of being buried in the Valley of the Queens, she was laid to rest in the Valley of the Kings.

The daughter of the pharaoh Thutmose I, Hatshepsut rose to power when, in keeping with royal tradition, she married her half-brother, Thutmose II. When he died, his son, Thutmose III (also Hatshepsut's nephew) was next in line for the throne. But he was too young to govern, and Hatshepsut ruled in his place.

When Thutmose III came of age, Hatshepsut, believing she had a stronger claim to the throne than her nephew, refused to yield it to him. Instead, she proposed that they rule together. Hatshepsut then took the title of pharaoh by declaring herself a man and by wearing the traditional false beard, headdress, and kilt of the pharaohs. She also declared herself the daughter of the great Egyptian god Amon-Re and claimed that her ascendancy to the throne was ordained by Amon-Re himself.

Hatshepsut and Thutmose III ruled their country together from 1489 to 1469 B.C.E., late in Egypt's Eighteenth Dynasty. During their reign, Hatshepsut fought battles against the Nubians and also increased trade with them. She established other trade routes as well.

She restored many of the Egyptian kingdom's ancient ruins and built beautiful new structures, including a breathtaking temple dedicated to herself at Deier el-Bahri near the Valley of the Kings on the west bank of the Nile River. She also honored her "father," Amon-Re, by installing pink granite obelisks in his temple at Karnak. Always the self-promoter, she ordered the royal stonecutters to carve inscriptions and images detailing her life into them, including scenes from a glorious trade expedition to the Land of Punt (Somalia) that she organized.

Unlike the reigns that preceded and followed her, Hatshepsut's rule was one of relative peace. This changed, however, following her death in 1468 B.C.E. Tired of years of kowtowing to his aunt, Thutmose III not only set Egypt on a more militant course, but he also halted all of Hatshepsut's building projects. In a final gesture of revenge, he defaced any structure having to do with Hatshepsut, erasing her name whenever and wherever he could.

Fulfilling a Prophecy: Jael

Like most ancient societies, the Israelites had to fight off a number of enemies. Not only that, they often had to battle oppressors sent by God to teach them a lesson when they ignored their responsibilities to Him. They were helped in one of these skirmishes by a woman named Jael.

The story of Jael is told through Deborah, one of a number of leaders, or judges, raised up by God to help the Israelites shake off their oppressors. In this case, the Canaanites were pestering the Isarelites, and Deborah decided to ask the Israelite general Barak's help in fighting them off. When she called on Barak with her request, she prophesized victory for all if he would join the cause. Barak agreed to do so, but only if Deborah would fight as well. She agreed to do so.

Hear Me Roar

Most blessed among women is Jael,
The wife of Heber the Kenite;
Blessed is she among women in tents.
He asked water, she gave milk;
She brought out cream in a lordly bowl.
She stretched her hand to the tent peg,
Her right hand to the workmen's hammer;
She pounded Sisera, she pierced his head,
She split and struck through his temple.

—From the Song of Deborah in Chapter 5 of the book of Judges

Hear Me Roar

So as regards these great obelisks,
Wrought with electrum (fine
    gold) by my majesty for my
    father Amon,
In order that my name may en-
    dure in this temple,
For eternity and everlastingness,
They are each of one block of
    hard granite,
Without seam, without joining
    together!

—Queen Hatshepsut

Barak and Deborah led the Israelites to victory over the Canaanites, who were led into battle by Sisera, the captain of the Canaanite army. After he lost the battle with the Israelites on the plain of Esdraelon, he fled for safety to the settlement of Heber the Kenite on the plain of Zaanaim. Heber's wife, Jael, received the fallen leader in her tent with apparent hospitality and gave him milk in "a lordly bowl."

After drinking the milk, Sisera laid down and sank into weary sleep. While he slept, Jael crept up to him, took one of the tent pegs in her hand, and drove it through his temple with a mallet. She then led Barak, who was pursuing the enemy leader, into her tent and showed him what she had done.

Jael's story is told in prose and in verse in the book of Judges in the Old Testament. In the verse version, also known as the Song of Deborah, the Israelite judge venerates her as the most blessed of women for her heroism in slaying the Canaanite general and insuring Israel's victory over his people.

A Woman's Place

Judith, another ancient Israelite, also played an important role in delivering her people from the enemy. Judith saved the Israelites from the Assyrians by assassinating Holofernes, the Assyrian king. She did it by disguising herself as an informer, which allowed her to infiltrate the enemy's camp. Once there, she was invited to join Holofernes for dinner. When the king got drunk and passed out, Judith chopped off his head and took it with her in a sack. She then showed it to the Israelites, whose morale had been dragging. The trophy gave them renewed desire to vanquish their enemies. They attacked the Assyrians, who had a hard time putting up a united front with their leader dead, and defeated them.

The Renaissance artist Artemisia Gentileschi, who was fond of painting heroic women, used the story of Judith for one of her most famous works, Judith and Maidservant with the Head of Holofernes.

Fighting for Her Country: Cleopatra

The oldest daughter of the Egyptian king Ptolemy XII, Cleopatra had it all—brains, beauty, and power. Although many of her actions appear motivated by her hunger for power, they were often driven instead by her desire to protect her kingdom from Roman annexation. Her fierce struggles for power, coupled with her legendary beauty, which she was clearly willing to put to its best use possible, made her the most famous Egyptian queen and an enduring icon to this day.

Whatever Cleo Wants ...

Cleopatra's rule began in 51 B.C.E. when, at age 18, she married her 10-year-old brother, Ptolemy XIII, following their father's death. It wasn't an auspicious time for the two young rulers; there was famine in the land, the Romans were threatening Egypt's borders, and there was plenty of familial strife going on. But Cleopatra proved to be a natural ruler. She greatly enjoyed the power she had as queen of Egypt, and she set out to expand her control.

From here, Cleopatra's life begins to read like a lurid soap opera. Just take a look at all the twists and turns that follow, the plotting and intrigue, all in the name of power and most of it orchestrated by the infamous queen of the Nile herself.

Hear Me Roar

Her form, coupled with the persuasiveness of her conversation, and her delightful style of behavior—all these produced a blend of magic.

—Plutarch

... Cleo Gets

In her thirst for power, Cleopatra sought assistance from the people she felt could best help her, whether they were enemies or not. When the Egyptian chief minister tried to remove her from the throne as co-ruler, she went straight to the leader of the civilization that was posing the greatest threat to Egypt at the time—the great Roman emperor Julius Caesar.

Much taken by Cleopatra's beauty and intelligence, Caesar decided to intervene on her behalf. In the battles that followed, Cleopatra's adversary, the chief minister, was killed.

A Woman's Place

According to legend, Cleopatra's first meeting with Julius Caesar took place after she was smuggled across enemy lines rolled up in some bedding. Some accounts have her wrapped in a carpet.

Down with Ptolemy

But there was still the matter of Cleopatra's brother, Ptolemy XIII. Two years of bickering between the two of them became a blood battle when he demanded his share in leading the country at age 14. According to legend, she had him poisoned.

And Up with Ptolemy!

Cleopatra then married another brother, Ptolemy XIV, who became her new co-ruler. But, in a surprise move, she decided to leave Egypt in her brother/husband's hands and followed Caesar to Rome. She cruised up the Nile in an elaborate barge provisioned with the finest food, wine, and jewels. Once in Rome, she moved into Caesar's villa and became his mistress.

And Down with Ptolemy Again ...

Caesar was assassinated on March 15, 44 B.C.E. (the famous Ides of March) by forces jealous of his power. A civil war broke out after his death, during which Cleopatra fled from Rome and returned to Egypt. She then had Ptolemy XIV drowned in the River Nile and made her son Cesarion, who may have been Caesar's son, co-ruler.

Enter Marc Antony

Cleopatra next took up with the Roman Marcus Antonius (Marc Antony), an ardent admirer and supporter of Julius Caesar's who visited her in Egypt, presumably to assess the possibility of turning Egypt into a client state of Rome. But Cleopatra used her charm and political skills and persuaded him to abandon this scheme.

The two began their famous love affair (which lead to the end of Cleopatra's dynasty, in 42 B.C.E.). After a few years in Egypt, however, Antony decided to return to Rome and married Octavia, the sister of Octavian, the future Roman emperor. But he couldn't stay away from Cleopatra's feminine wiles for long. They reunited in 36 B.C.E. during a military campaign that Antony lead against the Parthians. He divorced Octavia and married Cleopatra. They had three children together.

Cleopatra and Mark Antony remained in Egypt until the angry Octavian decided to avenge his sister's honor. Joining Antony in battle, Cleopatra stood by him until Octavian's troops defeated the Egyptian fleet at Actium in 31 B.C.E. Sensing their defeat, Cleopatra and Marc Antony fled to Alexandria. There, Cleopatra was taken captive by Octavian. Rumors of her death soon spread, and Antony killed himself. Rather than sharing her throne with Octavian or being held captive, Cleopatra induced a poisonous snake, or asp, to bite her. After Cleopatra's death, Octavian murdered Caesarion and claimed Egypt for Rome.

With Cleopatra's death came the end of true Egyptian rule, as Egypt became a province of the Roman Empire. Despite the fact that she was unsuccessful in keeping the Romans from conquering her homeland, Cleopatra's never-ending willingness to fight for her country endeared her to her subjects.

Zenobia the Land Grabber

One of the greatest female warriors of ancient history was the Roman queen Zenobia, who came to power in the second century C.E. Claiming to be a descendent of the legendary Cleopatra, Zenobia took after her possible ancestor with similar beauty and intelligence. She spoke four languages—Latin, Egyptian, Greek, and Aramaic—and studied philosophy and literature. She also had a certain fondness for such male pursuits as drinking, trading, hunting, and riding—skills that would come to serve her well.

Zenobia rose to power in 266 C.E. as *regent* of Palmyra, a Roman state, after the assassination of her husband, King Odenathus. At the time, Palmyra, located on the northern edge of the Syrian Desert, was an extremely prosperous region with important trade connections. Not about to let such valued booty fall into unfriendly hands, Zenobia took control of the area for her son, Vaballathus Athenodorus. She then used her beauty and wiles to expand her domain as far as she could.

Victory Through Deception

Zenobia's first military campaign came at a time when the Roman Empire was weak. This factor, coupled with some deception on her part—she continued to claim allegiance to the Romans—allowed her to seize control of neighboring Syria and part of Egypt in 269 C.E. without much resistance from those areas or from Rome itself.

In the following year, Zenobia continued to hide under her false cloak of loyalty to Rome. While doing so, she conquered neighboring Cappadocia and Bithynia, which gave her control over several key Roman trade routes.

With so much land under her control, Zenobia felt comfortable enough to break her ties with Rome. She even went so far as to begin minting her own currency. By then, however, the Romans smelled a rat. They decided to put the queen's rebellion to rest by attacking her troops.

Zenobia Exposed

In 272 C.E., Emperor Lucius Domitius Aurelian invaded Zenobia's realm and captured its outlying

Words for Women

A man or woman who rules in place of a minor child is referred to as a **regent.**

Yeah, RIGHT.

A Woman's Place

Rather than being borne in a litter or riding a chariot, as may have befitted a woman of her position and stature, Zenobia instead chose to ride into battle on horseback or march in on foot.

areas. He then lay siege to Palmyra, where Zenobia, who saw the writing on the wall, was hastily negotiating her surrender. When captured by Aurelian, Zenobia abandoned her former independence and blamed the men around her for the rebellion.

Aurelian left Palmyra in ruins. He took Zenobia with him to Rome, where he first displayed her as a captive and then imprisoned her on an estate in nearby Tibor. But Zenobia triumphed in the end. She later married a Roman senator and became the leader of one of Rome's most prominent intellectual circles, as well as a noted patron of the arts.

Bodacious Boadicea

Mediterranean and Middle Eastern empires weren't the only areas that the Romans had set their sights on conquering. Roman rulers staged numerous campaigns against other civilizations and lands, even marching troops as far north as the British Isles. They took Britain for their own in 60 C.E. and ruled there for another 400 years or so, but not without first encountering strong resistance from a tribal queen named Boadicea.

Boadicea was the wife of King Prasutagas, the leader of Britain's Iceni tribe located in what is now the county of Norfolk. But Prasutagas was a leader in name only, having conceded true rule to the Romans in 43 C.E. As part of his concession, Prasutagas struck a deal that allowed him to stay as regent under a Roman governor, Suetonius Paulinus.

Prasutagas died in 60 C.E., naming Nero, the emperor of Rome, as his co-heir along with Boadicea and their daughters. But the Romans refused to recognize Boadicea's inheritance and decided to take the regency away from her, first by seizing her personal property and that of the other Iceni royals, then by plundering all of Britain.

When the Romans came to take Boadicea's jewelry, they flogged her and raped her two daughters. A furious Boadicea recruited an army and planned a revolt. She successfully organized a huge army—estimates vary between 80,000 and 120,000—composed of her own tribe as well as members of neighboring tribes. Along with a good supply of chariots and weapons, they set out to overtake towns that had fallen to Roman rule. She successfully attacked the Roman cities of Camulodunum (Colchester), Londinium (London), and Verulanium (St. Albans), leaving tens of thousands of massacred Romans and their allies in her wake.

Hear Me Roar

If you weigh well the strengths of our armies you will see that in this battle we must conquer or die. This is a women's resolve. As for the men, they may live or be slaves.

—Boadicea, in a speech to her troops in 62 C.E.

When news of the battles reached Suetonius Paulinus, he immediately planned a counterattack against Boadicea's weary troops. Sensing defeat, Boadicea fled to her kingdom, where she and her daughters committed suicide—in their eyes a far better fate than becoming Roman slaves.

Almost always portrayed as a substantial, statuesque woman with flaming red hair, the role she played in English history is memorialized in a statue opposite Big Ben on the Thames Embankment in London.

Preserving Their Country: Trung Nhi and Trung Trac

Sisters and Vietnamese noblewomen, Trung Nhi and Trung Trac showed similar valor in their efforts to protect their country from Chinese rule. Without them, there's a good chance that Vietnam wouldn't exist today.

Trung Trac and her younger sister, Trung Nhi, were the daughters of a Vietnamese lord. The two were very close as girls and remained so as adults when Trung Trac married Thi Sach, another Vietnamese lord.

At the time, Vietnam had been under the rule of the Han Dynasty of China for more than 100 years. Things had been relatively peaceful under Chinese rule, but they became less so around 39 C.E. when some of the Vietnamese lords, tired of Chinese domination, began plotting to overthrow their Chinese rulers. Whispers of the uprising reached the Chinese, and they retaliated by killing Trung Trac's husband in an effort to keep the Vietnamese in submission.

Thi Sach's death lit a fire under Trung Trac and Trung Nhi. Sensing the growing unrest among their Vietnamese compatriots, they decided to avenge his death and mount a rebellion against the Chinese. Their instincts were correct, as more than 80,000 Vietnamese royals and peasants—men and women alike—joined in a vast army led by 36 women generals, including the sisters' mother.

The Trung sisters lead their army to the Chinese governor's home, where they attacked and defeated Chinese forces. Similar battles in other key sites followed, and the Vietnamese emerged victorious.

The Vietnamese people honored the Trung sisters by naming them co-queens. They started out as popular rulers and become even more so when they abolished the taxes imposed by the Chinese and restored the traditional Vietnamese form of government.

A Woman's Place

One of the women trained as a general in the Trung sisters' army was Phung Thi Chinh. A fierce warrior, she fought while pregnant and even delivered her baby on the battlefront. Shortly after giving birth, she strapped her baby to her back and continued fighting.

The Trung sisters retained control over Vietnam until the Han emperor sent forces to recapture the region in 42 C.E. This time, the Vietnamese forces were badly defeated by the Chinese. Rather than being taken captive by enemy forces, the sisters committed suicide in the traditional way by drowning.

As the heroines who led the first national revolt against the Chinese, the Trung sisters occupy a special place in Vietnamese history and lore to this day. Their heroism is celebrated by a national holiday, and they are honored in temples built in their memory.

Hear Me Roar

I want to drive the enemy away to save our people. I will not resign myself to the usual lot of women who bow their heads and become concubines.

—Trien Au

Trien Au

The threat of being enslaved to Chinese rulers inspired another Vietnamese warrior queen to fight against Chinese rule. Often called the "Joan of Arc of Vietnam," Trien Au was a third-century Vietnamese peasant who fought against yet another Chinese occupation of her homeland. Images show her mounted on an elephant and wearing golden armor as she led her troops into battle following the fall of the Han empire.

Sadly, Trien Au wasn't able to rack up the same successes as the Trung sisters did. Despite a lengthy and hard-fought battle, she and her army were defeated. Like the Trungs, she committed suicide rather than surrender to her victors.

The Least You Need to Know

➤ Many warrior queens, as well as their less aggressive sisters, came into power through their relationships with their husbands or sons.

➤ Of the five women who ruled Egypt as pharaohs, Hatshepsut was the most successful.

➤ Royal birth wasn't necessarily a requisite to becoming a warrior queen. Trien Au was a Vietnamese peasant.

➤ Honor was everything to the warrior queens. Many committed suicide in lieu of being captured by their victors.

Chapter 4

At Work

In This Chapter

➤ Keeping house

➤ Weaving a life

➤ Gaining freedom through slavery

➤ Making the "staff of life"

In the ancient world—and, frankly, in virtually every era that followed—being born female defined the work that women did. There's no denying that from the beginning of civilization, women have played an essential role in both the world's economy and in ensuring the survival of human kind. But from the beginning of recorded time, and even before, the chief functions and roles of women in society were primarily dictated by their gender.

As you'll see in this chapter, however, the work done by women has ranged far beyond rearing children and taking care of the house, even in ancient times. While a woman's primary duties were to her husband, her family, and to her home, her work there by no means kept her from other occupational pursuits.

First Work

As you read in Chapter 1, "A Woman's Life," the first work that women engaged in were tasks essential to keeping the tribe alive. Finding food was the most important, and women shared the responsibility equally with men. For the most part, the men hunted while the women gathered such things as plants, roots, berries, bird eggs, etc.

A Woman's Place

The early division of labor between men and women in nomadic tribes made for some interesting occupational choices as civilization continued to develop. The years women had spent messing around with roots, plants, and other organic materials gave them a unique body of knowledge that they would use years later as midwives, physicians, and even brewers.

At first, there wasn't an absolute separation of responsibility—women, for example, sometimes took part in cooperative hunts or went to the fields after small animals, while men sometimes foraged when game was scarce. But gender played a more important role as time went on. Childbearing and rearing, by necessity, kept women near the home. Since they were there, it made sense that they also assumed most of the responsibilities related to housekeeping.

As nomadic hunting/gathering evolved in agricultural societies, women at first shouldered most of the responsibility for raising crops and breeding livestock. Over time, as the agrarian lifestyle became more established and the necessity for hunting diminished, men took over these roles in most societies while women focused more of their efforts on the household.

While many women still worked in the field, and would continue to do so for generations, the expectation was that such work was in addition to their responsibilities in the home. This created an extremely long workday, and an extraordinarily busy one as well.

Hear Me Roar

She finds wool and flax and busily spins it. She is like a merchant's ship; she brings food from afar. She gets up before dawn to prepare breakfast for her household and plan the day's work for her servant girls. She goes out to inspect a field and buys it; with her earnings she plants a vineyard. She is energetic and strong, a hard worker. She watches for bargains; her lights burn late into the night. Her hands are busy spinning thread, her fingers twisting fiber.

—Proverbs 31:13–19

Working both in the home and away from it would become the standard in ancient societies for the vast majority of women. The exceptions to it were royal women and other women of the aristocracy, who traditionally hired other women to care for their children and help them run their households. Wealthy women rarely entered the marketplace as workers, as their marriage dowries assured their freedom from such labor. A handful of learned women and artisans were able to skip this double burden as well.

It was during the establishment of agrarian societies that the first tools for weaving and spinning were invented, almost assuredly by women, to fashion wool and flax from the field into cloth.

A Woman's Place

Greek women, in particular, became highly skilled at working with wool. Records show that women of all classes in Classical Athens spun and wove. Some women went so far as to make businesses of it and produced textiles for the market as well as ready-made clothing. Cloth goods were so valuable to the Greek economy that wives going through divorce were allowed to take half of what they had woven when their marriages ended.

A Common Thread

Working with fibers and fabrics was a role shared by virtually all ancient women, even those born to royalty. In many respects, it, too, became women's work as it was a good fit with other womanly work—the actions of spinning, weaving, and sewing meshed relatively well with raising children and cooking. It was fairly easy to feed a child or stir a pot while carding wool or spinning yarn on a drop spindle.

Women worked on looms of all sizes, both inside the home and outside in kitchen gardens or court-yards. Working outside allowed them to build larger looms, and it wasn't uncommon for women to work on them together, passing the bobbins

Hear Me Roar

By how much the men are expert above all other men in propelling a swift ship on the sea, by thus much the women are skilled at the loom ...

—Homer

back and forth between them. Girls learned how to spin and weave in preparation for marriage. Noblewomen often wove their own cloth from expensive yarns, such as wool colored with costly dyes—that other women couldn't afford.

Weaving began simply but became more complex as women gained new skills and experimented with weaves that created different patterns and textures. Over time, they unleashed their creative talents and created textiles of immense beauty, embellishing their work by:

➤ Weaving color-on-color stripes or patterned borders.

➤ Using wool from different sheep to create subtle patterns throughout the cloth (wool grows in various shades of white, tan, and blue, depending on the individual sheep's pigmentation).

➤ Braiding and fringing the edges of the fabric. They sometimes hung beads on the edges of the fabric as well.

A Woman's Place

Although most of the cloth woven in ancient times was used for clothing, not all was. Women also created pictorial pieces on large looms that documented important events or simple scenes from everyday life. These early woven illustrations were the forerunners of medieval tapestries.

Early woven pieces were either bleached or left in their natural state. As ornamentation grew in popularity, women drew on knowledge developed during their gathering days and experimented with dyes made from various plants and other substances. Saffron, for example, turned cloth sunshine yellow. The root of the madder plant transformed plain wool into a fiery orange-red. The indigo plant yielded a rich blue.

In China, the third millennium B.C.E. discovery that thread could be drawn from the cocoon of the Bombyx mori moth led to the development of silk and a whole new way of making textiles.

As trade routes were developed, cloth became an important commodity outside the household. The demand for it became so great that women were sometimes forced into producing it. Slavery was by no means unheard of in ancient Greek and Egyptian societies, and it fueled a growing textile industry that in time became controlled by men.

In Attendance

Midwifery was another profession that became almost the exclusive province of women. Like weaving, it was a natural fit for ancient women as most of them gave birth at home, attended by female family members or neighbors. Because most women refused to be attended by or examined by male doctors for modesty's sake, the work of midwives expanded to other areas of medicine as well.

It appears that women of all classes used midwives, although some babies in wealthy families were delivered by male doctors. Generally, male expertise was only called on in the most dire situations. Midwives were expected to know how to handle everything else. As they weren't allowed to study medicine, they learned what they needed to know by watching and assisting other women.

Accounts of midwifery and the women who practiced it are found throughout ancient records. Socrates' mother was a midwife. Several other Greek women became famous for their work in this profession. Among them are Elephantis, who treated baldness; Olympias of Thebes, who specialized in using herbs in contraception and abortion; and Salpe of Lemnos, who claimed she could cure fevers, rabies, numbness, and sunburn.

Many of the treatments employed by midwives again came from ancient knowledge of the actions of herbs, roots, and other substances collected in the fields. Midwives often guarded such information jealously. This furtiveness, coupled with what sometimes seemed like unusual powers (and maybe a little jealousy over them) led some people to think that midwives were of another world, and perhaps not a good one at that. As you'll read more about in Part 2, "The Dark and Middle Ages," when the witch hunts of the Dark and Middle Ages were organized, midwives often found themselves the target of such persecution.

For obvious reasons, hiring out as a wet nurse was another ancient occupation that was solely the province of women. Women in high positions in many cultures often used wet nurses as part of the childrearing process. For their service, which might extend for two years or even longer, wet nurses could receive board and a salary. In some cases, they took the babies to their own houses for the duration of their service and returned them to their parents' homes when they were weaned.

First Physicians

Women weren't entirely banned from the formal practice of medicine, but female physicians were definitely a rarity in ancient society. The Greeks, as could be expected, prohibited women from the profession until the fourth century B.C.E. There is evidence of the Egyptians, who took a more liberal stance in almost all aspects of women's rights, allowing women to study medicine at a school in Heliopolis as early as 1500 B.C.E. High-born women of all cultures were more likely to be allowed to study and practice medicine. The twelfth century B.C.E. physician Agamede, an herbalist, was the daughter of the king of the Epeans.

A Woman's Place

The first female gynecologist was a Greek woman named Agnodice. She had to disguise herself as a man both to study and to practice her profession. Following accusations by her fellow physicians that she was corrupting aristocratic women, Agnodice revealed herself as a woman and was arrested. Only through the pleas of her patients was she allowed to live.

The few female physicians in practice in ancient society were generally allowed to treat women only.

The Oldest Profession

While occupations like cloth making and midwifery were considered respectable jobs for both freeborn women and slaves, others were decidedly less so. The profession that often carried the greatest amount of stigma and contempt was prostitution.

Prostitution is by no means a savory subject, but it would be nearly impossible to talk about the history of women without mentioning it. As the oldest profession—yes, it's mentioned in the Bible—prostitution has played a certain role in most societies from the beginning of civilization. It wasn't as prominent in *polygamous* societies, such as those found among later Celtic and Germanic tribes where men simply took multiple sex partners when it suited them.

There is evidence of institutionalized prostitution, or brothels, in the earliest records of both the Greek and Roman civilizations. They were moneymakers for the government, which established them in the new city centers that developed as a result of expanding trade routes, and taxed them heavily. Most were run by men; some by women.

Prostitutes often came from the lower social classes as their status afforded them few other occupational choices. Other women—in fact, a large number—were forced into the profession through slavery. Economic necessity drove some women to it; for example, widows with no means of support would often turn to prostitution as it was better than starving to death on the street.

Prostitution was not only a way to make a living and keep a roof over one's head, it was also a means to an end for slave women trying to gain their freedom. If they were highly attractive, they might be able to use their sexuality to curry favor with their clients and improve their circumstances. If freedom eluded them, the role of a courtesan or mistress could ensure a secure and sometimes powerful future. In classical Athens, for example, only courtesans could accompany men to social occasions like dinners, speeches, and plays. You'll meet several of these high-powered hired ladies in Chapter 5, "Ground-Breakers."

Words for Women

Having two or more partners at the same time, or having plural marriages, is **polygamy.**

A Woman's Place

A woman didn't have to sell her body to be called a prostitute in ancient times. Using her sexuality to gain political favor or power could be enough to garner the label, regardless of her social rank. Cleopatra earned the epithet "regina meretrix," or "prostitute queen" from the Romans thanks to her sexual liaisons with Julius Caesar and Marc Antony.

Even prostitutes of the highest social standing, however, rarely enjoyed the rights and protection extended to other women. In many societies, men were forbidden to marry them. Any children they might bear were rarely acknowledged by their fathers. The amount of property they could own was routinely restricted, as were their legal rights. In most societies, men could beat or rape them without fear of prosecution.

In the Marketplace

The rise of city centers created a number of other opportunities for women to ply their skills outside of the home. The development of trade and the marketplace created an economy where excess goods were offered for barter or sale. Virtually anything that was created in the home—food, woven goods, pottery, etc.—could be made in greater amounts and sold or traded on trade routes or in city markets. Women clearly contributed a good share of the products and services that could be found there.

What women were allowed to do in the marketplace varied with their status, the culture, and the period —for example, women in early Greek society enjoyed a fair amount of freedom. They could move about freely and travel to the market to acquire goods for the house. By the fourth century B.C.E., however, they were banned from engaging in most monetary transactions and from owning anything beyond their personal property, which effectively eliminated them from the marketplace. Even shopping was believed to be more than their simple minds could handle.

Hear Me Roar

We have courtesans for our pleasure, concubines for our daily needs and wives to give us legitimate children and look after the housekeeping.

—Demosthenes

A Woman's Place

Some Egyptian women even worked as moneylenders. They were also allowed to borrow money, within limits, to fund their enterprises.

In ancient Sumeria, upper-class wives could conduct business on their own, including the buying and selling of slaves. At the beginning of the modern era, Roman women who were commoners worked as retailers, butchers, fishmongers, and stonecutters.

As previously mentioned, the women of ancient Egypt enjoyed some of the broadest privileges in ancient society. Their freedom extended to their activities in the marketplace, where they frequently bought and sold such goods as clothing, food, jewelry, and other trinkets. Since they were allowed a greater amount of personal property than women in other societies, they had the resources for entering into business contracts and buying property.

Brewers and Bakers

Experience at the hearth in the home also translated into work as food preparers and brewers for ancient women in many societies. Neither profession was the sole domain of women, but there's plenty of evidence to suggest that they played a prominent role in both arenas.

Bread was an essential part of virtually every ancient meal, and the people who made it were held in high esteem. Most was made at home, but it was produced commercially in bakeries outside of the home also and sold in the marketplace.

A Woman's Place

The Egyptians were particularly fond of beer and frequently made offerings of it to the gods and the dead.

Brewing both beer and wine was primarily done in the home, but records dating back to Hellenistic Egypt show the existence of commercial breweries that were operated by female brewers. Making beer was a natural adjunct to baking as making bread was a necessary step in the process. Egyptian women would grind fine barley into flour, moisten it, and knead it into loaves. After baking, the loaves were soaked in water and placed in a warm area to ferment. Once this process was complete, the precious liquid was drawn off by squeezing the bread through a cloth or sieve.

The Least You Need to Know

➤ While the work performed by women was often minimized or slighted, it nonetheless played an important role in the rise of civilization.

➤ As agricultural societies developed, women were expected to work in and outside of the home, but their responsibilities to husband, home, and family came first.

➤ The work women were allowed to do was often determined by their social status.

➤ Many women were able to express their creativity while making utilitarian objects for their homes, such as cloth and baskets.

Chapter 5

Ground-Breakers

In This Chapter

➤ Love and lust on Lesbos

➤ Socrates' inspiration

➤ Critical thinking in Ancient Greece

➤ The legend of the Amazons

Women have done amazing things since the beginning of civilization. They've been political leaders, inventors, artists, and poets. Their contributions to the world around us are undeniable—and often overlooked in traditional histories.

In this chapter, we take a look at some of the amazing women of antiquity. Some are familiar, others not, but they're a group of innovators and pioneering thinkers whose efforts remain a source of inspiration to this day.

Poetry in Motion: Sappho

The daughter of aristocrats, the Greek poet Sappho lived on the island of Lesbos in the Aegean Sea during the seventh century B.C.E. Detailed records of her life don't exist, so we know little about her personally. We do know she had a warm and loving family, which included three brothers. She was married and she probably had a daughter. We also know she was one heck of a poet—in fact, she is one of the greatest poets of all time.

Unlike girls living in other parts of Greece at the time, those growing up on Lesbos received a solid education. As the beneficiary of training not generally afforded to women at the time, Sappho drew on her lessons and became an educator herself, directing her efforts toward teaching young women.

As part of her work as an educator, Sappho wrote nine books of poems that discuss various aspects of women's lives, detailing such emotions as jealousy and love. Much of what she wrote was culled from her own experiences, and it's exceedingly intimate and personal in nature. As it was written by a woman for women, it also has an undeniably affectionate tone that impresses many as erotic.

Not all of Sappho's work is of an erotic nature—she also wrote lyric poetry, funeral dirges, and choral hymns. But it's her well-crafted verses on women's lives that have garnered the most attention and made her notorious. The great Greek philosopher Plato put her on equal footing with the goddess daughters of Zeus by calling her the Tenth Muse. When others speak of "The Poetess," there's no question that it's Sappho they're talking about. The poetic meter that she invented and perfected came to be called the "Sapphic."

After Sappho's death—possibly a suicide over a failed love affair with a sailor named Phaon—rumors erupted regarding her role in establishing a cult of young women who worshipped the goddess Aphrodite. Both the love affair and the cult were never proven to be anything more than speculation and rumor.

Hear Me Roar

Although they are only breath, words which I command are immortal.

—Sappho

Sappho's Work Lost

Of some 500 poems containing 12,000 lines of verse that Sappho penned in her lifetime, only about 600 have survived. There are several theories over why so many were lost. Some believe Sappho's work was burned by Christian popes and emperors furious over its erotic content. However, the more likely scenario is that it merely disappeared, as did many other documents, during the Dark and Middle Ages.

Even though the bulk of Sappho's work did disappear, enough of her poetry survived to inflame later generations, such as the Victorians, who found the poetry's homosexual content particularly disturbing.

A Woman's Place

The erotic nature of Sappho's poetry, coupled with the name of her island home, gave rise to the term lesbian.

Healing Hands: Acca Laurentia

Probably a figure more based in myth than reality—the lines between fiction and truth were often blurred in antiquity—Acca Laurentia was noted both for her healing abilities and her beauty in some accounts. In others, she is referred to as a mysterious, she-wolf-type figure with the nickname "Lupa," or wolf—hardly an attractive image. In either case, she is credited with nursing and rearing two abandoned babies who would go on to establish the city of Rome.

The non-she-wolf version of Acca Laurentia's life paints her as an obscure Roman goddess married to Faustulus, the royal shepherd of Amulius who found the twins Romulus and Remus after they had been abandoned by their mother, the Vestal Virgin Rhea Silvia. In one account, Acca Laurentia nurses the twins back to health. In another, Faustulus rescues the boys from the wolf that was nursing them and brings them to Acca Laurentia to be reared.

The she-wolf version of the tale portrays Acca Laurentia as Luperca or Lupa, the wife of Lupercus, who in the shape of a she-wolf suckled Romulus and Remus.

City Builder: Queen Semiramis

Noted as both a great sovereign and a great lover, the Babylonian Queen Semiramis, also known as Sammuramat, is renowned as a great architect of antiquity.

Semiramis was the wife of the Babylonian King Shamshi-Adad V, who ruled in the ninth century B.C.E. After he died, she first reigned as regent for five years while their son was still a minor. She then continued her rule for some 40 more years, during which time, according to the Greek historian Herodotus, she irrigated all of Babylon and supported her son's military campaigns against the Medes and Chaldeans.

Semiramis is venerated in Persian and Median folklore, which paints her as one of the greatest queens of all time. This makes it difficult to discern what her accomplishments really were. Older sources often credit her with rebuilding the city of Babylon, which had faded in glory under Assyrian rule. However, newer research discredits those earlier claims. Semiramis may also be responsible for some of the structures in the city of Nineveh, including its dams and irrigation systems. It's also said that she built the first tunnel below a river, linking the Babylonian royal palace with the Temple of Jupiter under the Euphrates River.

Semiramis is also noted for her lascivious nature. A lusty lover, she always found time for pleasure even when her agenda was full. Supposedly insatiable, she had a propensity for collecting lovers.

Hear Me Roar

She had gardens suspended between the sky and the earth.

—Herodotus (writing about Semiramis' famous hanging gardens of Babylon)

Since she was also believed to be an incarnation of Ishtar, the ancient goddess of love, she was allowed her wanton ways. In fact, she even presided as high priestess over Ishtar's cult.

It was during a festival honoring the great love goddess that Semiramis lost her city to her enemies. While presiding over sacred rights in Ishtar's temple, her chief minister staged a coup and removed her from her throne. By the time she emerged from the temple, the city was firmly under his control. With her status as queen now vastly diminished, Semiramis relinquished her throne to her son. Then, according to legend, she disappeared forever.

Alchemy: Mary the Jewess

Also known as Maria or Miriam, Mary the Jewess worked as an alchemist in Alexandria during the first century C.E. In the course of her work, she invented such devices as the tribikos, perhaps the first distillation mechanism; the kerotakis, an apparatus for creating metal alloys; and a prototype for the autoclave, fashioned from copper tubing made from sheet metal.

Mary the Jewess is also credited with developing many of the foundations of modern chemistry. Perhaps her best-known invention, however, is the double boiler, or bain-marie (named after her in some accounts, after the Virgin Mary in others). This simple device, which gently heats substances by suspending them over hot water, became a staple in virtually every laboratory and kitchen and remains so today.

Critical Thinker: Hypatia

She was the sole woman in a sea of men, espousing her beliefs in a civilization that emphatically believed that women should be seen and not heard. But Hypatia's innate brilliance elevated her beyond the customary role of women of the time and made her one of the most famous mathematicians and philosophers of ancient Greece.

A Woman's Place

While not true of all high achievers of antiquity, being born into learned or high-class families gave women a better chance of attaining an education and improving their social status.

Hypatia, who lived from about 365 to 416 C.E., had the incredible good fortune—especially in ancient times—of being the daughter of Theon, a philosopher and geometrician who taught advanced classes at Alexandria University. Unusually forward-thinking for his time, Theon schooled Hypatia in astronomy, plane geometry, mathematics, trigonometry, and philosophy. Her quick mind made it easy for her to grasp any subject and master it. Noting his daughter's brilliance, Theon soon expanded her training to include the philosophies of Plato and Aristotle, the most celebrated thinkers and scholars of the day.

Hypatia soon became known as Theon's "philosopher-daughter," and eventually replaced her father as head of his department at Alexandria University. Students from near and far came to hear her speak and came away impressed with her knowledge as well as her reputation for purity and chastity. While a notable beauty, Hypatia put her career before her personal life and never married. She may have indulged in a lover or two, but there was never as much as a mention of affairs or relationships that would have marred her reputation for purity.

As Hypatia's reputation and influence grew, her attempts to revive the ancient traditions of god and goddess worship and her views on the role of women in society drew the wrath of early Christian leaders. They eventually identified her as a threat to the Catholic Church. Hypatia gained a particularly powerful enemy in Cyril, the bishop of Alexandria.

When word began to circulate that the Greek government was seeking Hypatia's skills as an advisor, Cyril developed a plot to do away with her once and for all. He gathered a group of religious fanatics—some accounts identify them as monks—and commanded them to attack her as she made her way to her weekly lecture at the University. The fanatics pulled Hypatia from her chariot, dragged her into the cathedral of Alexandria, stripped her naked, and beat her to death. Cyril ordered her body burned, along with everything she had written.

Teacher and Debater: Aspasia

Like Hypatia, Aspasia had the rare benefit of a good education during a time when women were generally denied the opportunity. Living during the fifth century B.C.E., she became a noted scholar and orator, as well as a member of the *hetaerae,* a group of high-class courtesans who accompanied men to places other women were forbidden to go.

Aspasia's skills as a lecturer eventually caught the attention of Pericles, Athens's popular statesman and orator. They couldn't marry as Aspasia was a foreigner, but they did live together and she bore him a son.

Her association with Pericles brought Aspasia great power. As a non-Greek (she was born in Asia Minor) and a member of the hetaerae, she also wasn't constricted by many of the laws that governed the behavior of other women. She was allowed to open a school where she lectured on philosophy and taught debating. It is said that the most prominent men in Athens attended her classes, including Socrates, who, in some accounts, attributed his famous teaching and learning process—the Socratic method—to her.

Words for Women

The **hetaerae** were Greek courtesans of the highest class. The term comes from the word *heter,* meaning companion.

Because she wasn't Greek, Aspasia also had great latitude in what she was allowed to say. Many of her public comments were against the severe restrictions the Greeks placed on women, such as forbidding them to leave the home or to visit other women. She also spoke out strongly in support of providing Greek women with an education.

As could be expected, Aspasia's views didn't endear her to many Greek men. According to Plutarch, who chronicles parts of Aspasia's life in his *Life of Pericles*, attempts to discredit her included prosecution for keeping a brothel. She stood trial for this crime, but, thanks to an appeal by Pericles, was acquitted.

The event did tarnish Aspasia's already shaky reputation. It also didn't do Pericles' much good. But the two stayed together until Pericles died. About six months after his death, Aspasia stepped out of the public spotlight by marrying Lysicles, a cattle dealer.

Courtesan to Empress: Theodora

Like Aspasia, Theodora used sexual connections with the right people to elevate her beyond the role of prostitute. Unlike her high society courtesan sister, Theodora climbed all the way to the top.

The second of three daughters of a dancer and a bear keeper at the Hippodrome in Constantinople, Theodora also took to performing at a young age, joining her older sister as a dancer and mime when she was four.

Theodora's quick wit soon drew the attention of Roman society, and she became a popular performer, often working as a comedienne at private parties. She became the mistress of Hecebolus, a Roman provincial governor, and lived with him for several years in North Africa. After the relationship ended, she returned to Constantinople, where she met Justinian, the nephew of the Roman Emperor Justin and heir to the Roman throne.

A Special Marriage

Justinian quickly fell in love with Theodora and was determined to marry her regardless of her low-class status as a performer/prostitute. In order to do so, he had to amend existing laws that banned marriage between free men and prostitutes. He was successful and took Theodora as his wife in 523 C.E. Two years later, he succeeded to the throne and made Theodora his co-ruler.

By all accounts, Theodora and Justinian had a wonderful relationship. Justinian doted on her, giving her a court of her own, an entourage, and a royal seal. He also depended on her wit and brilliance to help him make state decisions, describing Theodora as his partner.

A Woman's Place

Theodora's intelligence and courage played a big role in Justinian's keeping his throne. During a popular uprising in 532 C.E., during which Justinian was preparing to flee from his palace, she told him that every man would die, but a man who became an emperor should not die as an exile. Justinian listened to her and stayed the course. He ruled for another 33 years, 17 more than his beloved wife.

Fighting for Courtesans' Rights

Even though Theodora was now an empress, with all the power and prestige such a position afforded, she never forgot her humble roots. She had a special place in her heart for prostitutes and women of all classes and established a convent for prostitutes who wanted to leave the profession.

Theodora also worked to pass legislation that mandated the death sentence in rape cases, gave prostitutes and other women greater property rights, protected them in divorce cases and from abusive husbands, and provided against parents paying off debts by selling their children into slavery.

True Believer: Nefertiti

Known for her great beauty, Nefertiti, in concert with her husband, the pharaoh Amenhotep IV, was an influential force in shaping Egyptian religion during the thirteenth century B.C.E.

Nefertiti encouraged Amenhotep to proclaim Atenism, a monotheistic cult based on the sun god Aten, or Aton, as the only acceptable religion in Egypt. In a land that worshipped hundreds of gods and goddesses, this was tantamount to heresy. Although it seems that some elements of Atenism had previously existed in other cults, including that of Amon-Re, which was still being practiced, replacing the

Egyptian pantheon with a single god rested poorly with many of the Egyptians, and especially with the Amon-Re priesthood.

To solidify the new cult, Amenhotep and Nefertiti moved from Thebes, which was the center of the Amon-Re cult, and established a new royal residence at a site on the Nile. To show their complete allegiance to Aten, Amenhotep changed his name to Ahkenaten, meaning "Servant of Aten." Nefertiti took the additional name of Nefernefruaten. They named the city they founded Akhetaten, or "Horizon of the Aten."

Akhenaten and Nefertiti had six children together—all girls. Because they were unable to produce a male heir, their religious innovations died when they did.

Nefertiti's great beauty is immortalized on a famous bust that is today one of the finest examples of ancient Egyptian art.

Mother of Military Invention: Penthesilia

No one is entirely sure whether the legendary matriarchal society of the Amazons actually existed, but there's no denying that Greek literature and art are full of stories about these mighty warriors.

The Amazons are believed to have descended from the inhabitants of the island of Crete, which factors prominently in legends and mythology as the home of matriarchy. When the Cretan civilization came to an end in 1200 B.C.E., many of the people living on Crete left and settled elsewhere. The Amazons were one of several groups that developed from settlements on the coast of Asia Minor.

A Woman's Place

The name Amazon is thought to derive from the Greek word *amazoi,* meaning "without breast" or "breastless." To the male–centered Greek civilization of antiquity, they symbolized everything that was non-Greek, and therefore barbaric.

They are almost always portrayed as locked in battle with men, often with one breast bare. According to legend, they also made it easier to draw their bows on the battlefield by amputating their right breasts. It was believed the Amazons maintained their female-only society by periodically mating with men of various tribes. They kept the female babies; the boys were shipped off to their fathers' tribes for rearing.

Of the Amazon queens, Penthesilia is one of the best known. Renowned for her bravery, wisdom, and skill in weapons, she is often credited with inventing the double-sided ax, or battle ax, although there is enough evidence to suggest that this device was actually independently invented by several cultures.

Legend has it that Penthesilia put her ax to good use on the battlefield while proving her prowess as a warrior. It may also have been what she used when she accidentally killed one of her fellow Amazons—Hippolyta—during a heated battle. With Hippolyta's blood on her hands, Penthesilia begged Priam, the king of Troy, to purify her of her crime. He did so, and Penthesilia repaid him by fighting for Troy during the Trojan War.

Penthesilia's life came to a sad end when she engaged in a battle with the mighty Greek hero Achilles. Legend has it that he fell in love with the beautiful Amazon queen as the two were locked in battle. When she died, Achilles was overcome with grief over having slain such a beautiful creature.

Giving Her Life for Her Faith: Perpetua

During the early years of the Christian Church, a number of women who were followers of the faith became martyrs when the Roman Empire persecuted them for their beliefs. (This was before Christianity was proclaimed the preferred religion of the empire.) One of the best known was a woman named Perpetua, for she left a detailed account of her thoughts and the incidents that took place prior to her death.

Perpetua was only 22, a new mother and a new Christian when she was imprisoned during the persecutions ordered by Emperor Septimius Severus in the first decade of the third century C.E. According to her accounts, she was terrified of the prison, having never been held in such a dark place. Although her father pled with her to forsake her vows during the questioning she was about to undergo, she refused to do so, telling him that she could not call herself by anything other than what she was: a Christian. Along with the other Christians who had been imprisoned, Perpetua made it clear that she was a follower of the faith by being baptized. They were all condemned to die by being fed to animals in an arena.

On the night before her execution, Perpetua had a series of prophetic dreams. She saw herself as victorious over her oppressors. She also caught glimpses of the eternal life that awaited her.

Comforted by her dreams, Perpetua calmly entered the arena the next day. Although she was knocked to the ground by a wild cow, she actually met her death at the hands of a Roman soldier. According to the unknown observer who recorded her final minutes, Perpetua even guided his sword to her when his first blow failed to kill her.

The Least You Need to Know

➤ The poetry of Sappho is still considered some of the finest love verse ever written.

➤ Many innovations related to distilling and metallurgy can be traced to the work of Mary the Jewess.

➤ The Roman Empress Theodora, a former street performer and prostitute, was responsible for enacting some of the most progressive legislation regarding women's rights in the ancient world.

➤ The Egyptian queen Nefertiti greatly influenced religious practice of her time by supporting the theory of one god instead of many.

Notorious Women

Women who loom a little larger than life—every era and every civilization has them. As you'll see in this chapter, there was a fair share of these notorious women in the ancient world as well.

In some cases, their deviousness, plotting, and scheming made them memorable. In others, they were just in the right place at the right time. Sometimes they became pawns in male power games. Regardless of the situation, their fortunes and failings are decidedly the stuff of legends.

Fu Hao

Also known as Wu Chao, she was the first woman in Chinese history to rule as emperor. A real battle-ax, she never let anything or anyone stand in her way during her quest for power.

Fu Hao was the daughter of a Chinese general who died when she was a child. When word of her father's death reached the royal court, Emperor T'ai Tsung, who admired her beauty, summoned her to his court and made her a royal *concubine*. While there, she managed to catch the eye of the crown prince, Kao Tsung, who was in line to ascend the throne when his father died.

Fu Hao remained in Emperor T'ai Tsung's court as a concubine until his death in 646 C.E. Then, in accordance with Chinese tradition, she and her fellow concubines were forcibly retired to a Buddhist convent. She didn't remain cloistered for long, however. Kao Tsung ordered her brought back to the palace, where she was again made a royal consort, but not the lead concubine. Within six years, she bore the emperor his first son, as well as three more sons and a daughter.

Words for Women

Concubines were common in many ancient societies. They lived with men they weren't legally married to, often as one of several or many women of the same status. Although they had no marital status or rights, their children were generally regarded as legitimate.

From Concubine to Queen

Now that she had proven her worth to the royal court, Fu Hao systematically plotted her rise in the imperial household. She accused the empress, who was childless, of murdering her second child, presumably due to jealousy over Fu Hao's childbearing capabilities. Even though the story was without merit, the emperor chose to believe Fu Hao and deposed the empress. A similar tall tale about the chief concubine removed her from the royal court as well. Fu Hao's path to the throne was clear.

Although plagued by illness (he died of a paralytic illness in 660 or 683 C.E., depending on the source), Kao Tsung was enchanted with Fu Hao and gave her control over his court. She ruled with more than an iron hand, quashing anyone who might pose a threat to her authority. But she worked hard on behalf of her country, endearing her to her subjects if not those closest to her.

Redemption Through Good Works

Fu Hao ended a long-standing war between China and Korea by ordering an invasion by sea. After the war was over, she negotiated an alliance between the former enemy countries. She reformed government, lowered taxes, and increased China's agricultural production. Although there were numerous plots against her for the duration of her reign, she was able to quell them thanks to the loyalty of her armies and her subjects.

After Kao Tsung died, Fu Hao extended her rule by exiling her son Chung and his wife. With her other son, Jui, she retained power until 690, when her ministers, angry over her earlier usurpation of the throne, put Crown Prince Chung back on it.

By this point, there wasn't much fight left in the 80-year-old empress. She retired to her summer palace and died there a few months later.

Messalina the Elder

The wife of Roman Emperor Claudius during the first century C.E., Messalina the Elder was another imperial plotter. As it turns out, however, she was nowhere near as successful as Fu Hao was.

Dissatisfied with Claudius, Messalina took a number of lovers in his stead and eventually conspired with one of them to kill her husband. They came up with numerous plots but were obviously not terribly good at concealing their plans. Eventually, Claudius got wind of her plotting and infidelities and decided to put her to death.

Claudius' soldiers stormed Messalina's chambers, where her mother was pleading with her to do the honorable thing and commit suicide. Messalina, however, stalled for time, holding her dagger to her neck and her chest as she debated the best angle for death by her own hand. While she hemmed and hawed, one of Claudius' men decided to cut the melodrama short and slew her.

The Black Widow: Agrippina II

Women who marry frequently only to bury their husbands in fairly rapid order are sometimes called black widows—they mate and they kill. Counting the spousal casualties of Agrippina II—she definitely deserves this title.

This is another tale of cunning and deception in the Roman court. No wonder the country fell.

The legendary power-monger Agrippina II was the daughter of a granddaughter of the Roman Emperor Augustus and his adopted grandson. After being reared in the royal court, where she cavorted with the children of other political leaders, she was married at age 13 to the son of a powerful consul. The two had a son 14 years later.

Agrippina's brother became the Emperor Caligula the same year. He sent Agrippina II and her sister into exile for four years; while there, Agrippina's husband died. A few years later, Caligula also died.

A Woman's Place

Daughters were commonly called by the feminine form of their father's name in classical Rome. In cases where there was more than one daughter, their birth order might be indicated by adding "the younger" or "the elder," as in Messalina's case, or by adding numerals, as was the case with Agrippina.

A Woman's Place

Legend has it that Agrippina hired a woman named Lucusta, who worked as a professional assassin, to assist her in her fiendish plots. Lucusta allegedly supplied the poison that killed Claudius. Agrippina's son Nero also used her to poison Britannicus, Claudius' son.

The road was clear for Agrippina to rise to power, and she returned to Rome to begin her quest.

Hatching the Royal Plot

In Rome, Agrippina II married her second husband, a wealthy senator who left her a fortune when he died. Agrippina used the money to finance her next political ploy: She made a bid for the new emperor, Claudius, who also happened to be her uncle. Presumably still mourning the death of his wife, Messalina (you met her earlier), he nonetheless agreed to make Agrippina his empress and fourth wife in 49 C.E. Because they were so closely related, Claudius had to receive a special senatorial decree before the marriage could take place.

Claudius was pretty smitten with his new wife and gave her tremendous power and authority, much to his detriment. He also adopted little Nero, her son. Five years later, Claudius was dead under suspicious circumstances. Rumor has it that he ate poisoned mushrooms and that Agrippina II may have given them to him. What was her motive? The throne for her son, of course.

Nero was 17 when he became emperor. He was old enough to take control of the empire, but Agrippina was the power behind the throne. Tired of his mother's iron rule over him, Nero rebelled by taking up with a slave mistress named Acte, much to the chagrin of both his mother, Agrippina, and his wife, Octavia.

The Plot Thickens

Agrippina began plotting to replace Nero with Claudius' son Britannicus. Nero learned of his mother's devious plan and had Britannicus poisoned. Agrippina stood trial for treason against the state and barely escaped execution herself.

Nero then hatched a plan to rid himself of his mother's smothering forever. Goaded on by Poppaea Sabina, his new mistress, he ordered his royal workers to build a boat with a breakaway section. The idea was to stage an accidental shipwreck whereby Agrippina would drown.

Things didn't go as planned. Agrippina survived the wreck and swam safely to shore. Her respite from her son's assassination attempts was brief, however, as armed guards soon showed up at her home to execute her. With the end of her life just minutes away, Agrippina opened her dress, bared her belly to the guards and commanded them to "Strike me here, in the womb that bore that monster."

Athaliah

There were two Athaliahs of antiquity. Both were vicious and bloodthirsty. The first Athaliah was the daughter of Jezebel, the legendary wife of Israel's King Ahab who instituted Baal as the official court god in place of Israel's Yahweh in the ninth century B.C.E.

Athaliah's reign as queen began in roughly 843 B.C.E. after the death of her husband, King Jehoram. After her husband and son died, she had everyone who might oppose her killed, including all her grandchildren. She then followed her mother's lead and introduced Baalism to her people, who were even less thrilled about it than the Israelites were. When she tried to enter the Israelites' temple, she was murdered by order of the high priest.

The story of the second Athaliah mirrors the first in so many details that its existence could be chalked up to a biblical transcription error. Four centuries later, this Athaliah became queen of Judah after her son died. She, too, insisted that her subjects worship Baal, in defiance of such folks like the prophet Elijah, whose railings against her exist to this day in the book bearing his name in the Old Testament.

The second Athaliah also protected her crown against the claims of any relatives by having all her grandsons killed. One managed to survive and mounted a rebellion against her. She was executed in 437 B.C.E.

Pheretima

Wife of Battus, king of Cyrene, and mother of Arcesilaus, the crown prince in line to the throne, Pheretima came into power in 624 B.C.E. when rebel forces assassinated her son. With the help of the king of Egypt, she wrested the kingdom away from her enemies and rounded up all the assassins. She planned to avenge her son's death by positioning the captured assassins around the city walls of Cyrene and crucifying them.

Most warmongers would stop here, but not Pheretima. She planned an additional surprise for her supposed assassins and decorated their crucifixion walls with the amputated breasts of their wives. Admittedly, she was aggrieved over her son's death. But even this was too much for her people.

According to legend, Pheretima met her justly deserved death in a way befitting her absolute cruelty. She was devoured by worms.

The Lemnians

Another female society much like the Amazons, you won't see much about the Lemnians, as there remains to this day significant doubt that they actually existed. According to legend, however, they lived for a brief time during the Bronze Age on the Greek island of Lemnos, put there by their husbands who couldn't stand their distinctive body odor. In an era where few people smelled that great, this is hard to believe, but that's the story.

Understandably highly irritated with men in general, the Lemnians plotted to kill every man on the island in one night, sparing only one—the father of Hypsiplyle, one of the Lemnian leaders. After the massacre, they then welcomed (in the biblical sense) the Argonauts, who visited the island during their quest for the Golden Fleece. They wanted the Argonauts to stay on the island, but, probably wisely, the sailors quickly boarded the *Argo* and resumed their quest.

Although the Argonauts departed in haste, they left a legacy. The children they fathered during their night of passion with the Lemnians repopulated the island following the massacre of its previous inhabitants.

Galla Placidia

The daughter of the Roman Emperor Theodosius the Great, Galla Placidia was born on the eve of Rome's downfall and was there to see its collapse. During the course of her life, she associated with some of the most notorious rulers of the time, both Roman and barbarian.

Placidia's whirlwind of a life kicked into high gear at age five when her father died. He left the throne to Flavius Honorius, her 11-year-old brother. Since Honorius was too young to rule, his guardians took actual control of the empire. Despite their efforts, the empire slowly disintegrated under their authority.

Rome was under attack from all angles, most notably by the Visigoth king Alaric. He managed to enter the city in 410 C.E., sacking it and kidnapping Placidia as part of his plunder. She was clearly a top prize, as she was then traded to Alaric's successor, Athaulf, whom she forcibly married in 414. After he was murdered, the Visigoths handed her back to the Romans.

Now back in her homeland, she was again forcibly married, this time to the Roman general Constantius. Despite rumors concerning what might be an incestuous relationship between Placidia and her brother, Honorius proclaimed her ruler of Rome in 421 C.E., naming Constantius her co-ruler.

When Constantius died, Placidia's brother exiled her to Constantinople and took her throne. Her son inherited the crown in 425, initiating Placidia's 15-year rule over the Western Roman Empire on his behalf.

After her son took over as Emperor Valentian III, Placidia turned her attention to her rebellious daughter, Honoria. She refused to let Honoria marry Attila the Hun, who had been threatening the empire for some time. But when Placidia died, Attila tried to claim Roman territory in Honoria's name; Rome refused to recognize the claim, and Attila invaded Gaul.

Helen of Troy

The most beautiful woman in an era full of them, Helen was the legendary Greek woman for whom a war was fought and a country lost. She's one of the best known of all the women of antiquity, thanks to her appearances in Homer's epic poems, the *Iliad* and the *Odyssey*.

According to legend, Helen was born to King Tyndareus of Sparta and his wife, Leda. But Homer asserted that she and her brother Pollux were actually the children of Zeus, who changed himself into a swan to impregnate Leda. (Morphing into a swan was nothing for a Greek god—anything to get the girl.)

Helen turned into a rare beauty at a very young age, which made her an object of desire among the young men of Sparta. But others wanted her as well, including the aging Theseus, the king of Athens, who wanted to have sex with a daughter of Zeus before he died. Theseus had Helen abducted and taken to Aphidna, a small city north of Athens, where she was placed under the protection of Theseus' mother, Aethra.

It's not known how long Helen remained at Aphidna, nor are the details of her relationship with Theseus clear, but we do know that he quickly tired of her once he accomplished his goal of sleeping with her. He left the now-pregnant Helen in search of his next conquest. Furious, Helen swore she would never again subject herself to such treatment by a man, and summoned her brothers to bring her back to Sparta. There, she gave birth to a daughter, Iphigeneia. Since Helen was still thought to be a virgin, she gave her daughter to her sister Clytemnestra (who was married) to raise.

A Woman's Place

Helen was not the only member of her family to figure prominently in the war between Greece and Troy. Her sister, Clytemnestra, was married to Agamemnon, who instigated the Trojan War. Her cousin, Penelope, was married to Ulysses, the king of Ithaca, who fought in the Trojan War (and, as you'll read later, has an interesting moment or two with Helen as well).

Competing for Her Hand

Although Helen had sworn off men, the men of Greece had other ideas. According to some accounts, her earthly father, Tyndareus, decided to find another husband for his daughter and invited seven suitors to Sparta whom he believed worthy of her hand—Achilles, Ajax, Diomedes, Menelaus, Patroclus, Teucer, and Ulysses—and told her to pick one. Other accounts describe a number of suitors arriving at Tyndareus' home on their own accord, driven by their desire to possess the gorgeous Helen.

Of all of her suitors, Helen appeared to be particularly taken with Ulysses, but the choice wasn't to be her own. Although the men were vying for her hand, in reality they were wooing Tyndareus. As Helen's earthly father, he would decide on a suitable husband for her.

For his part, Tyndareus was in a precarious position. The best and the brightest of Greece were in hot pursuit of his daughter. Choosing one of them, he feared, would cause the others to seek vengeance against him. Ulysses, with his fine tactician's mind, offered a solution in exchange for Helen's cousin Penelope, for whom he would happily settle. He suggested the suitors agree to stand behind whomever Tyndareus selected, and to be ready at any time to defend the favored bridegroom against any wrongdoing related to his marriage.

They all agreed, and Tyndareus quickly selected Menelaus, much to Helen's dismay. Although Menelaus had power and money, he was older than her other suitors and not much to look at.

Misery in Marriage

Helen's second marriage fared no better than her first. Menelaus, daunted by her beauty and fiery nature, had a hard time even approaching her and had to get drunk to do it. Not that Helen really cared. She had virtually no interest in her husband and thought it was dandy when he took up with other women. Although they rarely shared a bed, they did produce four children: Hermione, Aethiolas, Maraphius, and Pleisthenes. Some accounts add a fifth child, Nicostratus. While Menelaus' marriage was slipping away, his brother, Agamemnon (who happened to be married to Helen's sister Clytemnestra), was busily planning to go to war against Troy. Knowing the marital strife between his brother and sister-in-law, he set the stage for such action by plotting a royal ruse.

A Woman's Place

Another version of the Helen of Troy saga blames the goddess Aphrodite for starting the Trojan War. According to myth, Aphrodite promised to give Helen to Paris if he named the goddess as more beautiful than Hera and Athena, her fellow goddesses. Paris, of course, chose Aphrodite.

Agamemnon asked Menelaus to invite Paris, the son of King Priam of Troy, to come to Sparta for a visit. Menelaus welcomed the handsome young man, and without thinking much about it, presented Helen to him. It was a fait accompli. Helen immediately fell for the crown prince; he fell for her. They scurried away to Troy.

Now, Agamemnon had a reason to threaten war against Troy. He was avenging his poor brother's honor. Although attempts were made at negotiation, Helen flatly refused to restore her husband's standing and leave Troy. She was there, she said, because she wanted to be. That was all Agamemnon needed. He declared war.

Guilt and Blame

The Trojan War dragged on for ten long years. At times, Helen felt badly about being the cause of such strife, and she missed her home. Paris and his father, Priam, who loved Helen like his own daughter, comforted her as best they could.

But Helen lost her royal protection when Paris was killed. In the resulting tumult, Ulysses (the same Ulysses from her youth) mounted his final attack against Troy. It was the famous Trojan Horse, which Priam unwittingly allowed to be rolled into the city. Ulysses and his troops, who were hidden inside the horse, jumped out, took the city, and carried Helen away.

A Woman's Place

Although the details of Helen of Troy's life vary widely, there's no doubt concerning her childbearing abilities. In addition to the children she had by Menelaus, Helen also had four children by Paris—Bunomus, Aganus, Idaeus, and Helen. Some accounts even add a fifth, Corythus. The boys—Bunomus, Idaeus, Aganus, and Corythus—were killed when a roof fell on them during the siege of Troy. Although it's unclear what happened to the baby Helen, she may have been murdered by Hecuba, Paris' mother.

A Final Heartache

The accounts of what happened to Helen after the fall of Troy differ widely. One version has Menelaus transporting her back to his palace at Sparta after abandoning his plans to murder her. Supposedly, all it took was one look at Helen and her gorgeous body for him to forgive her for her indiscretions. Most accounts simply suggest that she lived out the remainder of her life in peace and comfort until the gods transported her to Elysium, the final resting place for Greek heroes and heroines.

A decidedly more romantic version has a weary and dispirited Helen returning to Menelaus'

Hear Me Roar

Certainly there is no cause to blame Trojans and well-grieved Achaeans if they endure lengthy hardships for such a woman. In her face she is amazingly like the immortal goddesses.

—Homer's thoughts about Helen of Troy, from the *Iliad*

palace at Sparta. Things were no better between them, and they both resumed their old habits. But Helen couldn't bear the thought of putting herself on the shelf just yet.

One day she decided to take a walk in a grotto she often visited in her youth. She met a beautiful young man there, who was more than willing to provide a few minutes of bliss to help erase the years of strife from her life.

After their tryst, she asked her young lover his name. When she heard it, she was handed the deepest regret of her life. The young man was Telemachus, the son of her cousin Penelope and her husband Ulysses. He could have been her son if things had gone differently with Ulysses, her only true love. Heartbroken, she left him in tears. He would be her last lover.

The Delicious Dido

Another epic figure of mythology—this time Roman—Dido is the legendary founder of Carthage who committed suicide when her torrid love affair with Aeneas went south.

The story of Dido has long been the subject of debate between mythographers and historians as two separate accounts exist of her. The best known is Virgil's, who apparently exercised some poetic license when writing the Aeneid by appropriating Dido's story and moving it from the eighth century B.C.E. to the twelfth century B.C.E. The tale of the real Dido, more properly called Elissa, has many similarities to the mythological one. Both deal with the founding of Carthage, but Virgil's version is far more dramatic.

According to the historical version, Dido was the daughter of the king of Tyre. Her brother, Pygmalion, was heir to the throne, but was too young to ascend to it when their father died. Until he was of age, Acerbas, the king's brother, ruled the kingdom. At some time during this period, Dido and Acerbas married.

By all accounts, Acerbas was a wealthy man and Pygmalion was jealous of him. When Pygmalion reached adulthood, he not only became king, but he also tried to grab Acerbas' money by having his uncle assassinated. Fortunately, Acerbas, who was suspicious of Pygmalion all along, had the foresight to hide his treasure. With the help of her friends and followers, Dido managed to find the secret cache. With Pygmalion's soldiers in hot pursuit, they then fled Tyre by boat.

Dido and the other refugees landed in a bay on the coast of Africa. When they came ashore, they spotted a place they believed would be ideal for a new settlement. As their leader, Dido struck an agreement with Hiarbas, the area's king. She offered to pay him for only as much land as a bull's hide would cover. Believing he had a great deal, Hiarbas agreed. Dido then cut the hide into small strips that, when stretched out, covered an immense area. She called it Byrsa, meaning hide of a bull. The area became the city of Carthage.

Virgil's account of Dido's life paints her as a friend of Aeneas. She fell in love with him when he visited her during his voyage. Although she adored him, the feeling wasn't mutual. His journey, ordained by the gods, was far more important. After living with Dido for some time in Carthage, he resumed his travels with little thought as to Dido's feelings. Her heart broken, she built a funeral pyre and burned herself to death.

The Least You Need to Know

➤ While some women came to power through husbands or sons, others used more nefarious methods to claw their way to the top.

➤ Many royal plotters and schemers paid for their behind-the-scenes politicking with their lives.

➤ Galla Placidia, the daughter of a Roman emperor, associated with some of the most notorious rulers of her time—often not by choice.

➤ Although most accounts blame Helen of Troy for causing the Trojan War, some ascribe that dubious honor to the goddess Aphrodite.

Part 2
The Dark and Middle Ages

The next period in our history of women begins with a dim era called the Dark Ages. Spanning some 400 to 500 years, it was a time of war, disease, corruption, and despair. For men and women alike, it was one of the worst times to be alive in all of human history.

However, better times did lie ahead. After none of the disastrous prophecies connected with the coming of the year 1000 came true (sound familiar?), Western civilization began moving forward once again. The next four hundred years are known as the Middle Ages, which ended as the Renaissance began in Italy and spread gradually to other countries, marking the beginning of the transition from the medieval world to the modern. Art, learning, and literature were rediscovered. There were fewer wars and far less disease. While peasants would never live as well as the higher classes, life got a lot better for everyone.

Chapter 7

A Day in the Life

In This Chapter

➤ The fall of the Roman Empire

➤ Fashion victims

➤ The king's rights

➤ Living the monastic life

Aristocrat or peasant—you were one or the other if you were a medieval woman.

The class consciousness that began in ancient times deepened significantly in the centuries that followed, dividing the population into a rigid hierarchy consisting of an upper class of aristocrats and royalty and a lower class of workers and peasants. Economic circumstances, legal rights, and living conditions were vastly different between the two.

For an aristocratic or high-class woman, there was privilege and chivalry and courtly love, or maybe a life of religious asceticism. For a peasant, there was the drudgery of field work or other lowly service and the knowledge that freedom was really another word for having nothing left to lose.

Civilization in Uproar

What made the beginning of the medieval period so bleak was the fall of the Roman Empire in 476 C.E. In the years following the empire's demise, the world it left behind crumbled. Trade routes dried up, hard currency became scarce, and organized government disappeared. Even the aqueducts, buildings, and roads that the emperors took such great pride in fell apart from disuse and neglect. Cities shrank and built walls to protect their parameters. People forgot many of the skills that had made the Roman world "civilized."

More than one historian has categorized the Dark Ages—the five centuries or so immediately following the fall of the Roman Empire—as one of the least productive in the history of human kind. All invention and innovation ground to a halt as people left behind such leisure pursuits as music and art to focus on the task at hand, which often simply meant surviving until the next day. It would be a number of centuries before certain trades, like bricklaying, became something other than a lost art.

Instead of advancing, civilization retreated during the Dark Ages. It was a less than lovely time to be alive regardless of your gender or social status.

Fighting for Their Lives

The years following the fall of the Roman Empire were a period of vast confusion and despair in every area that had been under Roman rule. People suffered through invasion after invasion as warring tribes fought over the riches of the now-lost Roman civilization. When one battle came to an end, another began.

A Woman's Place

The average life expectancy for women during the Dark and Middle Ages was 24. They were considered old if they reached the age of 30.

Populations once united under the Roman Empire were now alone and isolated, living in small villages or in tribes. Fights over land and power were common. Peasants huddled together in communal homes as protection from invasion by foreign powers or their own neighbors. Increasingly wary and fearful, they trusted only those closest to them. When it came time to marry, it was generally to someone from the same village or tribe.

As their isolation grew, communication with the outside world ground to a halt as no one spoke a common language. Local dialects were so incomprehensible that people living even a mile or two apart couldn't understand each other. People were afraid of strangers.

Floods and Famine

Everyday life posed significant problems for virtually everyone in the Dark Ages. Status was little if any protection from the disease and warfare that ran rampant during this period.

Even the weather seemed to conspire against the people of the Dark Ages. Extreme climatic changes brought about a series of extraordinary storms and floods. Such events may not have been catastrophes when the Roman Empire was in full swing, but they were big problems now as the empire's drainage system, like the rest of its crumbling infrastructure, was no longer fully functional. People drowned or died of exposure to the harsh elements. Crops and livestock perished, causing widespread famine.

A Woman's Place

Even during times when there was enough food, the average diet was far from balanced or complete. Women, in particular, often suffered from pernicious anemia caused by insufficient iron in their food. The anemia also made them vulnerable to a number of potentially fatal diseases. Coupled with the backbreaking work typical of the times (for peasants), and the lack of even rudimentary medical care (for all), such ailments caused women in the Dark Ages to die in astonishing numbers.

A Plague on Your House

Communal life offered protection to the peasants of the Dark Ages, but it also created substandard living conditions that became more dangerous than any thieves could be. Drinking contaminated water, living in filth, and breathing the fetid air in cramped quarters spread such devastating diseases as smallpox, diphtheria, influenza, and bubonic plague. As soon as one epidemic seemingly came to an end, another would rise up in its place.

No one was immune to the waves of illnesses that swept over Europe. Because people didn't understand what caused disease, they also didn't know how to contain or halt it. Those lucky enough to survive a round of pestilence often fell victim to other diseases like rickets, which weakened their bodies even further and put them at greater risk for getting sick during the next epidemic.

Preparing loved ones for burial became a sad facet of life for peasants and highborn women alike. If disease didn't cut life short, childbirth often did. Peasants might have been attended by midwives and aristocratic women by physicians, but mortality rates for mothers and their newborns were still extremely high. Children who lived through birth often died shortly thereafter.

A Woman's Place

Scourges like the plague continued well into the Middle Ages. The infamous Black Death of 1347 was a pandemic not seen since the sixth century. It was fueled by a deadly brew of three related diseases—bubonic plague, speticaemic plague, and pneumonic or pulmonary plague. In its most common bubonic form, a boil-like nodule, or bubo, formed in the victim's groin or armpit, along with dark blotches on the skin caused by internal hemorrhage. It caused three or four days of intolerable pain before the victim died.

Living conditions for people of higher classes, while somewhat less cramped, also afforded them little protection from the rampant disease and pestilence. Again, since so little was known about how sickness developed and spread, no one took issue when residences went without cleaning for months on end. Airing out the home was unthinkable—most castles didn't even have windows. Instead of taking measures to prevent vermin from entering the home, infested beds and other furniture were annually moved outside and beaten, usually in the spring.

A Woman's Place

Clothing color often indicated women's wealth and social position. Fine ladies generally wore brighter and richer colors such as scarlet, green, deep purple, and bright blue. Women of the working class wore more somber colors, such as dark blue or brown.

Fashion Disasters

Even the fashions worn by medieval women had the potential for spreading disease. In various forms, the soft flowing dresses of the Roman and Byzantine empires remained fashion basics for all classes. As time passed, however, they became nothing more than undergarments for the richer and more extravagant attire worn by women in higher classes.

Trains began as simple augmentation to the skirts of overdresses and grew longer as they became more fashionable. To balance the long sweep of a train, sleeves were also elongated until they swept the floor as well. Such expanses of fabric were impossible to keep clean. The dust, dirt, and other filth they collected did nothing to improve the conditions inside the home and more than likely contributed to the spread of disease and illness both inside and out.

This fashion excess prompted more than one ruler to pass sumptuary laws, legislation proscribing extravagant dress. Pope Gregory X banned women from wearing gowns with excessively long trains. In France, nobility were forbidden to own more than four garments. Unmarried women could own only one unless they were heiresses who had inherited castles.

Such efforts, however, often turned medieval apparel into even greater health risks. Lacking changes of clothes, most people wore the same thing day in and day out. Since clothing spent more time on the body than off it, there wasn't much opportunity to clean it. Medieval apparel became breeding grounds for fleas, lice, and other vermin that you don't want to know about. Skin diseases were rampant, especially among peasants. Aristocrats got them, too.

Nightclothes were virtually unheard of in medieval times. Unless they slept in the nude (some did) many people hit the sack wearing the same bug-infested shirts and shifts that they wore during the day. If the bed they slept on had just been deloused, it wouldn't stay that way for long.

Going for the Vote

In China, women suffered from health risks caused by one of the most onerous fashions in women's history—the binding of the feet. This tradition of mutilation began at the Chinese court around 900 C.E. Since the feet didn't stop growing after they were bound, the toes would curl under the foot, rendering them and the feet virtually useless. While crippling women in such a manner was thought to make them more attractive to men, women who underwent the procedure also suffered from circulatory problems, gangrene, and infections caused when their toenails cut into the undersides of their feet. Although the procedure originated in the Chinese court, it eventually became popular in all social classes.

Annual Baths

Common personal habits of the Dark and Middle Ages also afforded little protection against disease. Instead of bathing their entire bodies in water, women would wash their hands and eyes only and clean other body parts with various oils, removing them by scraping the skin with wooden sticks or small metal tools. They used cold water for this rudimentary bath, saving hot water for their annual bath.

During the Middle Ages, regular bathing became more popular, especially among the wealthy. Even in the Dark Ages, women of a certain size often bathed more often than their slender sisters did thanks to a popular medieval obesity cure that called for regular dunking in sea water. They followed this brine bath with a rubdown using cow dung dissolved in wine and a sit in a sauna-like enclosure to encourage profuse sweating. Another bath to "improve the circulation" capped off the routine.

Medieval women considered their hair an essential part of their beauty. The longer it was, the more beautiful they were. Bodies might go for months without bathing, but hair was washed more often—sometimes even weekly—to remove the buildup of oils and balms used in dressing it.

A Woman's Place

The infamous Lucretia Borgia (you'll read more about her in Chapter 12, "Infamy"), postponed a pre-nuptial trip to her fiancé's home to give her maids-in-waiting ample time to wash and style her hair.

Words for Women

Feudalism was the economic, political, and social organization of medieval Europe in which serfs worked the land and provided food to the manor in exchange for protection from feudal lords.

Highborn women often wore their long hair in intricate styles. It could take many hands and many hours to unplait the hair, wash it, and restyle it. Peasant women wore their hair more simply—often loose around their shoulders—but they still liked it long.

Medieval women continued to use the scented waxes and oils of ancient times to dress their hair and mask unpleasant odors. The wigs of yesterday, however, were nothing more than vague memories, transplanted by the passion for long, flowing locks. They used henna, saffron, calf's liver, or eggs to change the color of their hair. Superfluous hair on any part of the body was removed by rubbing the skin with a caustic substance called quicklime.

Life on the Fief

The majority of medieval women were peasants, or serfs, who worked the land as part of their family's duty to a feudal lord. As such, they were an integral part of *feudalism*—the reigning economic, political, and social organization of the day.

Feudalism evolved as a way to give the scattered villages and tribes caused by the fall of the Roman Empire some measure of order and protection. Peasant families worked on pieces of land—the feodum, or fief—that were owned by vassals or knights serving feudal lords. They turned over the first tenth of everything they grew or raised to the fiefdom. The peasants kept the rest, which they could sell if they had more than they needed. For their work, the feudal lord and his knights protected them from roving bands of thieves and foreign intruders.

In addition to provisioning the lord's house, serfs could be requisitioned for military service during attacks on the lord's holdings if additional assistance was necessary. During those times, the full responsibility for tending the fields and flocks fell to their wives and children. Women of the upper class had to be similarly prepared to manage the affairs of the fiefdom when their husbands rode off to war.

As you'll read more about in Chapter 8, "Medieval Rights," feudalism—especially in its earliest form—did little to advance women's rights. While both male and female peasants were legally free, they were actually little more than indentured servants to the vassals and lords, who effectively controlled every facet of their lives.

The legendary institution of chivalry, the mannerly way of treating women, which developed from feudal knighthood during the Middle Ages, primarily focused on higher-class women. While it espoused courtly love and such lofty ideals as protecting and cherishing the female sex, only a small portion of the female population actually benefited from such attention. Many historians believe that chivalry had a far greater influence on men and women in later periods than it had on medieval life.

Such barbaric practices as the *droit de seigneur* gave a feudal lord the right to deflower any of his female serfs. While parents could often pay a fine to exempt their daughters from what basically constituted legal rape, many young women still had to submit themselves to their lords prior to marriage.

If a knight's wife became widowed, the feudal lord could protect the fiefdom by commanding her to remarry, usually to a man he felt fit to inherit her dead husband's fief. In situations where an unmarried girl was left behind when a father or male guardian died, the lord had the authority to arrange the girl's marriage, again to ensure control over the fief.

Words for Women

The **droit de seigneur** (the lord's right) was established by King Ewen III of Scotland. It's also called the *jus prima noctis*, or law of the first night.

Marriage: Let's Make a Deal

As in ancient times, a woman's worth during the Dark and Middle Ages largely depended on the size of her dowry, and after that, on her abilities as wife and mother. Marriages were little more than agreements made by men to exchange their daughters and other female relatives for land and other property. They bore little resemblance to the institution as we know it today.

Marrying off their daughters was one of the easiest ways feudal lords could increase the amount of land and property in their control. Whether it was for a few acres or vast ancestral holdings, fathers and other male guardians arranged the marriages of their children and female relatives at the earliest possible age. In cases where the exchange of girl for land was especially propitious, it wasn't unusual to see a girl of 12 marry someone three or even four times her age. Nor was it considered scandalous.

Going for the Vote

Some societies gave women freer rein when it came to selecting a spouse. Although Viking women couldn't look for husbands on their own, they could reject any potential spouses their parents chose for them. If a girl went with the parental pick, the husband-to-be paid for the privilege of marrying her.

Islamic women had to consent to marriage and couldn't be offered as property to another man. Nor did they need their parents' approval to marry. Grooms, not brides, provided the marital dowry; in cases of divorce, the wife returned the dowry to her husband.

Arranged marriages were particularly prominent in noble families, again because they had the most to gain from it. The Catholic Church's age of consent for marriage was 12 for girls and 14 for boys, but they were often wed well before these ages, consummating the relationship as soon as they were biologically able to do so. Among royalty, property rights might be sewn up by marrying children as soon as they were able to talk.

From the sixth and seventh centuries on, women were portrayed as lascivious and able to lead good men astray. Until the eleventh century, polygamy was practiced and concubines were acceptable. Even priests married and had concubines. However, as men acquired wealth during the Middle Ages, they became very concerned about permanence and inheritance.

The Catholic Church and secular men of wealth and power tried to control the sexual activities of women. Church and state acted together to give the sacrament of marriage greater importance. The ceremony, now conducted in a church with a priest, became more elaborate as it also became more public. It took a long time to get people to change their ways, but by the eleventh century the push to make monogamous marriage permanent and indissoluble was successful. Although the exchange of property continued to be the most important aspect of marriage, it was now necessary to have the union blessed by a member of the clergy to make it legal.

Marital fidelity was rarely a problem as it—and monogamy—was backed by both the law and the church. The punishment for stepping outside of marital bounds were often severe for both involved parties. In the upper classes, where women often enjoyed more rights, their virtue might be protected by a chastity belt—a metal barrier that covered the genitalia, leaving only a small opening for bodily functions.

There was little place in feudal society for women who did not marry. About the only alternative was life in service to the church.

Married to the Church

Christianity, established by the Roman Emperor Constantine in 325 C.E. as the official religion of the Roman Empire, was one of the few elements of the vast civilization to survive its downfall.

Christianity competed with still popular pagan beliefs in its earliest days. Converts to the new faith found it difficult to part with their familiar pagan gods. Even Constantine prayed to the goddess Tyche when he christened Constantinople, the city he built in his own honor.

In time, however, the basic tenets of the Christian faith—redemption and the promise of a better life ahead—won out over paganism. Christian emperors began suppressing goddess worship in all forms in the fifth century C.E. The last temple devoted to such worship officially closed in 560 C.E.

Church leaders believed that Christianity could bring unity and peace to the former Roman Empire. Missionaries traveled great distances to introduce the faith to local rulers. Those who became believers—and there were many—saw to it that their subjects became Christians as well. As you'll learn later, a number of these people would lose their lives during the holy wars, or crusades, mounted by their lords—and sometimes their ladies—on behalf of the church.

Monasteries were established throughout Western Europe to house those who chose to dedicate their lives to the church. Over time, more than a dozen monastic orders developed. Some segregated the sexes. Others had branches for women as well as men. Many of these double monasteries, especially those in Anglo-Saxon England, were led by women.

A Woman's Place

Helena, Constantine's mother, may have been the driving force behind her son naming Christianity the official religion of the Roman Empire. She was a renowned conversion evangelist who tirelessly promoted the faith through conversion, building churches, and preserving sites associated with Jesus' life.

Living the Monastic Life

Monasteries and the other religious institutions that developed during this period—nunneries, convents, abbeys, and the like—gave women a viable alternative to the uncertainty and despair of feudal life. Joining a religious order did mean withdrawing from the secular world to a large extent, but it didn't mean being branded as an outcast. Instead, the women (and men) who chose the monastic life were widely respected for their dedication to serving the church and for their role in educating the illiterate, providing wise counsel, and tending to those in need.

Many women who joined religious orders were the daughters of upper-class parents who had limited prospects for making a good marriage. They were often members of large families and had a number of siblings preceding them, making their chances of inheriting land or having a decent dowry poor at best. Other women consciously made the decision to serve God, rather than to marry and serve a husband. Often these women had to fight the objections of their families—who wanted to marry them off advantageously—to answer their calling to be members of a religious community.

While certain aspects of church work may have resembled the same servitude they would have experienced in the secular world, the women who "married the church" (as their commitment to the faith was often described), actually led fuller and more satisfying lives inside their church homes than they would have in the outside world. They were respected for their dedication to the faith. They learned how to read and write—skills necessary for fulfilling their responsibilities as teachers and scribes. They developed their innate intelligence and gained a healthy self-image, something rarely seen in women of the day. Many became leaders of their institutions, which gave them immense power and authority within their order and, sometimes, even in the outside world.

Some of the most influential women of medieval times were affiliated with monasteries or received their training in them. You'll read more about them in Chapter 11, "Trailblazers."

A Woman's Place

As part of their daily lives, women and men in religious orders copied books and other documents for use in monastery schools. Their work saved hundreds of scholarly and scientific texts from being lost.

The Least You Need to Know

➤ Social standing largely dictated the lives of medieval women.

➤ As in ancient times, many women died young due to childbirth and disease.

➤ Men still traded their daughters and female relatives for land and property.

➤ Joining religious orders gave women with poor marriage prospects the chance to live rewarding lives.

Medieval Rights

Women of medieval times shared many things with their sisters of antiquity, including the rights they did—or in most cases didn't—enjoy. Many of the philosophies and beliefs governing a woman's inheritance, property, and personal rights were the legacy of previous civilizations. As such, they hadn't changed much over time.

Gender, class, and marital status continued to govern what women were allowed to do and how much control they could have over their lives. While higher-class women and the nobility could and often did wield a great deal of power and influence, subordination to male authority remained the order of the day for most.

Laws from the Ancients

The rights women did have during medieval times were largely shaped by two factors: ancient tribal customs and Judeo-Christian beliefs. Both influences gave men superiority over women for roughly the same reason.

As you read in Chapter 2, "Ancient Rights," the belief that woman was both inferior and evil—a true instrument of the devil—was a cornerstone of early Jewish beliefs. Although it doesn't appear that Jesus held these views, other influential men of the early Christian church clearly did. The writings of such early church leaders as Paul in the first century C.E. and Augustine in the fourth and fifth centuries left little doubt that women were to be considered as inferior beings and treated accordingly.

Thanks to such constrictive beliefs, the prevailing wisdom regarding the majority of the female population was that their limited intelligence and lack of good sense (both of which, of course, caused Adam's downfall) made it impossible for them to make good decisions on their own. Most of the common practices of medieval times prevented women from being able to even try.

Women were generally excluded from making any decisions that would affect either their own situations or impact the world around them. If they were unmarried, they had male guardians who controlled every aspect of their lives. If they were married, their husbands had the same role.

Women couldn't hold public office. Nor could they serve in the military or practice law, although they could at times appear in court to represent their husbands. As a rule, however, they couldn't give testimony unless another witness could support their evidence, or unless the case involved issues that were purely feminine. Nor could they serve as *oath-helpers* or jurors. Even in trials involving women, these roles were restricted to men.

For noble and high-class women, however, these were often restrictions in theory only. Money and education let these lucky ladies slip the boundaries of convention and enjoy greater freedoms than their lower-class sisters could in many areas. They could be judges and rulers, military leaders, and estate managers. Tongues might wag, but the special status and influence these women enjoyed protected them from most harm.

The rights of unmarried women were often less constricted than for those who were married, especially when it came to civil matters. In some regions, they could enter into contracts on their own, draw up wills, and even borrow money. Unlike their married sisters, they could appear in court in some areas, although they often were required to have a male guardian or relative appear with them.

Hear Me Roar

Let your women keep silence in the churches: for it is not permitted unto them to speak; but they are commanded to be under obedience, as also saith the law. And if they will learn any thing, let them ask their husbands at home: for it is a shame for women to speak in the church.

—First letter of Paul to the Corinthians, 14:34–5

Words for Women

Oath-helpers acted as witnesses in early courts. They also collected evidence for presentation to the court.

When it came to criminal matters, married and unmarried women had the same rights. They could press charges for rape and battery. However, if a woman conceived and had a child as a result of a rape, her case could be denied as it was then assumed that she was a willing participant. A woman could also press charges if her husband was murdered.

Where a woman lived also determined her rights. Legal regulations varied from country to country and even from district to district. In northern Europe, Germanic tribes like the Burgundians, the Lombards, and the Anglo-Saxons had a heavy-handed tradition of male authority in the family that put more constraints on what women were allowed to do.

In France, women were considered to be under the perpetual guardianship of their fathers or husbands. In some cases, even their sons were given guardianship, which sometimes put small boys in control over elderly women. In southern Europe, influenced by more liberal Roman beliefs, women enjoyed greater freedom in matters of inheritance, property, and guardianship.

Women living in more urbanized areas often enjoyed freer rights than did those living in the country. Since they were often active in trade—some even ran their own businesses as *femmes soles*—these women made an important contribution to the economy. Their ability to pad city coffers overruled the standard strictures of the time. While the laws that governed them were often put in place to protect their husbands in case they did anything foolish, they had the net affect of improving the status of the women that were bound by them.

A Woman's Place

A thirteenth-century Germanic law called the *Sachsenspiegel* required a wife to relinquish all of her property to her husband and to obey him in all matters.

Words for Women

Femmes soles—literally, "women alone"—was a medieval legal term used to describe women who carried on businesses independent from their husbands or other male family members.

Ensuring Obedience

Almost every medieval society had laws designed to ensure that wives remained obedient to their husbands. Many condoned physical abuse as an acceptable disciplinary measure as long as the woman wasn't killed or seriously maimed in the process. The legal code of Aardenburg in Flanders allowed men to beat their wives literally within an inch of their lives if they could nurse them back to health. Eleventh-century

Anglo-Saxon women caught in the act of adultery lost their noses and ears and had to forfeit all their property to their husbands.

Even the church approved beating as an acceptable way for a husband to correct his wife's behavior. It was so prevalent in medieval times that men who didn't manhandle their wives, or who allowed their wives to dominate them, risked similar punishment. It was only natural that some of the tougher cookies of the time took things into their own hands and gave their husbands a return wallop or two. If the authorities found out, both parties could be punished—the wife for whacking her husband, the husband for allowing himself to be whacked.

Property Rights

As in ancient times, a woman's most important possession in medieval times was her dowry. This was true of women in all classes, as every woman brought some assets—tangible and not—with her when she married.

The amount of control a woman could have over her dowry largely depended on her social status and where she lived. In some European countries, the dowry was added to the husband's estate and managed jointly by both parties. In others, men and women retained the rights over the property they had prior to the marriage. Only property acquired while they were wed was regarded as belonging to both of them.

In most cases, women couldn't sell or exchange her own property—even personal items like clothing or jewelry—without her husband's consent. She couldn't use the property as pawn or take out loans against it. In Brittany, the property of widows was confiscated after their husbands' deaths as women were thought too weak and empty-headed to be able to handle property matters.

Frankish law, however, introduced in the sixth century, limited a husband's rights to his wife's property. He could administer it, but he couldn't sell it. Nor could he control the dowry, or marriage portion, as it now was given to the bride instead of her parents or close relatives. Women could dispose of clothing and jewelry, commonly included in their dowries, as they wished.

Owning the Land

As you read in Chapter 7, "A Day in the Life," during the Dark and Middle Ages land was often organized into fiefs that were controlled by vassals, or knights. Originally, kings or lords granted fiefs to the knights to honor them for their military service. Later on, such service was provided in exchange for the fief.

Since women were banned from military service, they couldn't receive fiefs from lords. But they could inherit them if they were married to knights or born to a noble family. Among the higher classes and nobility, land continued to be a significant part of a woman's dowry.

Widows often received fiefs as their part of their dead husbands' property and were allowed to keep their land for the rest of their lives. If there were ruling powers attached to the fief, they were also allowed to assume these roles. When they died, the property was passed along to their children or to the husbands' relatives if there were no children.

A daughter's right to inherit a fief from her mother or father varied from country to country and wasn't uniformly recognized by any of them. In the countries that upheld the principle of *primogeniture,* a younger brother might usurp her inheritance even if she was the oldest of the children. Only if there were no brothers would she be guaranteed her inheritance. In some cases, the oldest daughter would receive the ancestral home while the land was divided among her siblings.

Words for Women

Primogeniture is the legal right for the first-born male to inherit.

The Salic Law, an early French penal code developed during the sixth century C.E., mandated that land and any buildings standing on it could only be inherited by sons. If there were no sons, a daughter might inherit, but as a rule, she could only inherit the parts of the property that her parents had acquired while they were married. Premarital property couldn't be passed on.

In their earliest form, these laws effectively kept women from occupying the French throne. As time passed, however, French laws restricting the daughter's right to inherit gradually eased, as evidenced by the large piece of southern France that Eleanor of Aquitaine (you'll read about her in Chapter 9, "Royal Warriors") inherited from her father in 1137. English laws also became less restrictive and allowed women to own and lease their own land and to represent themselves in matters pertaining to such ownership.

A woman's rights regarding her control of the fief also varied. In some countries, they were allowed to exercise full authority over their land. In others, they had to call the shots from behind the scenes.

A good number of women inherited fiefs from their husbands or families during the Middle Ages. The death rate for noble men was high. Fighting for their lords, marching off to crusades, defending their ladies' honor through duels and jousting—it all had a devastating affect on life expectancy for medieval men. Wives lost spouses, but they gained land.

Personal Rights

While the feudal system did put more land into the hands of women, it did little to advance their rights in other areas. The personal rights of both men and women of the peasant class were tightly controlled by the vassals and lords. When a lord died, his vassals usually inherited their fiefs free and clear. But the peasants remained under the vassal's control. When a peasant died, the vassal, who considered a peasant's family as his assets, retained control over them. In effect, they were indentured servants who could never work off their debt to their master.

As mentioned in Chapter 7, the *droit de seigneur* allowed feudal lords to take any of the female serfs under their control to bed. If a vassal tried to usurp the lord's authority by doing the deflowering himself, he could face substantial legal penalties. Kings had the same right and could impose the same punishment on anyone who challenged their shot at a young virgin.

A Woman's Place

The king's power to arrange the forced remarriage of wealthy widows didn't end until the passage of England's Magna Carta in 1215.

In England, feudal control extended right up to the king. He could force wealthy widows, who were placed under his protection when their husbands died, to remarry against their will. Not only did this rob them of their personal freedom, but it also put their children's inheritances at risk, as they would also be forced to turn over their land to their new husbands.

Some widows paid large fines to the crown to avoid having their bodies and wealth transferred to someone chosen for them by the king. Kings and feudal barons often reaped sizable income from the fines paid by heiresses and widows who wanted to purchase the right to marry as they chose—or not to marry, as the case may be.

The Particular Plight of Widows

Widows had it especially tough during the Dark and Middle Ages. Not only did they lose their spouses, but they also often lost control over their property and their destinies.

The dowry provided by a girl's family when she married became her widow's portion to inherit if her husband died before her. As previously mentioned, many women outlived their husbands, so the widow's portion became particularly important. Unfortunately, a widow was often left either extremely wealthy or impoverished. Either condition put her in peril.

If the widow's portion wasn't enough to support her, her last years might be spent in poverty unless she could remarry or find some other means of support. If she had a little money left, she might be able to live in a monastery for a small monthly fee. If she had large holdings, she often wasn't allowed to retain sole control of them for very long.

Virtually every medieval society had laws that placed widows in the protection of male guardians who would watch over their holdings. As previously mentioned, they were protected by the king in England, who could force them to remarry against their wishes. Saxon tribal law, prominent in northern Central Europe, placed widows in the custody of their brothers-in-law or other male relatives on their husband's side. Lombardian laws were more liberal. While widows still had to answer to male relatives on most matters, they were allowed to remarry someone of their own choice.

Although little documentation exists that reflects how widows felt about the control others had over them, we do know how their children felt about it. The noisy custom of the *charivari,* used today to embarrass the heck out of a couple on their wedding night, was originally developed as a mock celebration by the sons and daughters of medieval widows who wanted to protest their mothers' remarriages—and, presumably, their displeasure over possibly losing their own inheritances.

Words for Women

The noisy and raucous **charivari** was a fourteenth-century invention designed to express displeasure when a widow remarried. It was usually staged at the woman's home by her children on her wedding night. Bachelors, envious of those who were embarking on a second marriage while they were still single, sometimes joined in as well.

The Least You Need to Know

➤ Ancient philosophies and beliefs largely shaped women's rights during the Dark and Middle Ages.

➤ Laws governing inheritance varied from country to country and often weren't evenly enforced.

➤ Even in countries where primogeniture wasn't practiced, the estates left to girls rarely matched those that boys received.

➤ Widows and girls left fatherless could be forced by male guardians to marry against their will.

Chapter 9

Royal Warriors

In This Chapter

➤ Defenders of country and faith

➤ Good King Tamara

➤ The queen's gold

A good number of royal women during the Dark and Middle Ages followed the precedents set by their ancient ancestors and advanced both kingdoms and personal agendas through their intelligence, cunning, and bravery. Their actions not only shaped their immediate circumstances, but they also helped set the course for important political developments to come.

Ironically, while these women often wielded great public power, they generally didn't have much control over their personal lives. Like women in lower classes, these queens and regents were considered as property—highly prized, of course—and their greatest worth to their families was in securing land deals and insuring the future of the kingdom. But the majority of them rose beyond chattel status and ruled as well, if not better, than their male counterparts did.

Defender of the Faithful: Queen Bathilde

The daughter of royal *Anglo-Saxons,* the beautiful seventh-century French Queen Bathilde also possessed a generous heart, an innate intelligence, and a humble spirit. These were saintly qualities for a woman who would become one.

Words for Women

Anglo-Saxon describes the people of two Germanic groups—the Angles and the Saxons—who lived in England before the Norman Conquest in 1066.

The record of Bathilde's life begins with her serving the wife of Erchinoald, the mayor of the palace of Neustria, that land that comprised the western part of Francia, or Frankland (roughly modern day France). According to many sources, Bathilde had been abducted from her family and taken there as a slave. Erchinoald bought her in about 641.

Bathilde's intelligence and virtues didn't escape Erchinoald's notice, and he gave her control over many areas of his household. When his wife died, he wanted to marry her.

Bathilde wanted no part of this and fled, staying away from Erchinoald until he married again. She then returned to her employment in Erchinoald's home, where she met Clovis II, the son of the great Frankish king Clovis I. Greatly impressed with her beauty and grace, he bought her freedom from Erchinoald and married her.

Clovis II wasn't in good health. Some accounts portray him as mentally ill, which might be why Bathilde had such tremendous influence during her husband's reign. Among other things, she controlled his court when he was incapable of doing so and determined how charity money would be allocated.

Clovis II died in 657, leaving Bathilde with three sons—Lothair, Theoderic, and Childeric. Lothair, the oldest of the three, was named king under the regency of his mother.

While serving as regent, Bathilde carried out a number of reforms. Chief among them was the ban on the sale of Christian slaves. Her other work had a charitable focus as well. She helped found a number of charitable and religious institutions, such as hospitals and monasteries. She also tried to unite Francia, the largest of the successor states to the western Roman Empire which had been partitioned and reunited numerous times. Along with her advisors, she arranged to absorb Burgundy, in south Francia, and installed her son Childeric as prince of Austrasia in northern Francia. Although she made few missteps as a ruler, Bathilde's great desire was to enter religious life. She had always been close to the Church and was deeply involved with the new discipline of monasticism. Her responsibilities as regent kept her from realizing this goal until her sons were of age. Once they were old enough and had firmly established themselves in their respective territories, Bathilde left the court and withdrew to her favorite Abbey of Chelles near Paris, which she had helped found.

Bathilde renounced her royal status when she entered the abbey and found great joy in serving the poor and infirm. She continued her humble service in the abbey for another 15 years until her death in 680 C.E. She was buried in the Abbey of Chelles and was canonized by Pope Nicholas I.

Eleanor of Aquitaine

Under French feudal law, women could inherit their family's holdings if there were no male heirs. The most renowned woman to benefit by this law was Eleanor of Aquitaine.

The daughter of William of Aquitaine, a feudal baron, Eleanor was the prize catch of the medieval period. She had it all—looks, intelligence, and riches. In her case, the riches were the vast kingdom of Aquitaine—about a third of modern France—which she inherited from her father when he died.

This was fief land, under the ultimate control of the French king. With such a large area at stake, the pressure was high for Eleanor to make a marriage beneficial to the crown. Fortunately, Eleanor's father had arranged a match to keep his daughter from becoming a political pawn. In his last will, he stipulated that Eleanor would marry Louis, the son of King Louis VI and the heir to the French crown. The two wed in 1137 when Eleanor's father died. She was 15; Louis was 17. They would become king and queen soon after when Louis' father died.

While a grand merger, the marriage was no love match. Louis was pious and reserved, and he paid a little too much attention to his mother; Eleanor was full of life and sought excitement and adventure. She got her chance at both when she accompanied Louis when he joined the *Second Crusade* in 1145.

It was common for women to join their husbands on crusades, but Eleanor's involvement reflected a greater passion, primarily fueled by an inspiring speech she had heard by the great Cistercian cleric Bernard of Clairvaux. She did more than merely ride along on the two-year crusade; she pledged vassals from her own land in support of the effort and helped nurse the wounded.

Work on the crusade satisfied Eleanor's need for excitement and adventure, but Louis still wasn't fitting the bill. While still on crusade, she began to push for a divorce. Despite the best efforts of both church and state—in this case, the pope and Louis—she obtained an annulment of her marriage in 1152. Under French law, her vast estate remained her own property.

Eleanor then made another royal match, and the timing on it suggested that she had been planning it during her first marriage. Just two months after she received her annulment, she wed Henry Plantagenet, the heir to the English throne.

Words for Women

Crusades were military expeditions launched by the Catholic Church during the eleventh, twelfth, and thirteenth centuries, with the goal of recovering the Holy Land from the Moslems.

A Woman's Place

A number of strong women worked to preserve their families' power and kingdoms during medieval times by ruling as regents on behalf of their sons or brothers until they were old enough to succeed to the crown. Among them were Margaret (or Margrethe) of Denmark, who married Haakon VI of Norway when she was just 10 and ruled over both countries on behalf of her young son Olaf after her father died in 1375 and her husband in 1380.

Margaret of Anjou, the French wife of King Henry VI of England, worked tirelessly to ensure her son Edward's succession to the throne after the king was declared mentally unfit to rule. During the War of the Roses, which pitted the House of Lancaster (King Henry's family) against the House of York (his relatives), she raised troops to fight the Yorkists on Edward's behalf. Her efforts, however, were thwarted as she was disliked by the English and too aggressive in her approach. The throne instead went to another Edward, the son of Richard of York.

Anne of France, the oldest daughter of Louis XI, served as regent after his death. Her most difficult task was preserving her father's kingdom by making peace with all the people he had alienated during his rule. With her husband's help, and some fancy political maneuvering, she was able to do so until her brother, Charles VIII, was old enough to ascend to the throne.

There was a significant age difference between Henry and Eleanor—she was older by 11 years—and Henry's somewhat coarse manner was far from the refinement that Eleanor had experienced with Louis. Her latest marriage turned out to be as disharmonious as the first, especially when the two started fighting over Rosamund Clifford, Henry's mistress. Tired of Henry's philandering, Eleanor left Henry and Rosamund to their fun and retired to her estate, where she maintained a lavish court largely supported by the "queen's gold," a special tax she was allowed to collect from Henry's subjects when he inherited the throne in 1154.

Eleanor had been unable to bear male heirs for Louis, but she gave Henry five of them. Two of her sons—Richard and John—went on to be kings. In 1173, Eleanor backed her sons' efforts to overthrow the unfaithful Henry. Henry, furious with her disloyalty, imprisoned her. Although he pardoned his sons, he kept Eleanor locked up for 15 years while he attempted to divorce her and gain full claim to Aquitaine. Eleanor successfully fended off his efforts while in prison.

Henry died in 1189. Richard—called Richard the Lionhearted when he was king in recognition of his bravery—became king and immediately freed his mother. When he left for the Third Crusade, Eleanor managed England's affairs in his absence, at one point putting down a rebellion against the throne by her son John. Weak, mean-spirited, and cruel—the opposite of Richard in almost every way—he was called John Lackland or John Softsword when he ascended to the throne after Richard's death in 1199.

A skilled and cunning politician throughout her entire life, Eleanor not only negotiated Richard's release when he was captured during the crusade, but she also made peace between Richard and John afterward. She remained involved in affairs of state until her death in 1204.

Eleanor's great beauty and intellect fueled some of the most famous ballads sung by medieval troubadours. She was a strong influence on the culture of the era and helped shape or found a number of the period's educational and religious institutions, including Fontrevault, the joint monastery which became one of Europe's leading houses of religion as well as her place of retirement. Eleanor was also something of a fashion plate and was the first to adopt the medieval fashion of dresses with long trains and flowing sleeves.

A Woman's Place

By retaining control over her ancestral lands, Eleanor was able to safeguard the privileges of the people who lived on them. In 1199, she upheld laws that allowed peasants the right to freely choose their daughters' marital partners and removed regulations forcing the daughters and widows of peasants to remarry spouses chosen for them by the feudal lords.

A Woman's Place

Eleanor remained fiery to the end. Her signature on her last public document read "Eleanor, by the wrath of God, Queen of England."

Tamara of Georgia

As queen of the Empire of Georgia during the thirteenth century, Tamara's brilliance as a statesman and military strategist guided her country to the height of its power.

During the course of her 24-year reign, she overcame both foreign aggressions and rebellions led by her ex-husband, riding into battle against Turks, Persians, Armenians, and Russians so aggressively that her troops addressed her as "King Tamara."

Tamara's daughter Rusudani, who ruled over Georgia after the death of her brother, Giorgi IV, showed a similar passion for battle. Her troops also referred to her as king, not queen.

A Woman's Place

Georgia, which borders the Black Sea, became an important trade destination during Tamara's rule. Her efforts to build her country's economy and culture led to her being named a saint by the Georgian Church.

Words for Women

Castile is a former kingdom of central Spain.

Blanche of Castile

Before she died, Eleanor of Aquitaine traveled to Spain to visit her daughter, also named Eleanor, who had married Alfonso VIII of *Castile*. While there, she also arranged a cease-fire (temporarily, anyway) between England and France by finding a suitable wife for the future French king.

Her choice was Blanca, the daughter of Alfonso VIII and Queen Eleanor. Although raised in one of the less-civilized areas of Spain (years of attack by various forces had stalled the area's cultural and economic development), Blanca had received a more worldly education than was common at the time for royals, thanks to the knights and troubadours who frequented her father's court.

This may have made Blanca more willing to leave her native country for uncharted waters—not that she had much say in the matter. Like so many royals, hers was an arranged marriage, a political contract more than anything else. While the hope was that she would find her intended husband a suitable match, it really didn't matter that much.

Blanca accompanied her grandmother on the rest of her journey and married the future King Louis VIII on May 23, 1200. Both were only 12 at the time, but their match proved a good one. Unlike many royal couplings of this nature, they were happy together and well-suited to each other.

As the queen of France, Blanca, now called Blanche, displayed much of the same spirit and intelligence as her grandmother did. In fact, she came to be known as the wisest of all women of her time. When Louis died during a crusade in 1226, Blanche became regent for her son, the future King Louis IX, who was still a young child. The French nobility and the King of England immediately challenged her authority, one of many noble conflicts she was to battle in the years to come. She succeeded in suppressing all of them until Louis came of age.

A Woman's Place

If it seems like many of the families in this chapter were related in some manner, your perception is correct. There were many advantages to royals marrying royals, and trying to untangle the genealogy charts of the world's great ruling families is proof that such advantages were recognized early on. Medieval parents were experts at arranging marriages for political and familial gain, and the unions that took place during this period in history established some of the most powerful alliances in Europe. Eleanor of Aquitaine and King Henry II had three daughters, in addition to their five sons, and married each of them to royalty: Eleanor to Alfonso of Castile, Matilda to Henry of Saxony, and Joan to William of Sicily. Isabella of Castile and Ferdinand of Aragon did the same when they married their four daughters to members of Europe's leading dynastic families: Catherine (you'll read more about her in Chapter 15, "Early Modern Rulers") to the English heir Arthur (she also married Arthur's brother Henry when Arthur died), Juana to Philip of Hapsburg, and Isabel to Manuel, king of Portugal. Their fourth daughter, Maria, also married Manuel after Isabel died.

When Louis IX rode off to the Crusades, he honored his mother's wisdom by choosing her over his wife to rule the country in his absence.

Isabella of Castile

The future marital alliance of another Spanish royal, Isabella, would form one of the largest and most powerful empires in Europe.

Isabella was the only daughter of King John II of Castile. Born during his second marriage, she had a younger brother, Alfonso, and a half brother, Henry. When John II died, Henry IV sent Isabella and her family packing.

Although Henry was only Isabella's half brother, by law he had a fair amount of control over whom she would marry. The two bickered for some time over her prospects, with Henry arguing for a man he had already chosen for her. But Isabella was determined to make her own decision. In fact, she had already made it.

Without Henry's knowledge or permission, Isabella met a number of times with Ferdinand, her second cousin. He was under similar pressure to make a match that pleased his family, but he, too, didn't agree with their choices. While their personalities weren't well matched, they shared a similar devotion to the Catholic Church. They also knew their marriage would have great political potential. She was in line to inherit Castile; he was the heir to *Aragon*.

The two finally got their way and wed in 1469. Henry died ten years later, but the throne didn't immediately go to Isabella. There was another contender, Henry's daughter, who was believed to be illegitimate. But Isabella's claim to the throne was stronger, and she had the combined influence of Castile and Aragon propelling her to it. She seized the treasury and proclaimed herself queen. She then rallied the support of her nobles and solidified her power by promising to restore order to the kingdom.

Words for Women

Located in the northeastern region of Spain, **Aragon** was a separate kingdom during medieval times.

Isabella and Ferdinand maintained separate authority over the land they each brought to the marriage. Together they ruled Spain, which became the largest kingdom in Europe after their marriage.

Isabella proved to be a capable and ambitious ruler. While some of her actions, such as her support of the Spanish Inquisition, have not held up well over time, she is still regarded as the most influential Spanish queen of all thanks to efforts to advance her country's fortunes and her support of education, religion, and the arts.

While admirable, her efforts in these areas pale in comparison to the decision that made her famous: underwriting Christopher Columbus' quest to find a passage to the Far East and India.

Queen Jadwiga

Called the "peace queen," Jadwiga of Poland was one of a number of royal women who were devout Christians and who used their positions and influence to help spread Christianity throughout Europe during the Middle Ages.

Going for the Vote

Christianity was brought to Russia in the early tenth century by Olga, the widow of Prince Igor, when she converted to the Greek Orthodox faith. She later became the first Russian saint of the Orthodox church.

The daughter of Louis d'Anjou, the king of Hungary and Poland, Jadwiga was betrothed at age four to Duke William of Hapsburg. She ascended to the Polish throne after the death of her father in 1384. Hungary went to her sister, Maria, who became that country's queen.

Jadwiga was then pressured by nobles who wished to unite the countries of Poland and neighboring Lithuania to forego her commitment to Duke William and instead marry Jagiello, the Lithuanian king. As part of the bargain, Jagiello, who was a pagan, had to agree to convert to Christianity and make Lithuania a Christian country. Duke William was given a large sum of money for agreeing to the plan. The union between pagan and Christian took place in 1386. Jagiello took the Christian name of Wladyslaw (or Ladislaus) II and honored his commitment to bring Christianity to Lithuania by building a Catholic cathedral on land that once held a priceless stand of ancient oak trees.

Jadwiga and Wladyslaw, who was 20 years older than she, ruled together for 13 years. Their union marked the beginning of the renowned Jagiellian dynasty, noted as one of the greatest eras of Polish history. Sadly, Jadwiga died in childbirth in 1399 when she was just 28. To this day, she is revered as one of the great rulers and saints of Polish history. 28.

A Woman's Place

In addition to her work on behalf of the Church, Jadwiga was a noted patron of the arts and supported the work of many artists, musicians, and scholars. She also helped establish the University of Krakow.

The Least You Need to Know

➤ Royal marriages during the medieval period were often arranged to merge noble interests or quell battles between countries.

➤ Love wasn't a requisite for royal couplings. Most of these marriages lacked this element.

➤ Parents or other advisors arranged most royal marriages. Rarely did the involved parties have much control over whom they married.

➤ Even though they often had little control over most aspects of their lives, many royal women were able to make the best of their situations by advancing their own agendas and making life better for those around them.

Chapter 10

The Working Life

In This Chapter

➤ Saying hello to bye work

➤ Serving the rich

➤ Working in the big city

➤ The rise of guilds

Women of all classes worked—and worked hard—during medieval times. In the Dark Ages, the main focus of their efforts was keeping the people and the animals of the fief alive and well. Whether they were peasants working in the field or ladies managing feudal estates, women played an important role in the feudal economy. In times of war, they assumed even greater responsibilities for keeping the home fires burning when their husbands were called away from the fief and into battle.

Trade and commerce, which had greatly decreased during the turmoil of the Dark Ages, were reestablished during the Middle Ages. As both expanded, women played an even more essential economic role. They worked in cities and towns, on farms and fiefs, primarily driven, as they had been in ancient times, by economic necessity. If they were single, they needed to earn a living. If married, they were expected to supplement the household income by working as assistants to their husbands in their trades, or by taking part-time jobs such as spinning or brewing, either in the home or away from it.

Working the Fiefs

Throughout the Dark and Middle Ages, the majority of women lived and worked as peasants on medieval fiefs.

These women were expected to share equally in their husbands' workloads, which meant spending many backbreaking hours in fields and pastures. There was no pay involved in any of this work for men or women, and none expected, just the right to remain on the land and under the protection of the feudal lord.

In the field, there was little division of labor between men and women of the fief. The idea was to get the work done; it mattered little who actually did it. Women sowed, reaped, threshed, raked, and winnowed the fields. They sheared sheep and milked cows. About the only field work women were sometimes exempt from was plowing, which involved the use of implements often too heavy for them to easily employ.

In addition to their work in the fields, they also had a full regimen of chores related to keeping house. They fed the chickens, hauled water from the well, churned butter and cheese, and grew vegetables in the home garden. They cooked, cleaned, spun, wove, and made clothes. They even helped build their homes, usually small, simple structures made of timber and stone.

A Woman's Place

Demographic records show that at least 90 percent of European women lived in rural communities until the beginning of the nineteenth century.

Bye Industries

In the later Dark Ages and early Middle Ages, many peasant women living on fiefs began supplementing the family income by doing craft work either at home or in workshops called *gynaecea* that were established and overseen by feudal landlords.

Also called bye industries, such work generally fell into two main categories: activities related to textiles and clothing and those connected to the production or sale of food and drink.

When women began moving to medieval towns and cities in the later Middle Ages, they often took these "cottage industries" with them and continued working at them in their new homes.

While men were generally encouraged to choose one profession and make it the focus of their efforts, it

Words for Women

Gynaecea (singular, gynae-ceum), were rooms for women to work and live in.

wasn't uncommon to find women working busily away at two or even three *bye industries* in addition to their other chores.

Early Enterprise

Thanks to the expansion of trade, demand for textiles was huge. Most peasant women worked in this area, providing cloth to their feudal lords and for sale to others. Over time, textile production became one of the chief occupations for women in England, the Netherlands, northern France, and Italy. The "piecework" they did at home or in the gynaecea eventually evolved into one of Europe's first commercial enterprises.

As was the case in ancient times, women worked in virtually all aspects of textile production, beginning with combing, carding, and spinning the raw fibers and ending with woven cloth and finished articles made from it. By about the middle of the eleventh century, however, when business leaders decided to organize bye work into more commercialized enterprises, men were hired and trained to do most of the weaving and dyeing. Women confined their weaving to the fabrics they'd use in the home.

Spinning, however, either on a drop spindle or the newly invented spinning wheel, remained almost entirely the province of women. Since it took five spinners to keep one weaver supplied, there was plenty of work to go around. Lacemaking also became almost exclusively a women-only enterprise. Women liked it as, like spinning, it was hand work that could be done while attending to other chores around the house. By the sixteenth century, lacemaking had become a regional specialty in France, Belgium, and northern Italy.

Words for Women

Bye industries, in which women produced cloth or food and sold it for extra money, were the equivalent of part-time jobs in the Middle Ages.

A Woman's Place

For some reason, spinning was almost always done by single women. Maybe they had more time for it than their married sisters did. In any case, it provided so many of them with a livelihood that people began using the term "spinster" to describe an unmarried woman. In the Middle Ages, it didn't carry the negative connotation that it does today.

Nursing and Healing

Such occupations as midwifery also remained almost exclusively women's work during the Dark Ages. By the Middle Ages, however, women wishing to work in the healing profession could seek broader employment.

While their numbers were by no means large, records show that some women were able to receive the training necessary to allow them to work as physicians, surgeons, barber-surgeons, and apothecaries (pharmacists). Eight women doctors appear on Paris tax roles dating from the late thirteenth century. Similar records from Germany, Italy, and England show women working as surgeons, performing such activities as bloodletting, amputation of limbs, and abortions. The renowned twelfth-century German abbess, Hildegard of Bingen, whom you'll read more about in Chapter 11, "Trailblazers," clearly had some medical training and wrote extensively on medical issues during medieval times.

Gaining the requisite training for working as a physician, apothecary or surgeon was no easy accomplishment. Men fought hard to keep the practice of medicine to themselves, often forming guilds (more about them later) or other protective societies that controlled who could practice and under what conditions.

By design, the rules and regulations of these guilds often excluded women from medical professions. For example, a university education was deemed necessary for working as a physician. Since universities in Christian Europe didn't accept women as students, their abilities to become physicians were limited. As you'll read more about later in this chapter, apprenticeship was another way in which women could gain the requisite training to allow them to work as surgeons and apothecaries.

Going for the Vote

About the only country in which women were allowed to study during the Middle Ages was Italy, which had remained more intellectually active than other parts of Europe due to its ties to the Moslem world. There are records of Moslem and Christian women working side by side in Italian universities. Women professors and doctors taught in a number of cities in the Moslem world, including Bagdad, Cairo, Constantinople, Cordova, and Toledo.

Another way women could enter the world of medicine was by continuing the work of their deceased husbands or fathers, which some guilds allowed them to do. According to city records from Frankfort in the fourteenth century, the daughter of the city physician took over his practice after he died. Several payments to her from the city council reflect that she treated mercenary soldiers. Other women simply called themselves healers and practiced medicine without any formal training.

As was the case in earlier times, even women who had full medical training and credentials were generally restricted to working on patients of their own sex. Tradition and morality prohibited the examination of women patients by male doctors, and vice versa. Women's health was still women's business.

Midwifery became increasingly more professional as the demand for midwives swelled. To meet the health care needs of their citizens, a number of cities employed both physicians and midwives. Some municipalities even paid the midwives regular salaries and exempted them from paying taxes. In other cities, midwives had to charge their patients for their services, which often meant that the poorest citizens were denied medical care or received inferior treatment.

To help curb abuses, city councils began to regulate midwifery by passing written codes that specified the qualifications for midwives and the conditions they had to meet to practice their profession. By the late Middle Ages, most cities in Europe had such regulations. They specified the training and qualifications that midwives were required to have. They also made midwives moral gatekeepers by requiring them to report all illegitimate births and all suspicious infant deaths.

Urban Workers

By the Middle Ages, the fief was no longer the center of the universe for medieval society. It was still important for agricultural production, but inefficient for large-scale craft production. As the demand for nonagricultural products grew, a number of nonagrarian urban areas sprang up. In time, they served as centers for the expanding craft industries.

Developing towns like Cologne, Venice, Naples, Paris, and London offered new environments for both men and women in which to work and live, and they moved to these areas in droves.

A Woman's Place

The *Livre des Métiers*, or *Book of Crafts*, written by a royal judge named Etienne Boileau in the latter half of the thirteenth century, contains a list of 100 occupations practiced in Paris at the time. Women worked in 86 of them, including some occupations that were exclusively female, such as silk spinning, making hats and purses, and other trades related to the manufacture of clothing.

Some women moved with their families to towns like these and many others that developed during this period. Others, especially the young daughters of peasants, came by themselves in search of a different (and better) life than what living in the country as a serf could offer. After working in town for a year, they could even earn their freedom and end their obligation to their fief lord.

These women made substantial contributions to the economies of medieval towns. Workers were in high demand, and most of the available jobs weren't restricted to men. If a woman was unskilled, as many were when they first came off the fief, she could work as a washerwomen, bathhouse attendant, gatekeeper, or in other professions that didn't require an education. More skilled women worked as shopkeepers or managed hotels and taverns. Many women rented out homes or made and sold food in markets and fairs. Some continued the tradition of the bye industries and did piecework for the textile industries.

A Woman's Place

Tax records from fourteenth-century London show that women comprised 4 percent of the town's taxpayers.

Living the Domestic Life

A number of young girls who immigrated to the cities replaced the families they left behind by taking jobs as domestic maids or servants in the homes of the rich. Such jobs were extremely plentiful, both in the towns and in rural areas. But they didn't carry much status—in fact, servants comprised the lowest of the urban labor classes. This kept the wages paid to servants low and made it possible for families with even middling incomes to afford hired help, both in towns and in the country.

It's estimated that more than half of the young women who worked in medieval towns did so in the service of wealthy families. These were by no means cushy jobs, regardless of their setting. Servant girls rose at the crack of dawn and worked well into the evening hours to do their mistresses' bidding. In the towns, their work was often confined to such household tasks as cleaning and straightening, cooking, setting tables, and washing clothes and dishes. Servants working on country estates would often see their duties expanded to include gardening and tending the household's domestic animals, such as chickens and goats.

A Woman's Place

Domestic service remained the leading area of employment for European women well into the twentieth century.

Alewives

Working as a brewer, or alewife, was a common practice for women in Western and Central Europe. This trade grew out of the area of bye industries that dealt with the preparation and sale of food. As in ancient times, beer was an extremely popular beverage. Since it was still closely linked to making bread (also a woman's job), it continued to be something women could do without much interference or questions about it being an appropriate job.

Brewing was closely related to house and property rights, which meant that women wanting to ply this particular trade had to first establish themselves as house or land owners. Once they did, they could ask the town council for a brewing permit—and pay a big price for the privilege. As they comprised a large portion of the town's budget, the fees for such permits could be steep.

Female brewers were often widows who had inherited their homes and land from their husbands. It was a trade that virtually guaranteed a solid income for them and their families, as beer was in strong demand almost everywhere. Brewing, in fact, was so profitable that the wills of brewers would stipulate in great detail who would inherit the specific elements of the brewing apparatus—the vessels, vats, and the brewing house itself.

Because it was so profitable, brewing became a guild trade in many areas, especially if beer was being produced for export. As was the case in a number of other guild professions, women could continue to work in the trade after a guild was formed but only in certain positions, generally as assistants to their male relatives who were the guild members.

Guild Workers

Guilds began in the twelfth and thirteenth centuries as casual associations that brought together women and men who lived near each other and worked in the same crafts or trades. By the late Middle Ages, they had evolved into formal organizations that served many purposes. They trained apprentices and regulated trade and industry. They established standards of quality and set prices.

A Woman's Place

Brewing was one of several trades practiced by the fourteenth-century autobiographer and mystic Margery Kempe (more about her in Chapter 11). She used the money she made to buy better dresses than what she would have ordinarily been able to afford. She also used her brewing profits to help pay her husband's business debts.

Words for Women

Guilds, or gilds, joined together people who worked in the same trade or craft for mutual economic, social, and religious benefit. They were the first formal organizations to protect the interests of skilled workers.

Guilds were also important social institutions. Medieval families celebrated birthdays and marriages with other guild members. They also turned to the guild for comfort and support—both emotional and financial—in times of distress. Guilds looked after the families of sick or deceased members, providing burial money and other financial assistance. But they were more than economic organizations. They participated in religious processions and feast days and had political clout—membership in a guild was often a prerequisite for voting.

There's no denying that guilds played an important role in protecting their members against competition and the loss of livelihood. But as far as most women were concerned, the primary function of the guild was to limit their access to the more highly skilled professions of the medieval period.

Women had no trouble gaining employment in professions deemed too low in status for guild organization. Jobs as domestic servants, shopkeepers, midwives, even as prostitutes—none were considered skilled labor, and as such, they were never organized into guilds.

More skilled crafts and trades—even in the textile industry, which had been the province of women for centuries—eventually came under the control of men who had the power and authority to make them into profitable industries. Merchant guilds were the first to be developed. Craft guilds soon followed. By the fourteenth century, most urban trades were organized and represented by guilds. The majority of them prohibited women from full membership, relegating them to second-class status.

A Woman's Place

Women who worked in low-status, low-paid jobs could have formed guilds, but as a rule they didn't. They may have resisted guild formation because they liked things as they were. There wasn't much regulation or organization in these professions, which suited the temperament of many who chose them. They may also have resisted since they knew that once a guild was organized, domination by men soon followed.

Boys' Clubs

Guilds were membership organizations. Because men had developed them for the most part, they also called the shots on who could be members and the rights those members would have. Some guilds were completely closed to women. Others permitted women members but gave them fewer privileges than their male counterparts received.

Some trade guilds, especially those in the textile trades, awarded apprenticeships to a very small number of young women. The training they received rarely matched that given to male apprentices. More often than not, the master's wife, instead of the master himself, took on the responsibility for training them.

The female students might actually get a better education from the master's wife, but it would still be considered inferior to the training their male counterparts received from the master. In fact, when the young women finished their training, they rarely moved on to the next rung of the guild ladder. Instead of becoming fully independent journeywomen, they often remained with their masters, working in unofficial servitude until they married.

A Woman's Place

Although most guilds were organized and run by men, not all were. In Paris, the high social status of the women working in the silk manufacturing trade afforded them the ability to form guilds in this industry. Organized along the same lines as male-dominated guilds, these organizations allowed their members similar privileges. They could take on and train apprentices and employ whomever they chose, including their own children. Most of these guilds, which flourished during the fifteenth century, were women-only organizations. Men were allowed to join just one—a guild that represented small spindle silk spinners.

If the female students were lucky, they married a guild member. If they did, they often obtained many of the privileges denied them in their unmarried state. As the wives of guild masters, they could work with their husbands and could sometimes even be granted membership as a "sister" of their husband.

Men rarely opposed extending guild privileges and membership to their wives as doing so still gave them control over what women members in general were allowed to do and the rights they were given. For the most part, the men appreciated the help their wives could give them. It was far better, and easier, to keep the family's trade in the family than it was to take on apprentices and train them.

Very few women achieved guild membership based on their own status and skills. But they often got it when their husbands died. Some guilds would allow membership to transfer to the widows of members so they could carry on the work of their deceased spouses. These widows were often given the most extensive guild privileges women could have. They were allowed to take on apprentices and journeymen and could supervise their own workshops. They could participate in most social and religious celebrations but were banned from taking part in any aspect of guild politics.

Unfortunately, the guild could also control their personal lives. Widows wishing to remarry were strongly encouraged to pick someone within the guild, as outside marriages could erode the guild's power and authority. If they insisted on marrying someone outside of the fold, they could lose their guild memberships and their workshops—two important assets that they would rather pass along to their children. If they chose the life of "chaste widowhood" espoused by the Church, the guild could alter how they ran their businesses by requiring them to hire journeymen as assistants. It's impossible to know how many women were coerced into living compromised lives thanks to guild strictures, but many clearly did. A less-than-satisfactory personal life was still far better than losing precious status and property.

The Least You Need to Know

➤ Many crafts that were once the province of women became important commercial enterprises in the later Middle Ages.

➤ The growth of cities and trade gave women broader employment options.

➤ While guilds protected the rights of workers, they also limited women's access to most of the better professions.

➤ Widows who received guild membership and privileges when their husbands died were discouraged from marrying outside of the guild as doing so could weaken the guild's power.

Trailblazers

Being a ground-breaker or a trailblazer—truly being first at something—is a distinction few can claim. Frankly, the women in this chapter probably can't claim it either. As far as we know, they were the first to do the things we give them credit for. But we don't know for sure.

What we do know is that these women were in a class by themselves when they were alive. They were cultured and well educated in an era when women generally weren't. They were artists, mystics, and scholars. They left behind an important body of work that shows us what they thought and felt and what their lives were like. Maybe that's all it takes to blaze a trail.

Royal Historian: Anna Comnena

Hoping to save the deeds and character of her famous father from historical oblivion, Anna Comnena wrote what remains to this day one of the most important documents in Medieval Greek history.

This highborn daughter of the Byzantine Emperor Alexius Comnenus was born late in her parents' life. She was much loved by her father, who saw to it that his intelligent daughter had an education befitting her talents. Her studies ranged from the work of classical authors to military affairs. She also knew history and medicine, which would help her in her future pursuits.

A Woman's Place

Anna's knowledge of medicine was put to good use when the First Crusade came to Constantinople in 1096. She ran the city's hospital of 10,000 beds that her father had built some years earlier and worked as a physician at a time when most women weren't permitted to do so. She also wrote a book on gout.

Words for Women

Troubadours were poets and minstrels who lived in Provence, Catalonia, southern France, and northern Italy in the eleventh, twelfth, and thirteenth centuries. They wrote poems of courtly love—the "gay science," as it was called—and acts of chivalry.

Anna was promised in marriage at age eight to Constantine Ducas, then the heir apparent to the throne. Presumably, her future as a Byzantine royal was assured. Then came the completely unexpected birth of her brother John in 1091. His arrival displaced Constantine's position as heir. Constantine died in 1094 when Anna was just 11, before they could be married.

When she was 14, Anna married Nicephorus Bryennius. She spent a good deal of her time trying to convince her father to make her husband heir apparent in place of her brother John. She continued her efforts even after her father died in 1118, but to no avail. John ascended to the throne. Unless he died young and without children, Anna had no chance of ever becoming queen.

She had every right to be angry with her father, but she instead channeled any feelings of resentment she might have had into penning a masterful book, the *Alexiad,* which documented her father's reign.

Alexiad is much prized by scholars and students of medieval Greek history, both for its great detail about Alexius Comnenus and for Anna's similarly detailed accounts of the Byzantine world.

Female Troubadour: Marie de France

Since *troubadours* came from knightly ranks, most were men, but Marie de France (so called because she once wrote about herself that her name was Marie and she came from France) was regarded as one, thanks to her lyrical voice and her gift for storytelling.

Most likely the illegitimate daughter of an English nobleman, Marie became a fixture in the English court of Henry II as a minstrel at a fairly young age. An accomplished poet, she took contemporary stories of love and honor and turned them into romantic poems set to music.

Lais, a collection of songs based on ancient Celtic legends, is Marie de France's best-known work. While the stories were not original, her treatment of them was. She showed strong talent for bringing the stock characters of these oft-repeated stories to life. She also was gifted at creating realistic portrayals of relationships between men and women. Through her imagery, she encouraged women to take the first step in lovemaking, a responsibility she felt should be shared equally between the sexes. Unlike that of many authors and artists of the time, Marie's work became popular while she was still alive and was translated into a number of languages, including English, French, Italian, and German.

The First Novelist

The credit for writing the first work of fiction belongs to a woman of medieval Japan. Although her true name is no longer known, we do know her as Murasaki Shikibu, a pen name probably derived from the name of the principle heroine in her book.

Murasaki Shikibu was a member of the noble Fujiwara family. Her branch of the large family was literary and included a number of well-known poets. Her father was a provincial governor and a learned man. When he discovered his daughter's interest in literature, he saw to it that she received an education similar to her brother, which was somewhat unusual for the time.

Shikibu lived at home in Kyoto until she was 27. She then married a long-time suitor, Fujiwara Nobutaka, a distant cousin 20 years her senior. He was already married—in fact, he had a number of wives, concubines, and children. Why she consented to the marriage is unclear, but it appears that her husband might have helped advance her work by proudly reading aloud her letters to him.

The two were married just three years before Nobutaka died. Their daughter, born a year before Nobutaka's death, would follow in Shikibu's footsteps and become a respected poet.

Shikibu fielded many offers for remarriage before she decided to devote her life to literature. It was a propitious decision—she was a member of a prominent feminine literary society that was renowned for its famous members. Her membership in this esteemed group helped her gain the imperial court's notice, and she was asked to become a lady-in-waiting.

She used the events around her as inspiration for *The Tale of Genji,* the book she began writing when she was about 35. Originally meant to be read aloud, it presents the adventures of a prince named Genji in grand style, spanning three quarters of a century in 54 chapters containing more than 1,000 pages.

Although its form is vastly different from modern novels, it's the first written work to resemble this literary form. Some found its personal detail too provocative and revealing. Others loved its intricate stories that pitted good against evil, with good coming out on top.

Visionary, Saint, and Scientist: St. Hildegard of Bingen

A renaissance woman hundreds of years before the era began, it is impossible to describe the *Benedictine* nun Hildegard of Bingen as anything other than truly remarkable. Possessing one of the greatest minds of her time, Hildegard's talent ranged far beyond her vocation in the church. She was a renowned scientist, composer, mystical theologian, and playwright. She also advised popes and kings and wrote visionary works and scientific treatises, among her many accomplishments.

Born in 1098 to aristocratic parents in Bokelheim, Germany, Hildegard realized her future vocation at a young age. She began seeing visions as early as five, and at age eight was sent to live with a mystic named Jutta. Here she was taught reading, writing, and Latin.

Hildegard became a nun when she turned 15 and later became the leader of the small religious community when her teacher Jutta, who founded the community, died in 1136. Some 10 years later, Hildegard started an independent Benedictine monastery—St. Rupert—at Bingen and served as abbess of the monastery. She would spend her remaining life in service to the church in various capacities and would earn the sobriquet "the Sibyl of the Rhine" for her legendary visions.

Words for Women

Benedictines are members of the monastic order founded in the fifth century based on the teaching of Saint Benedict. Although its numbers are greatly diminished, the order exists to this day.

Hildegard, who believed that God commanded her to write what she saw and heard, was a prolific author and spent a good amount of her time working on texts on subjects ranging from medicine to morality. Her greatest visionary work, *Scivias* (short for *Scito vias Domini,* or *Know the Ways of the Lord*), begins with her visions related to the Creation (where she perceives the Creator as a woman) and ends with an accounting of what might happen on Judgment Day. In 1148, she was verified as a divinely inspired prophet by an ecclesiastical commission.

Hildegard's other works include books on the Gospels and the Benedictine Order. She also wrote close to 100 musical pieces, including hymns, funeral dirges, and the first European opera. Much of her work has survived and is performed and recorded to this day.

Throughout her adult life, Hildegard was intimately involved in Church politics. She helped organize support for the Second Crusade and called for women to take more responsibility in the Church to help abate the wealth and corruption that she felt was the result of its masculine leadership. She advised no less than four popes, two emperors, both King Henry II of England and Eleanor of Aquitaine, and Bernard of Clairvaux.

A Woman's Place

Among Hildegard of Bingen's many written works are two scientific treatises related to medicine. In *Causae et Curae (Cause and Cure)*, she analyzes the causes and treatment of 47 diseases, including diabetes, ailments of the circulatory system, and gynecological problems. In *Physica*, she details numerous types of animals and rocks, and gives medical uses for some 300 varieties of herbs.

Feminist: Christine de Pizan

France's first woman of letters and history's first professional female writer and feminist, Christine de Pizan had the courage and intelligence necessary to mount an eloquent argument against one of society's prevailing beliefs regarding women. Most people during the Middle Ages—well, men, anyway—held that women were inferior to men. Some thought them downright evil. Christine begged to differ.

An Italian by birth, Christine moved to Paris with her family at age four when her father was engaged as the astrologer for the court of Charles V. Although she grew up in a scholarly environment and was obviously intelligent, she received no formal education.

Christine married a young notary named Etienne de Castel when she was 15. They had a happy and successful marriage, which unfortunately came to an early end when Etienne died of the plague 10 years later. Just 25 at the time of his death, Christine was left with the responsibility of supporting three children, her mother, and a niece.

Christine decided she'd support her family by writing. She set about learning how by reading just about anything she can get her hands on. Soon she was putting her own words onto paper in the form of love ballads. People enjoyed her work, but this was just the beginning. She branched out and wrote prose histories, allegories, and instructional texts. She also wrote manuscripts on military strategy, international law, and the political problems of France.

Hear Me Roar

There is not the slightest doubt that women belong to the people of God and the human race as well as men, and are not another species or dissimilar race, for which they should be excluded from moral teachings.

—Christine de Pizan, *The Book of the City of Ladies*, 1405

She also proves to be a champion of women. Her *Book of the City of Ladies* is the first history of women by either sex. In another work, *Letter to the God of Love,* she sparked a heated debate over the treatment of women in Jean de Meung's popular poem "The Romance of the Rose." The arrows slung between de Pizan and de Meung constituted one of the great literary debates of the time.

Other noted works by Christine de Pizan include *Le Debat de deux amans,* a debate between two lovers about love; *Le Livre dudit de Poissy,* a recap of a trip she made to a Dominican convent; and *Le Livre de la Mutacion de Fortune* (*The Book of the Changes of Fortune*), a work containing more than 23,000 verses that took her 3 years to complete.

Autobiographer: Margery Kempe

One of the better contemporary accounts of life in the later Middle Ages exists today in the autobiography of Margery Kempe. (What makes Margery's account unique is that it is written by an ordinary middle-class woman.)

The daughter of John Brunham, the mayor of King's Lynn in Norfolk, Margery married a well-known merchant named John Kempe and proceeded to have fourteen children by him. Unfulfilled by her role as wife and mother and wanting to wear finer clothing than her budget allowed, she also worked outside of the home.

A Woman's Place

Margery's financial independence also put her in good stead to pay off her husband's debts, which she agreed to do in return for his agreeing to join her in vows of chastity necessary for the pilgrimages Margery wanted to make. Before she left for her first trip, she had her parish priest make a public announcement from the pulpit that she would personally settle all claims against her spouse.

The specific details of Margery's work life vary. Some sources have her working alongside her husband, whose family were millers and brewers. In others, she runs a brewery and a mill independent of her husband.

A Woman's Place

Margery Kempe was one of two English mystics of the late Middle Ages. The mystic known as Julian of Norwich also put her visions on paper, hoping to encourage a more inclusive religious attitude than what was prevalent at the time. Her description of God the father and the mother and her comparison of God's love to that of a mother helped fuel later attempts to admit women to the clergy.

In her later years, Margery became something of a mystic, visions and all. This caused some people to accuse her of heresy, but her husband remained by her side and even traveled with her on several pilgrimages. In all, she visited Europe, the Holy Land, and other areas of England. On one of her last journeys, she dictated her memoirs to a priest. This account of her life was lost for many years but finally emerged in 1934 as *The Book of Margery Kempe*. It contains descriptions of her travels and her life, as well as details on her divinely inspired visions.

The Least You Need to Know

➤ In her effort to pen a tribute to her father, Anna Comnena wrote one of the best documentaries of the Byzantine Empire.

➤ Divine visions fueled the writing of Hildegard of Bingen, Margery Kempe, and Julian of Norwich.

➤ Although not a feminist per se, Christine de Pizan was one of the greatest champions of women in the late Middle Ages.

➤ Affairs at court provided Murasaki Shikibu material for writing the first novel.

Infamy

Unlike the plotters and schemers you read about in Chapter 6, "Notorious Women," the ladies here gained their infamy through actions that made them a little suspect … and sometimes more than a little! In some cases, their efforts were righteous but misunderstood. Like Jessica Rabbit, they weren't necessarily naughty. They just seemed that way. In others, they were bad girls through and through.

Lady Godiva

If you grew up in the 1960s, you probably knew of Lady Godiva through popular song lyrics—"Seventeen, a beauty queen …" She was all of that, and she obviously wasn't ashamed of it. Nor was she afraid to use her beauty to get what she wanted.

The famous naked rider of Anglo-Saxon England, Lady Godiva (also known as Godgifa) was the wife of Earl Leofric of Mercia. She asked her husband to lighten the taxes paid by the people of Coventry. He said he'd do it if she would ride naked through the marketplace. He figured she wouldn't, so his income was assured.

But the comely Lady Godiva called his bluff. She made her infamous ride covered only by her long hair. The earl made good on his promise.

Joan of Arc

A simple peasant girl led to glory by the voices only she could hear, Joan of Arc remains one of the foremost military heroes of French history.

The future kingmaker was born around 1412 in the village of Domremy in the French province of Lorraine. Her father was a plowman; her mother, a housewife dedicated to family and God.

In her early teens, Joan claimed to hear the voice of God, which told her she had been chosen to do great things. A few years later, she said she was hearing the voices of Saint Michael, Saint Margaret, and Saint Catherine. They were all telling her to come to the assistance of the *dauphin,* Charles of France, the son of the French king who was being kept from the throne as a result of France's ongoing battles with England.

Words for Women

Dauphin was a title used from 1349 to 1830 by the oldest sons of kings. It was originally given as a proper name in noble families living in the province of Dauphine.

The English had, by then, managed to occupy a good part of northeastern France, including the town of Reims, which was the traditional site for royal coronations. If the siege of Orléans, located on the southern edge of the area occupied by the English, was halted, the French army could possibly march to Reims and reclaim it, thereby permitting a proper coronation. It was a daunting task by any measure, but Joan's voices told her she was the girl who could do it.

Fulfilling Her Destiny

Joan decided to go to the dauphin and explain what she had been commanded to do. For protection, she cut her hair short and donned men's clothing. She made her way to the northernmost town still under French control. There, she asked the commander of the French troops for permission to see the dauphin. Joan was a small thing, and her new haircut made her look even younger than she was. The commander saw her as a silly young girl—maybe even a witch!—and sent her back home.

Joan returned the following year. This time, she managed to convince the commander that her motives were true and in everyone's best interest. She was allowed to travel to the royal castle and was given six soldiers to protect her journey. When Joan finally got her audience with Charles, things didn't go as she thought they would. He, too, thought she was a witch at best and a heretic at worst—at least at first. As she explained her divinely inspired plan to restore him to the throne, his skepticism faded. Still, he insisted that she undergo several weeks of intense questioning to make sure she was not a heretic. So assured, he equipped Joan with the necessary arms and troops—including two of her brothers—and sent them on their way.

Joan and her troops marched to Orleans. Although they met strong resistance there and were outnumbered by enemy forces, Joan and her group entered the city in triumph a week later and secured it for the crown. Joan returned to Charles to tell him the good news and to escort him to Reims for his coronation. First, however, she insured Charles' safe trip by returning to the battlefield and liberating a few more cities.

Fall from Grace

Joan's victory on behalf of the dauphin proved to be her greatest one. She continued to fight the English and took many towns from their control. But the greatest prize—the return of Paris to French control—eluded her. In May 1430, while attempting to free more land in the area from English control, she was captured by rebel Burgundy troops and sold to the English. Joan was tried for heresy and witchcraft in a church court in Rouen. She maintained her innocence through five months of interrogation, harassment, and browbeating. Joan's persecutors, who tried their best to get Joan to admit to heresy or some other evil, fell far short of their goal. But they had to do something to get such a rabble-rouser out of their midst. They condemned Joan for the dubious crime of wearing men's clothing. For this, she was burned at the stake in late May 1431.

Charles, now the king of France, did nothing to help Joan during her trial and execution. However, when the French recaptured Rouen some 20 years later and seized the records of her trial, he ordered a new trial, this time in a secular setting. In 1456, Joan's name was cleared when the previous verdict was overturned. She was canonized by the Catholic Church in 1920.

A Woman's Place

Medieval witches practiced healing by magic, made effigies to use when casting spells, and used their knowledge of herbalism to make love potions and other concoctions.

Be Witched

Joan of Arc wasn't a witch, but her uncommon beliefs and actions were suspicious, and that was enough for medieval people to make the next jump and ascribe such a description to her.

There were witches during the Dark and Middle Ages just as there were in previous eras. Magic, or witchcraft, was a facet of many ancient and pagan beliefs. The people who practiced them naturally learned to cast spells or recite chants to cause good or harm.

The prosecution of people like Joan of Arc as witches began in the late Middle Ages and increased significantly during the *Reformation*. In fact, the greatest incidences of witch prosecution didn't take place until the sixteenth and seventeenth centuries. But the precedent for them was set during the Middle Ages with the publication of what was seen for the next two hundred years as the definitive guide to witch-hunting.

The Witches' Hammer

It figures that the handbook for hunting down witches was written by two German monks. First of all, they were men, and witchcraft was decidedly a gender-based practice. While there were some male witches, and some men accused of being them, the majority of people prosecuted as witches were women. And men did the prosecuting.

Second, they were representatives of the Church, an institution that had more to do with witch prosecutions than any other. Since witchcraft was a holdover from paganism, Church leaders felt it was necessary to eliminate it, along with all other vestiges of pagan worship, to ensure the success of the Church. In fact, Pope Innocent VIII had, just two years before the publication of the famous witch-hunting manual, published a papal *bull*, the *Summis desiderantes affectibus*, which detailed the Church's official stance on witches (they did exist) and dictated the measures to take (get them).

Malleus Maleficarum (*The Hammer of Witches*) was written by the aforementioned monks—Jakob Sprenger and Heinrich Kramer—in 1486. In it, they describe in great detail the proper procedures for identifying, trying, and burning witches at the stake, including …

➤ Using torture as an investigative tool (highly recommended).

➤ Stripping the suspect to search for the "devil's mark," supposedly left somewhere on the body when the suspected witch was seduced into evil by Satan.

➤ Poking and prodding various body parts to cause pain. Witches supposedly couldn't feel it and wouldn't weep when hurt.

➤ Throwing them into the water. A definitive sign of guilt was the ability to float. Since a woman's higher body fat percentage virtually ensured that she would, this was a particularly damning test.

Equipped with this handbook, witch-hunters prosecuted an estimated 100,000 people for witchcraft during the 200 years that followed its publication. About 60,000 were executed. An overwhelming majority of them were women.

Charges Against Witches

People suspected of practicing witchcraft could be charged with causing the deaths of people or animals, destroying harvests through storms, droughts, or floods, or making people and animals ill, sterile, or impotent. In fact, they could be the scapegoats for virtually anything bad that happened—business failures, other misfortunes, you name it. It was easy to point a finger at craggy old women or men who might behave a bit oddly and accuse them of casting a spell.

Having a particularly strong or mesmerizing personality could be enough to draw suspicion of witchcraft. Hearing voices, as Joan did, could definitely make someone suspect.

Sprenger and Kramer advised forcing confessions by offering amnesty to the accused but stressed that keeping such promises wasn't necessary. Since these offers were generally made after several rounds of torture and questioning anyway, confessions were often made without any promise of leniency.

More than anything else, witchcraft trials were a convenient way to do away with people who were suspect in some way or another, who didn't fit society's mold, or who were felt to be a threat to others in their actions or beliefs.

Prosecuting Midwives

Because midwives often kept the details of their practice very close to the vest, they also became a prime target for prosecution. It didn't help matters much that Sprenger and Kramer railed against midwives in their book, accusing them of all sorts of pacts with the devil and worse.

This not only made it difficult for midwives to practice their occupation, but it also denigrated the profession of midwifery in general and eroded peoples' confidence in it. Midwifery became more and more suspect as the witchcraft hysteria grew, and secular and nonsecular authorities alike sought ways to impose restrictions on its practice. This made it easier for male physicians to establish themselves as the medical experts and keep the practice of medicine to themselves.

Hear Me Roar

The woman has spells for getting a husband, spells for marriage, spells before the child is born, before the christening, after the christening ... Men, it is much marvel that ye lose not your wits for the monstrous witchcrafts that women practice on you.

—From a 1250 sermon preached by Berthold of Regensburg, where decrees regulating the work of midwives were passed in 1452

In a world with narrow boundaries, witchcraft hysteria easily spread. By the mid-1500s, few doubted its power or existence. Even if they did, they didn't talk about it as they could bring accusations of heresy on themselves if they showed any signs of allegiance with the devil. By 1700, more people had been prosecuted and put to death for witchcraft than at any other time in history.

Baddest of the Bad

One of the most infamous women of all time, the mere mention of Lucretia Borgia's name evokes images of wanton sexuality and easy morals.

The achingly beautiful Lucretia was the daughter of Pope Alexander VI and his mistress, Vannozza dei Catanei, who was, in fact, the daughter of another of the pope's mistresses. (Back then, chastity wasn't an absolute for a pope, although the Church preferred them to be chaste.)

Lucretia proved to be beautiful and brilliant. She was taught Tuscan, French, and Spanish, read classical Greek and Latin, and wrote beautiful poetry. She also showed herself to be her father's daughter when it came to sex. Whether she came by it naturally or had to be taught to be bad remains in question. But there's no denying that Lucretia had sex young, often, and in as many different ways as she could.

Her lascivious life began when she was married at age 13 to Giovanni Sforza, lord of Pesaro and a member of a powerful Milanese family. Lucretia's father made the match as part of a political settlement, one of several that involved Lucretia. He used her as a chess piece, moving her from one liaison to another when it was advantageous for him to do so. By all accounts, Lucretia was a willing participant, spending the time between her marriages getting to know the young men of Rome.

Lucretia's marriage to Sforza came to an abrupt end when Pope Alexander decided it was time to move his chess piece daughter again. He publicly denounced Sforza as impotent—a grave insult in Italy—and filed for Lucretia's divorce. Sforza furiously fled Rome and headed for Milan. Protected by distance, he in turn accused Alexander of something even worse—that the divorce was instigated by the pope's desire to have his daughter in his bed, not in someone else's.

This was a scandalous claim, but hardly a surprise to the Romans. Alexander's nefarious ways were legendary, and they'd been witness to his less-than-popely behavior and activities for years. Rumors like this had been floating since Lucretia was a little girl. What they didn't know was that Sforza's claim was true. Daughter and father were lovers and had been for some time. He wanted her back home.

Brotherly (?) Love

Now the Romans began to think the rumors they'd been hearing might be true. Then, another story surfaced that was even more shocking. It turned out that

Lucretia couldn't come home because she was involved in another relationship—with Juan and Cesare, her two brothers. It was whispered that she liked them both in bed. For their part, they both wanted their sister for themselves.

Soon after, Juan's corpse was discovered in the Tiber River. He'd been stabbed to death, cruelly mutilated by a dagger. Fingers immediately pointed to Cesare, who already had the reputation of a killer. The question of who had done it was never solved. While Cesare was an obvious suspect, Juan was known to have other enemies. Regardless of the outcome, Lucretia's tarnished reputation was then beyond redemption. The baby she had roughly nine months later added little to the public's scorn.

Living the Pious (?) Life

Lucretia had entered a convent when she found out she was pregnant, hoping to keep her condition away from public eyes. Of course, she brought one of her young lovers along. But her secret slipped out when her father, who had arranged for a ceremonial annulment of her marriage to Sforza, brought her to church for the ceremony. She was obviously pregnant, and the pronouncement by the church judges that she was intact—a virgin—sent wails of laughter throughout the building—and later, throughout Rome.

The baby boy, named Giovanni, was clearly illegitimate, but the question remained: Who was his father? Lucretia wasn't sure—it could have been her remaining brother or her father. For his part, the pope tried to legitimize the boy by passing two papal bulls. One identified the boy as the son of Cesare and an unnamed, unmarried woman. The other acknowledged the pope and the same anonymous woman as the parents.

Lucretia's actions in later life redeemed her slightly. After her second arranged marriage ended when Cesare killed that husband as well, she married Alfonso d'Este, the duke of Ferrara, and devoted her remaining years to the education of her son and to religious work. However, she died at age 39 of syphilis, never knowing whom she caught it from.

Clerical Scandal: Heloise and Abelard

The story of the passionate love affair between this brilliant student and her tutor overshadows the fact that she was also the most learned woman doctor in France during the twelfth century.

Heloise was born in 1101 in Paris and was schooled in the convent of Argenteuil, receiving an education far beyond what was common for the period. While she was studying at Argenteuil, her uncle Fulbert, a *canon* at Notre Dame of Paris, introduced her to Peter Abelard, a famous teacher of philosophy who had established his own school just outside of Paris.

In addition to teaching, Abelard was also a canon at Notre Dame and was pursuing a career in the church. He also had a roving eye, which had fallen on Heloise more than once. Wanting more than just pleasant eyefuls of the young girl, he asked Fulbert whether his young niece needed a tutor. Unaware of Abelard's ulterior motives, Fulbert said she did, as she was studying medicine, surgery, theology, and philosophy at the graduate level.

Words for Women

A **canon** is a clergy person on the staff of a cathedral.

Abelard became her tutor. Then he tried to become more. At first the young Heloise was shocked by her tutor's advances and tried to defend her honor. Then, flattered by the attention from such a learned and famous man, she yielded to him. They were soon embroiled in a passionate love affair that they hid behind the pretense of lessons, opening books and strewing papers about to show how hard they were "working."

The Heat Is On

Abelard hadn't planned on his relationship with Heloise being much more than a fling, but he soon became obsessed with her. Distracted and flustered, he was unable to concentrate on his teaching. All he could do was write sappy love songs, some of which later became troubadour ballads.

Abelard's students knew what was going on, but Uncle Fulbert refused to believe it until he came home at an odd hour and found the two in bed. Furious, he banned Abelard from his house and forbade Heloise to see him.

But Heloise and Abelard couldn't stay away from each other. And Heloise was now pregnant with Abelard's child. She wrote to him to give him the news, and the two made plans to elope. They waited until a night when Fulbert was out for the evening. Then, Heloise snuck away from the house and traveled to Brittany with Abelard, where they stayed with his sister. When their son Astrolabe was born, Abelard headed back to Paris, where he assured Fulbert he would marry Heloise.

Fulbert was less than pleased about the baby, and even less supportive of the marriage, although he agreed that it was the right thing to do. But Abelard faced bigger problems. While there were married canons and priests at the time, the church was beginning to frown on this practice and was moving toward banning it. Canonical law still allowed Abelard to take a wife because he wasn't ordained, but if he married, he couldn't teach. Having a wife could endanger Abelard's chances of climbing clerical ranks. The two agreed to keep the nuptials a secret.

Abelard probably should have consulted with Heloise before he even opened his mouth. When he returned to her, she informed him that she didn't want to get married, didn't want anything to do with the institution. In fact, she believed that marriage was designed to separate humans from their relationship to God.

This notion wouldn't work for Abelard, who was concerned about what would happen to both of them if word of the deception leaked out. Marriage was the only choice, he told Heloise. She agreed to it, but only if they kept the nuptials a secret, as originally planned.

The End of the Affair

Abelard and Heloise lived apart after their quickie Paris wedding. But word soon leaked out that the famous teacher had married his young pupil. In the interest of safety, Heloise returned to the convent at Argenteuil. But she continued to see Abelard. According to some accounts, they even made love in a dining hall dedicated to the Virgin Mary. Fulbert caught wind of these developments, but he didn't get the whole story. He thought Abelard had abandoned his niece, and he set out to avenge her honor. Late one night, he crept into Abelard's bedroom with a few of his friends and castrated him. It didn't take long for the story of what happened to the great teacher, and why it happened, to spread throughout Paris. Shamed, and with his life forever altered, Abelard entered the abbey of Saint-Denis and became a monk.

In the eyes of the Church, Heloise's offenses were far less onerous than Abelard's. She actually moved upward in the hierarchy of the convent, eventually becoming a prioress (head nun) at Argenteuil. At the same time, Abelard's fortunes were declining. Some of his more radical theological notions had raised the ire of Church leaders, who in 1121 forced him to renounce his work and sentenced him to prison for a short time. A year later, he left Saint-Denis and built a small chapel on a parcel of land that he had been given. He called it the *Paraclete*.

Although Abelard intended to withdraw from public life forever, his friends and former students pulled him back in. He worked for a time at a monastery in Brittany, which is where he heard word of Heloise's abbey being disbanded. In 1129, he contacted her and offered her Paraclete and the land surrounding it for a new convent. Heloise readily agreed to her former lover's offer and became the abbess of the new facility in 1131 after Pope Innocent II confirmed the convent's charter.

Hear Me Roar

The title of wife may seem more sacred and binding, but for me the title of friend will be ever sweeter, or, if you will permit me to say so, of mistress or whore ....

—Heloise, *Epistola II*

Words for Women

From the Greek word *parakletos*, meaning "advocate or intercessor," the term **Paraclete** is sometimes used in the Christian Church in reference to the Holy Spirit.

We know of Heloise and Abelard through their letters, of which there are many. Although they clearly could never have been lovers again, they expressed their affection for each other in correspondence that lasted from roughly 1128 until Abelard's death in 1142. Heloise lived for another 21 years and was buried beside him.

Virtually every account you'll read about Heloise gives great detail about her life with Abelard. Rarely is mention made of the fact that she was a brilliant scholar in her own right. She knew a number of languages and was widely read both in the classics and theology. She was renowned as a mathematician and for her knowledge of medicine. Often referred to as a second Hypatia, she taught medicine and practiced it later at Paraclete.

The Least You Need to Know

➤ Although not a witch, Joan of Arc's mystical ways led many people to think she was.

➤ The witchcraft prosecutions that began in the Middle Ages were launched by papal authority and fueled by the publication of *The Hammer of Witches*.

➤ Lucretia Borgia and her family set the standard for lascivious behavior in the late Middle Ages.

➤ An Hypatia of the Middle Ages, Heloise is best known for her affair with her older tutor.

Part 3

Rebirth and the Beginning of the Modern World

The Renaissance, which began near the end of the Middle Ages and continued into the sixteenth century, marked the rebirth of western civilization. Instead of moving backward, civilization could now move forward, and it did so in leaps and bounds. Learning, culture, the arts—all the long-lost passions—began to flourish. The ways of the lords and manors were cast aside by new governments run by kings and queens with greater and more centralized power than ever before. There were lots of changes during the sixteenth, seventeenth, and eighteenth centuries, which span some critical periods in world history: the tail end of the Renaissance, the Reformation, the discovery of the Americas, and a couple of revolutions—the American in 1776 and the French in 1789. This is also the period in which some women ventured forward into a really brave new world and set sail for the new freedoms and privileges across the Atlantic.

These centuries comprise what historians call the Early Modern period. It gave birth to our modern world.

Sigh...

Chapter 13

Daily Life

In This Chapter

➤ Courtly fashions

➤ Deadly beauty

➤ Life as a Beguine

➤ New opportunities in the New World

The circumstances of daily life for a woman at the beginning of the Early Modern period weren't much different from what they were at the end of the Middle Ages. As before, she was either a commoner or an aristocrat of some sort—either royal- or noble-born—and her status largely determined the life she would have. There still wasn't much in between—in fact, the class-consciousness of earlier eras had continued to evolve, causing even greater differences between the haves and have-nots.

But this was a time of great change. By the end of the eighteenth century, many aspects of daily life changed dramatically for women all over the world. Although most societies remained structured along rigid class lines, common women had greater opportunities to slip the bonds of their heritage than ever before.

Living the Common Life

If an Early Modern woman was a commoner—and chances were great that she would be—she'd be a member of the lowest class on the social ladder. She'd also have a lot of company there. This was still the largest group in the world's population, comprised of generations of people who could trace their heritage back to medieval serfs. As was the case for their ancestors, they were the laborers, the field-workers, the salt-of-the-earth folks who made the lives for those of better social status far easier and a great deal more comfortable.

A Woman's Place

Even wealthy women and members of royalty were expected to take an active role in the management of their homes. The Spaniard Juan Luis Vives, who wrote the *Instruction of a Christian Woman* for England's Queen Catherine of Aragon, said women of privilege should avoid idleness by retaining hands-on control over the management of their homes, no matter how many servants they had.

Words for Women

The **Victorian Era** is named after Queen Victoria, who ruled England from 1837 from 1901. It was characterized by middle-class values that defined respectability and often resulted in prudery and bigotry.

Even in this broad class, however, lives were defined by such factors as gender, age, wealth, and marital status. Where a woman lived was also fast becoming a defining factor. As the urbanized society that began developing during the late Middle Ages continued to expand, so, too, did the difference between life in the country and life in one of the new city centers.

Dedication to Home and Hearth

During the Early Modern period, a woman's life, regardless of her class, was still primarily organized around meeting the needs of the household and the family. Unlike women of the Middle Ages, however, what now constituted a home might be vastly different than before. Instead of a small hut in the country, it could be a room in a common house in a city like London, Venice, Paris, or any of a number of bustling burgs that were now developing.

City life was increasingly becoming an option for people during this period. The city held many attractions, especially for the young: more job opportunities, greater access to job training, and more chances to meet potential spouses. Most important, however, was the opportunity to earn a good living. As you'll read in Chapter 16, "Employment," working to supplement the household income was still a necessity for women during the Early Modern period. It would continue to be the norm until the beginning of the *Victorian Era*.

The opportunities cities offered outweighed the fact that the living conditions in them were usually abysmal. Most had developed in a haphazard fashion with little thought given to infrastructure or planning. Neighborhoods were crowded, with buildings of various sizes and purposes squeezed into extremely narrow quarters. There was no indoor plumbing of any type—getting rid of household waste consisted of little more than throwing it out the window into the street below.

Such squalid conditions meant that disease and death were rampant. Systems to meet the sanitary needs of growing populations had yet to be developed, which meant that death rates in the cities were far higher than in the country. Overcrowding and poor sanitation remained problems even in cities where deaths outnumbered births.

One-room dwellings were the standard for most working-class families, and those rooms were packed to overflowing. Families of this era were large and extended. Putting all family members in one room made privacy and cleanliness virtually impossible.

The State of Marriage

Because the center of the world for most women continued to be home and family, marriage also continued to be a top priority for women of the Early Modern period. As in past eras, it was almost unthinkable not to be married and certainly unthinkable to be single by choice.

As you'll read in Chapter 15, "Early Modern Rulers," even royal women like the fiery Elizabeth I and Sweden's Queen Christina couldn't escape the public's disapproval when they chose not to yield to convention and join up with a guy. As royals, they got away with it. But they, and a handful of women like them, were the exceptions to the rule. Most women, regardless of their status and class, were unwilling to endure society's wrath by deviating too far from the norm, regardless of how they actually felt about the institution.

What did change about marriage, however, was the relationship between man and wife. The traditions of yesteryear were still very much in place, with the sexes coming together for many of the same reasons they had in the Middle Ages. Marriages, especially among aristocrats and royalty, were still largely based on the exchange of land and property. (You'll read more about their legal basis in Chapter 14, "Defending Our Rights.")

But now marriage had a new and extremely important component—love. While it was always acceptable for couples to care for each other and be affectionate toward one another, the knights and troubadours of medieval times had made love into a lofty ideal. Since it was what they sought after, it couldn't possibly be a component of such a mundane institution as marriage. As chivalry faded away, love gained its rightful place as part of the marital bond. It was now acceptable for people to find compassion and happiness in their marriages—and to love one another.

What Women Are Wearing

Fashions during the Early Modern period reflected the changing times and became far more lavish than they had been in the past. While the most opulent fashions and fabrics were reserved for the men and women of the royal courts, people of all classes adopted the styles of the court in some way.

In general, fashion during this era defined the body. Bodices were tight—or at least they were until the eighteenth-century French Queen Marie Antoinette expressed her preference for a looser, flowing style—and emphasized a good bust line and a tiny waist. Corsets fashioned of fabric and wood created a good waistline if a woman lacked one of her own. To make the waist appear even narrower, the Spanish developed the farthingale, which encircled the lower body with a series of hoops in the shape of a cone. To accentuate the look, skirts were trimmed to just barely off the floor, which made women look like floating bells when they walked.

Words for Women

Stomachers were padded undergarments that resembled duck breasts. Because they artificially extended the length of the torso, women found it nearly impossible to sit down when wearing them.

A Woman's Place

The elaborate costuming of the Early Modern period, coupled with all the powdering and perfuming that went with it, could take as long as four hours, especially for those dressing for the royal court.

French dressmakers modified the farthingale into a roll of felt called a bourrelet. It had the same waist-narrowing effect as the farthingale but was supposed to make walking easier (it didn't). Another common dress style incorporated a *stomacher,* which eliminated the waist and bust completely but accentuated the hips.

Ruffs were another common aspect of fashion. Dating to the sixteenth century, they were insanely popular with both men and women and were widely altered and copied. Made of fine linen and often adorned with lace, they started small but soon became extremely wide. They were always stiff and were heavily starched so they'd keep their shape. Like stomachers, they were extremely uncomfortable to wear. Men gave them up first. Women stuck with the fashion longer, probably because some royalty still liked it.

For the French, especially during the reign of Louis XIV, it was impossible to dress too extravagantly. Elegant women added a third skirt to the two they already wore. Made of brocade, and often of gold, silver, or another metallic thread, this skirt was open in front so it could display the others and pulled back to the hips with knotted ribbons, pins, or buckles.

Another decidedly French fashion was the false beauty spot, which was applied to various parts of the face—cheeks, nostrils, even lips. They were fashionable, but they also served a purpose if applied to cover a blemish.

Hairstyles were also very grand, with each having its own name. They also changed continuously according to the whims of the hairdressers. One of the wildest fashions was the Mesmer, which was inspired by the work of a Doctor Mesmer. Of German origin, he claimed to be able to cure illnesses through hypnotism. The hairstyle that bore his name was very high and strewn throughout with small magnets and little figures of the men and women he had cured. Small hats often perched on top of the elaborate 'dos.

In the eighteenth century, after Louis XIV died, styles became much simpler, with little of the excess ornamentation that burdened the body in earlier years. They would become even more spartan during the French Revolution, when such things as silks and brocades were abolished altogether.

In the New World, styles were considerably simpler. Both necessity and choice defined what men and women wore in the new settlements. There was little room on the ships for finery, or wardrobes, for that matter, which meant that the first task for women settlers was often making their clothes. Religious sects like the Puritans dressed more simply as a part of their religious beliefs.

As the colonies became more established, clothing did become more elaborate, especially in urban centers, but it rarely matched the extreme ornamentation seen in European styles of the time. Women read European style books and copied the fashions they contained for their own use. They still used homespun for many of their garments as finer fabrics were still in short supply.

A Woman's Place

When the American colonies boycotted British goods during the Revolutionary War, women formed spinning societies to provide much needed cloth. Wearing clothing made of homespun was not only practical, it was politically correct as it indicated a commitment to the war effort and freedom.

Perfuming

Personal hygiene was uneven at best during the Early Modern period. With no adequate water supply, attaining even minimal cleanliness was an immense task. The daily toilet often consisted of little more than a wipe of the face in the morning. As in earlier times, sponge baths were a weekly occurrence; full body baths took place annually. Masking personal odors with perfume was still a necessity. Favorite scents included lavender, violet, and musk. Each royal court had its own perfumer, with concoctions made by the Italians and the French especially prized.

A new form of perfume made its debut around the sixteenth century. Invented by two brothers from Italy, it consisted of bergamot flowers, lavender, rosemary, neroli, and the peels of oranges and lemons mixed with water and alcohol. The inventors called it Cologne after the city they were living in.

Health

Good health was still a rarity for Early Modern women. Diets were far from balanced and diseases caused by malnutrition were common. Food was often scarce due to harvest failures caused by bad weather. The styles of the day even caused a fair share of health risks. To effect a fashionable pallor in the 1500s, women either powdered their faces with a substance made from lead—which causes brain damage, or ingested arsenic—which damages blood circulation. Schoolgirls were often deprived of fresh air, adequate food, and exercise to give them the desired thinness, languor, and pallor.

Body lice and other bugs still wreaked havoc with skin. Tight corseting was practiced even on young children. At best, it stunted their growth. At worst, it squeezed their small lungs so tightly that they suffocated to death.

Childbirth was still deadly and killed one woman out of every twenty until the 1880s. The death rate for infants remained high as well. Poor women faced increased risks related to childbearing due to poor diet and health. They often worked until they delivered and then farmed out their babies to wet nurses so they could go back to work. Infanticide was common as women often had too many children to take care of.

Such diseases as smallpox, typhoid, typhus, malaria, and tuberculosis swept through cities and decimated families. Cholera, caused by drinking water contaminated with sewage, infested European cities until the third quarter of the nineteenth century. Infections of all sorts were common and largely went untreated.

School Days

Girls during the Middle Ages didn't get much of a shot at an education. Even when they did, what they commonly received was far inferior to what boys were taught. The situation wasn't much better throughout most of the Early Modern period. In fact, in some cases it was worse. Not only was a quality education denied to most girls, what they were taught was designed to emphasize their inferiority to men.

The prevailing wisdom—among men, at least—was that education should suppress what they believed to be the negative aspects of a woman's nature—intelligence, independent reasoning, logic and whatnot—which, if left unchecked, could make a girl dominant, prideful, and sinful.

Such works as the *Instruction of a Christian Woman,* published in 1523 by the Spanish humanist Juan Luis Vives, suggested that girls should learn how to read so that they could be rescued from ignorance. In fact, they should be allowed to read some of the most serious authors of the time and the most important works—the Bible and the writings of early Church leaders among them—but only certain parts of the Bible, and only certain writings, only those that underscored subordination and obedience to familial duties and virtues.

Girls were denied the right to read most secular texts. Instead, they were subjected to the misogynist writings of the apostle Paul and of St. Augustine, another early Church leader who felt that women were evil and corrupt and blamed them for his early life of debauchery among them. They also read accounts of the lives of classical heroines like Penelope, Virginia, and Lucretia. While interesting, they also were good examples of the dutiful helpmate that subordinated her own needs to those of her husband.

Women in Religion

As was the case during the Dark and Middle Ages, the Church continued to offer many women the chance at a better life than they would lead in the secular world. Some sought the peace and dignity offered by cloistered life as an alternative to marriage. As in the past, convents also were havens for young women with poor prospects of making good marriages. Widows of all ages joined them as well.

Service to the Church was still noble work and women could still gain a fair amount of power and authority in the various orders that developed over time. However, when the Protestant Reformation began in the early 1500s, nunneries lost much of their purpose and status and began closing due to lack of financial support. More than 3,000 women lived in English convents in 1350; by 1534, less than 2,000 resided in 13 fewer convents. Numbers shrank in other parts of Europe as well. Many Protestant reformers saw it as their duty to liberate nuns from their convents. The great reformer himself, Martin Luther, led the way by opening the convent doors in his city of Wittenberg. He even married a former nun.

Religious communities like the Beguines, which had organized in the late Middle Ages, and the Ursulines, named after St. Ursula, the legendary English martyr, offered women the opportunity to live a pious life outside of the convent. The women who formed these groups came together under no formal rule, pooled their property and other resources, shared residences or lived at home, worshipped together, and performed charitable acts.

A Woman's Place

Juan Luis Vives' beliefs on the education of young women were echoed by the seventeenth-century French churchman and educator Francois Fenelon in his *Treatise on the Education of Daughters*. In it, he urged against women becoming "ridiculously learned" and advised them instead to train their talents on creating beautiful and comfortable homes for their husbands and families.

Hear Me Roar

Learn to obey, for you will obey forever.

—Madame de Maintenon, a long-time companion to Louis XIV of France (she helped raise his children from his other liaisons, of which there were many) and the founder of St. Cyr, a school for poor girls of aristocratic birth

131

They took vows of chastity and poverty, just as they did in the convents. Many groups started schools exclusively for girls.

At first allowed to operate without much male interference, these communities grew so large both in numbers and in membership that members of the male clerical establishment knew they had to step in. They did so by imposing the same rules that governed life inside the cloister. Some women rebelled against the restrictions. Others learned to work within them.

New Freedoms

The Reformation—the religious movement that established Protestantism—both offered women new vistas and constricted them. Those who wished to live a cloistered life found it less easy to do so as the Protestants distrusted single women and female communities and worked to close them. Married women, on the other hand, actually had the chance to live richer spiritual lives thanks to the reevaluation of marriage as a companionable and honorable state. Where once they were prohibited from praying with their husbands or studying scripture with them, they now could do so.

Wives could even discuss theology with their spouses, but they couldn't preach it. Developing sects like the Quakers, Puritans, and Calvinists gave women more rights, but only to a certain extent. They couldn't be clergy members; in fact, they were prohibited from all positions of authority. If they preached or debated theology in public, they could be whipped or beaten. As Anne Hutchinson found out, such punishment was even doled out in a new society supposedly founded on religious tolerance.

A popular Boston midwife, Hutchinson began holding women's theological meetings in 1636. All went well until men starting attending them. They leaked word of the meetings to the Puritan establishment, who didn't cotton to the idea of a woman teaching theology.

Hutchinson was hauled before a church council and her theology denounced. She was then tried for verbally attacking the colony's ministers. Found guilty, she was banished from the settlement.

The message remained loud and clear: Stick to your place. Stay within the boundaries set by men.

Hear Me Roar

We do not mean to discourse with those of your sex.

—Massachusetts Governor John Winthrop to Anne Hutchinson during the inquiry against her

Coming to the New World

Anne Hutchinson and other women like her were lured to the New World by the chance of greater religious freedom and broader economic opportunities. To gain it, however, many of the earliest female settlers had to indenture themselves as servants to pay their way. Such agreements could bind them to their masters for as long as seven years. Once they served their term, they were free to marry.

Other women gained passage to the colonies by agreeing to be auctioned off to prospective husbands when they got there. In 1620, 90 new arrivals went on the auction block at Jamestown. The opening bid was 120 pounds of tobacco. It took just a few minutes for the anxious men to snap up all 90 of the "tobacco brides."

Like the Reformation, the New World was a mixed blessing for women. Their capacity for hard work was greatly appreciated—and the work was unbearably hard in the colonies. But they were also bound by many of the same legal strictures they thought they had left behind. Women's rights were still a thorny issue. As you'll see in the next chapter, even the founding fathers were loath to address it.

The Least You Need to Know

➤ Most women of the Early Modern period were commoners.

➤ The likes and dislikes of royalty determined the fashions of the time.

➤ Ill health still plagued many women. If a disease didn't kill them, childbirth often did.

➤ Women in the New World still lived by many of the rules they thought they had left behind.

Chapter 14

Defending Our Rights

> ## In This Chapter
>
> ➤ Taming women's tongues
>
> ➤ New rules for property rights
>
> ➤ Speaking out
>
> ➤ Equal rights for all?

By this point, we've studied women's history over the course of more than three thousand years. Many things have changed during that time, both for the world in general and for women in particular. One thing that hasn't changed much, however, is women's status in society.

With some notable exceptions, which you will read more about in this chapter, the rights women had during the Early Modern period were still far from being equal to men's. Women were still in a position of subservience to men and were expected to remain there.

As you'll see in this chapter, women living during the Early Modern period actually lost ground in several important areas when it came to the control they had over their lives. But by the end of this era, a number of women were fed up enough to begin raising some serious questions regarding their status and rights.

The most important thing that happened in this period in Europe was the shift from a God-centered world to a man-centered world. Called Humanism, this new way of looking at life began in Italy in the 1300s. Humanists rejected the medieval view of man's inherent sinfulness. This changed how both men and women lived and set the stage for the world we know today. Economically, for example, it encouraged consumerism, which fueled a commercial economy.

The second most important development in Europe at this time was the Protestant Reformation, an outgrowth of Humanism. By emphasizing a personal relationship with God, Protestant theologians encouraged literacy and reading of the Bible.

Both of these ideological shifts meant that individuals, whether male or female, became more important. By the end of the seventeenth century, society had shifted from one based on kin allegiances, where personal preferences were subordinated to the group's welfare, to one in which people could choose their own spouses and delight in affectionate relationships.

The Rule of the Patriarchs

As the feudal systems of the Dark and Middle Ages faded away, the power of the manor lords had passed to two entities: the new, centralized states run by royalty and the male heads of households.

Kings and emperors had authority over their own families and put laws into place that governed how commoners were to run theirs as well. In these families, it was now up to the man of the house to assure the proper transfer of property between generations by protecting his family's bloodlines. In the past, such authority had varied depending on the area and was rarely codified by the courts. But the new legal systems gave common men the legal right to act in such matters.

Men's authority made obedience by their wives, families, and servants unquestionable. It was considered acceptable to physically reprimand anyone who offered anything less than complete loyalty. Men governed everything, from how the resources of the house would be used to the household's position in communal politics. It was unthinkable for a woman to represent her home in such matters, even if her husband was away.

The primary function of the ideal wife, as defined by the leading thinkers of the day, was to keep her husband happy by insuring that her household ran like clockwork. A wife was to carry out her husband's wishes in all areas and make sure that household expenses were kept in check. While the head of the

A Woman's Place

Early modern men may have been authority figures in theory, but when it came time to exercise their influence, they often had to turn to the courts for enforcement. Records from sixteenth-century court proceedings reflect more than one case brought by a husband against his wife for disrupting his life in some way, usually by scolding or cooking bad meals.

household was responsible for hiring servants, their training and supervision were always left to the wife. The Holy Family was the model for every family, and the Virgin Mary, the exemplar for all women, as she was obedient (unlike Eve), asexual, silent in her suffering, courteous, and humble. A good woman had four roles in her life: daughter, wife, mother, and widow. Still, women never shook the taint of Eve's bad choice.

Early modern wives were under tremendous pressure to create perfection. Their actions reflected on their husbands and their families. A dutiful wife brought honor to her family and her husband. If she misbehaved or erred in any way, she brought disgrace upon herself and on her husband, who could be chastised for his inability to educate his wife or for not choosing a wife more capable of being trained. Until 1790 in England, a husband was legally responsible for any crime his wife committed.

A Woman's Place

In England and Scotland, wives who scolded their husbands or in other ways were found verbally offensive could be made to wear a particularly onerous device called a scold's bridle. It was a metal cage placed around the head with a sharp or spiked plate that wounded the tongue when the wearer attempted to talk. Women condemned to wear them were further humiliated by being placed on public display.

The intellectual movement called Humanism had much to do with the increased subordination of women during the Early Modern period. The movement had reawakened interest in studying the classics, and it had in fact improved access to education for women in its earliest stages. However, as it developed, it not only relegated women's education to the few subjects their supposedly feeble, emotional minds could handle, but it also reaffirmed other ancient attitudes about them.

Traditional beliefs that women were by nature evil and inferior and had to be controlled and subordinated robbed them of the gains they had made in such areas as education and legal rights. They also fueled the *Querelles des Femmes,* or the Debate over Women, a heated discourse that began during the Renaissance and lasted throughout the Early Modern period. This was the debate, in fact, that Christine de Pisan had joined in the 1400s when she wrote *Book of the City of Ladies* and *Letter to the God of Love,* in which she argued against woman's inferiority to man.

Men had launched the debate, with arguments for their natural superiority far outweighing those against. Still, there were some men who couldn't ignore the obvious. Women were clearly capable of greater participation in the public arena and occupying a greater role in society, and men argued for it, in such works as *Admission of Women to Civic Rights,* written by the French Marquis de Condorcet in 1790; and *On the Civic Improvement of Women,* penned by the German Theodor von Hippel in 1792.

As the dispute wore on, women such as Mary Wollstonecraft (you'll read more about her in Chapter 17, "New Ground"), who wrote *A Vindication of the Rights of Woman,* and Josefa Amar y Borbon, a Spaniard who wrote *Discourse in Defense of Women's Talent and Their Capacity for Government and Other Positions Held by Men* in 1786, argued against those who said that women's subordination was inevitable and natural.

Hear Me Roar

There are some loopholes out of which a man may creep, and dare to think and act for himself, but for a woman it is a Herculean task, because she has difficulties peculiar to her sex to overcome which require almost superhuman powers.

—Mary Wollstonecraft, *A Vindication of the Rights of Woman*

A Woman's Place

During the 1700s, English law dictated that husband and wife became one person through marriage, effectively eliminating any independent rights for wives.

Marriage and the Law

Old customs and traditions regarding marriage continued to flourish during the Early Modern period. Women still had little to say about the matter, and getting married still meant the loss of their separate identities and most, if not all, of their independence.

As mentioned in Chapter 13, "Daily Life," marriage partners and terms were almost always set by the parents with little input from their daughters. Negotiations could be lengthy and involved, especially among royal and aristocratic families, as such unions almost always entailed the exchange of large sums of money as well as land and titles.

Marriage among royal families helped large dynasties grow even larger and more influential by solidifying key social and political connections. It was important to make the best matches, and royal parents went after them almost ruthlessly. Their actions made it clear that what their families could gain from marriage was far more important than the needs or feelings of those being mated.

Families of lesser social status obviously had less to barter with but worked just as hard to preserve their limited holdings through bargaining and matchmaking.

At the beginning of the sixteenth century, most upper-class families felt that choosing a marriage partner was too important to be left to the bride and groom. Some families abused this practice, marrying off children to children. In other cases, young people eloped, or the prospective bride fled to a nunnery.

Aristocratic families, which had so much to lose if their children decided to exercise their independence, turned to secular and religious authorities for support. Both entities passed laws and issued decrees that enforced arranged marriages and prescribed various punishments for any son or daughter who dared to go against their parent's wishes. To insure that everyone understood the rules, families in France and England had to publicly announce impending marriages by posting *banns*. To insure against challenges to the marriage, weddings had to be held in churches where witnesses could watch as vows were exchanged.

Other laws made it illegal to elope and allowed parents to disinherit their children if they married without parental consent. In seventeenth-century France, fathers could ensure against such actions by confining their daughters to convents until they were married.

But from the mid-seventeenth century on, things began to change. Sons and daughters had more choice in who they could marry, although parental counsel still weighed in heavily. Voluntary consent and affection between the individuals involved were acknowledged as important ingredients of a good marriage.

Property Rights

The end of the feudal or manor system also influenced women's rights to inherit. In the past, such rights varied by region and often within regions. Now, royal rulers, as heads of nations, and their courts enacted uniform laws that superseded the existing hodgepodge of regional legislation. Since royalty had always placed such a high emphasis on producing male heirs, the new rules favored the rights of sons, and especially first-born sons, above all others.

The kings and emperors of the Early Modern period believed that the new system of inheritance, which included the laws of primogeniture and *entail*, would better protect ancestral holdings and eliminate many of the squabbles of the past. Leaving everything to one heir—and preferably a

Words for Women

Banns were announcements that stated a couple's intention to marry. They were posted and generally announced in church on three successive Sundays.

Words for Women

Entail limits property inheritance to a specific line of heirs so that it can never be legally transferred outside of the family.

139

male who could defend it against the claims of others—was thought to be the best way to keep a family's holdings intact.

The new principles of inheritance, which now heavily favored a single male heir, often made it difficult for noble and royal families to provide adequate dowries for their daughters as they had in the past. To ease the financial burden, these families began combining their daughters' dowries and inheritances and made just one payment at the time of betrothal that reflected the value of both.

Another common practice, again used to make the financial burden on the wife's family a little less onerous, was using land and property that had been borrowed against to satisfy the widow's portion of the dowry. Theoretically, the mortgages and other obligations would be satisfied by the time the woman had to exercise her rights over this property. In reality, they rarely were, which meant that the widow had title to the land but no right to any income derived from it. The title was all she could pass along to her children until the debt was paid.

The laws during the Early Modern period restricted what a wife could do with her property regardless of how much she received and how encumbered it was. In many cases, the marriage contract agreed to on her behalf (but without her consent) stipulated how her holdings would be passed on after her death. Children other than first-born sons might inherit them, but this wasn't always the case. Laws so favored the right of first-born sons to inherit that widows often had to take their sons to court to gain their rights over their widow's portions after their husbands died.

Going for the Vote

Men in fifteenth-century Russia controlled women by confining them to *terem*, or women's quarters. For the most part, they were virtually imprisoned in their homes, allowed to go to church only occasionally and to visit friends even more rarely. Such control was exerted over them until they were too elderly to present much of a concern.

The Female Body

Humanistic theories and new inheritance laws elevated chastity to almost surreal importance during the Early Modern period. Humanism held that women must be protected from their own evil natures. Even the suspicion that a child's father might not be a wife's husband threw a monkey wrench into the carefully crafted code of laws designed to insure clear inheritance and pure bloodlines. Both influenced a societal standard where a woman's body belonged first to her family and then to her husband.

Daughters were kept at home under extremely close supervision. Even a momentary lapse in guardianship could have serious consequences and irretrievably damage both the girl's and the family's honor. Something as innocent as allowing girls and boys to play together could be misconstrued as loose behavior and call a girl's chastity into question. The best thing was to marry her off at an early age.

As previously mentioned, chastity assured future husbands that their bloodlines would be pure and their heirs legitimate. It also protected their family's reputation. Fathers of daughters whose honor had been broached in any way could seek recourse and compensation either from the responsible male or from the courts.

Marriage was about the only way in which young women who had lost their virginity could reestablish their honor. Artemisia Gentileschi, a sixteenth-century Italian artist, was one of many who took this approach.

In Italy, a number of cities gave women a second chance at marriage and reentry into polite society by giving them jobs in institutions established specifically for this purpose. In rural areas, peasant girls sometimes got pregnant to prove their fertility. Although their chastity was clearly past history, memories grew conveniently faulty if they augmented their pregnant state by tying the knot.

Voices of Change

There has always been a cadre of women who took the contrarian's view of the world around them, who spoke out against injustice and worked for change, often at great risk to themselves and their families. In the past, most of these women had been high born—if not royal or noble then certainly high class—whose elevated social status gave them greater freedom to do what they wished. During the Early Modern period, women of the lower classes lifted their heads, saw what was going on around them, and joined the fray as well.

By the seventeenth and eighteenth centuries, the number of women railing against society's conventions and injustices had significantly swelled. Tired of relinquishing their voice to men, which basically meant their opinions weren't expressed at all, they began speaking up for themselves. They were still vastly in the minority—most women gave little thought to their particular situations, and even if they did, they generally put up and shut up—but there was no doubt that they were there.

There's no denying that women in the Early Modern period had a great deal to complain about. Civil wars in England and France had made their lives more difficult by taking away their husbands and their livelihoods, delivering more women and children than ever before into poverty. Restrictive legislation had placed even greater control in the hands of men, who had effectively excluded women from virtually all economic activities beyond making a living.

At the same time, people were fighting for—and winning—new rights both in Europe and in the Americas. Religious sects like the Puritans that had developed after the Protestant Reformation were now asserting the right of people to have a say in how they were governed by their church and by the state. It was hard not to notice what was going on and hard not to ponder whether such reforms should extend to all people.

Rallying the Forces

The invention of movable type in the mid-1400s had revolutionized the written word and made it possible to spread news and opinions more easily and widely than ever before. Some women printed and circulated pamphlets and petitions to galvanize greater numbers of their compatriots into action.

A Woman's Place

Two women, identified as Mary Tattle-Well and Joan Hit-Him-Home, Spinsters, published a pamphlet in 1640 titled *The Women's Sharpe Revenge*, which attacked anti-feminist writings being circulated at the time.

English women presented a number of petitions to Parliament during the seventeenth century. Maids in London, in protest of unreasonable working conditions, petitioned Parliament in 1647. In 1649 a petition with 10,000 signatures asked for women's rights to voice their opinions in how the country was run. They were told that they didn't quite understand the matter and remanded back to their homes. Women again petitioned Parliament in 1651, seeking reform of England's debtor prisons.

Rights in the Colonies

Another huge change for Western society during the Early Modern period was the discovery of the New World—North and South America. Emigration to new countries expanded economic and personal opportunities for both men and women.

While some women chose to work for reform in their home countries, a large number decided to leave the old order behind. Some went as single women; others dutifully followed their husbands. Male colonists not only needed all the bodies they could get, but they also greatly appreciated the efforts of the women who chose to join them, and they showed their appreciation by giving women colonists almost equal footing in the New World.

Not only were women allowed to speak for themselves in the courts, they could operate businesses, manage plantations, and even practice medicine. In Virginia, the land grants made to women were equal to those received by men. In New Amsterdam, soon to become New York, Dutch women played a key role in developing overseas commerce and trade with the Indians.

When it came to women's legal rights, however, things were often not much different in the New World. As was the case in English common law, women were expected to turn over all her personal and property rights when they married. But New World judges often ruled against tradition and gave wives control over their money and land. Eventually, concerns over women's newfound freedom led many men to call for legislation to restrict it.

Going for the Vote

In the New World, colonists were exposed for the first time to powerful women who called the shots in virtually every situation. With a long heritage of matriarchy, many Indian tribes of the New World were still matrilineal, especially the League of the Iroquois in New England, with which early settlers had many dealings. They were led by powerful Indian women who assumed many of the responsibilities filled by men in European societies.

Since both men and women were so accustomed to men calling the shots in public arenas, few thought much of it when women weren't allowed to sit on village councils or participate in the other forms of government that were developing. But as the colonies developed, other rights enjoyed by the earliest female settlers began to dwindle. They were no longer given equal land grants. As more male settlers came, many of the important roles women had filled when populations were low went to men as well. After having a taste of what it was like to be regarded as equals and have their work highly valued, going back to narrower roles similar to what they had left behind held particular rancor for many women.

Legislating Change

The revolutions of the eighteenth century did much to expand the rights of many people, but did little for women. Women in France had raised their voices in protest throughout the eighteenth century and had staged a number of rallies and protests during the French Revolution, even going so far as to march to Versailles to bring the king to Paris to see how bad things really were. The ruling elite was clearly aware of their protests and was concerned enough to do something about it. Rather than consider the basis of the complaints and possibly put some reforms into place, however, they instead passed laws that were even more restrictive than before.

Hear Me Roar

Do not put such unlimited power into the hands of the Husbands. Remember all Men would be tyrants if they could.

—Abigail Adams to John Adams, 1776

Women in the American colonies took up arms and fought side by side with men during the American Revolution. They won freedom for their country, but their own status and rights changed little.

The notion of freedom and liberty for all was a grand one, but hardly inclusive. The founding fathers chose their words carefully when they wrote that all men were created equal in the Declaration of Independence. All men, yes. But what about slaves and women? Weren't they created equally as well? Those were thorny issues that the drafters of the Declaration and the Constitution that followed it were unwilling to address.

But they also were issues that women weren't about to drop. As you'll read about in Part 4, "The Nineteenth Century," the questions they raised would carry forward into the reform movements that developed during the nineteenth century.

The Least You Need to Know

➤ An ideal wife put up, shut up, and did her husband's bidding without question.

➤ A woman's behavior in all areas could affect not only her reputation but also that of her husband and family as well.

➤ In the Early Modern period, when mankind assumed center stage and the group became less important than the individuals who made it up, women had more say in some areas of their lives, such as choosing marriage partners.

➤ Women's rights expanded during the early days of American colonization but soon receded to pre-colonial levels.

Hail To the queen, baby!

Chapter 15

Early Modern Rulers

> ## In This Chapter
>
> ➤ The object of a king's obsession
>
> ➤ Married to her country: Elizabeth I
>
> ➤ Small but mighty: Catherine de Medici
>
> ➤ Living a boy's life

The women you'll read about in this chapter share a common bond: They were all queens. That's about where the similarities between them end, however.

Many queens of the Early Modern period gained their thrones in the old-fashioned way—their families traded them to other families in exchange for land, wealth, and power. It was still rare for a woman to ascend to the throne in her own right, although two of the women in this chapter did exactly that. One stayed; the other decided she wasn't much cut out for the royal life and left it to someone else.

Regardless of the circumstances, each of the women in this chapter had a profound effect on the histories of their dynasties and their countries.

Anne Boleyn

All King Henry VIII wanted to do was produce a male heir. His first wife, Catherine of Aragon, disappointed him by failing to do so. But Henry believed Catherine's lady-in-waiting, the lovely Anne Boleyn, might be the one who could deliver the goods.

Anne Boleyn had joined the royal court as a lady-in-waiting to the queen in 1522 when she was just 15. She immediately caught Henry's eye, which actually wasn't any great feat as it was roving long before she got there. In despair over Catherine's infertility, his goal was to find a suitable wife to replace her. In the interest of decorum, he waited five years before he secretly began seeking annulment papers. It was toward the end of those five years that he met Anne.

Henry petitioned the pope for six years for his annulment, but his pleas were ignored. Weary of his quest, he decided to let the chips fall where they may and marry Anne. The two wed in 1533. When word of the union reached the pope, he excommunicated Henry.

The excommunication gave Henry the room to do what he pleased regarding his marriages and his heirs. He had Parliament pass the Act of Succession in 1534, which declared his marriage to Catherine invalid and proclaimed Anne as the new queen. It also made questioning her marriage to Henry a capital crime and required all of Henry's subjects to swear their loyalty to him.

A Woman's Place

The Boleyn women weren't lacking when it came to libido or comeliness. Both Anne's mother and her older sister shared their beds with King Henry before his attention turned to young Anne.

Poor Anne didn't prove any better at producing male heirs than her predecessor was. Nor did the impatient Henry give her much of a chance to succeed. She delivered her only child—Elizabeth—the same year she married the king. Three years later, he beheaded his lovely young wife and moved on to his next victim.

Henry's decision to marry Anne resulted in England's break from the Catholic Church. He also wasn't done with the Boleyn family—his fifth wife, Katherine Howard, was Anne's cousin.

Elizabeth I

She had her father's fiery red hair and his legendary temper, but Elizabeth I would prove to be a far better ruler than dear old dad. Henry VIII had married Anne Boleyn in hopes of producing a male heir. Elizabeth appeared instead in September 1533. Three years later, her father lopped off her mother's head, leaving the young Elizabeth with no family to speak of. Considered a bastard child after her mother's death, she was raised in Hertfordshire, far from Henry's court.

While her future prospects were less than positive—the chances of her inheriting the throne were remote—Elizabeth nonetheless received an excellent education for the time, even for the children of nobility. She learned French, Italian, and Spanish—all languages that would serve her well in the future. She also proved to be an able musician, a confident horsewoman, and a superb dancer.

In the years following Henry's death in 1547, Elizabeth lived as quietly as possible and as far away from the public eye as she could. From various vantage points far removed from the royal court, she watched the controversy and scandals swirl around the reigns of her sickly half-brother—Edward VI, born to Henry and Jane Seymour, whom he had married after he beheaded Anne Boleyn; and her vehemently Catholic half-sister Mary Tudor (see Chapter 18, "Reign of Terror"), the daughter of Catherine of Aragon, Henry's first wife. When Mary died in 1558, it was Elizabeth's turn at the throne.

As queen, Elizabeth immediately restored Anglicanism as the official religion of England. Fearing that Spain and other Catholic countries might try to oust her, she also worked to accommodate the needs of the country's remaining Roman Catholics.

A good politician, she also managed to pressure the French into withdrawing from Scotland. She was unsuccessful, however, in returning Calais, which her predecessor, Mary Tudor, had lost to the French in 1555, to English control.

Elizabeth's reign was characterized by peace, prosperity, and cultural advancement. Although she was often distracted by the antics of her cousin Mary, Queen of Scots, she created a magnificent court that attracted some of the finest talent of the time, including Francis Bacon and William Shakespeare.

With the assistance of her counselors, most notably Sir William Cecil, the prime minister who worked closely with her for 40 of her 45 years as queen, she managed to quell a number of insurrections and made England into one of the world's supreme powers. She also supported the adventures of Sir Walter Raleigh, his explorations and colony in Virginia (named after Elizabeth, the virgin queen), and Francis Drake, who sailed the world in her name.

A Woman's Place

Writers and pamphleteers defended and attacked women and their nature throughout Elizabeth's reign. To make herself more acceptable to those who questioned the propriety of a female ruler, Elizabeth positioned herself as a spouse to her realm and a mother to her subjects. Like the Virgin Mary, she was both virtuous and maternal.

Refusal to Marry

As queen, Elizabeth was expected to marry so she could produce an heir. If she could have married her true love—Robert Dudley, the Earl of Leicester—she possibly would have done so. But Dudley was a poor pick as he had a number of enemies and a shady past, including at least one prior marriage. Thus denied her shot at happiness, Elizabeth entertained a number of other royal suitors but ended up saying no to all of them. Her possible availability ended up being a good political bargaining chip, but Elizabeth saw no reason to share her throne unless it was absolutely necessary.

Elizabeth's earlier concerns over possible attack by Catholic countries became reality in 1588 when King Philip II of Spain sailed his armada against hers. But Elizabeth was ready, and she had the better fleet. Philip's slow and pokey ships were bested by Elizabeth's smaller and faster ones.

Elizabeth's later years were spent promoting the arts and further building England's role in the world arena. She had to put down a few more uprisings, including one staged by her favorite courtier, the Earl of Essex. With great sadness, she signed his execution papers in 1601. The feisty queen, who often said she was married to her country, died two years later.

Hear Me Roar

I have long since made choice of a husband, the kingdom of England ... charge me not with the want of children, forasmuch as everyone of you, and every Englishman besides, are my children.

—Elizabeth I in a speech delivered to Parliament in 1558

Catherine de Medici

The daughter of the Duke of Urbino, one of the richest bankers in Florence, and niece of Pope Clement VII, Catherine de Medici had power and political connections, which she used to her family's best advantage.

Both of Catherine's parents had died when she was an infant—her mother, a Bourbon princess, just 15 days after giving birth to Catherine; her father five days later. That left marriage arrangements to her uncle, the pope. He began looking for a suitable husband for his young niece when she was just five. When she was 14, she married Henry, the duke of Orléans and son of King Francis I of France. Although Catherine wasn't much to look at, she brought a lot to the table, including the towns of Pisa, Livorno, Reggio, Modena, and Rubiera, as well as a considerable sum of money, which the pope had given her. And, of course, she had considerable political clout, thanks to her uncle.

Short, thin, with bulging eyes and a hooked nose, Catherine couldn't keep her young husband's eye from roving. He was secretly in love with another woman anyway—Diane de Poitiers—who was older than he was by 21 years. Henry's passion for his mistress kept Catherine in the background of events at court for many years, and Catherine always felt like she was competing with Diane for his affection. Even still, Catherine managed to bear 10 children in 12 years. Seven survived to adulthood.

Catherine's political career began when she helped assure her husband's control of the throne by acting as regent for him from 1553 to 1559 when he was away from France. A year later, Catherine was left a widow at age 41 when Henry died in a duel with the Comte Gabriel de Montgomery. She wrested the power away from two aristocratic factions that assumed they could rule in her child's name and took over as regent. She also forced Henry's mistress to return all the money he had given her. She then threw Diane out of the royal court.

Although she put the interests of her children above all else, Catherine showed little hesitation over taking back the reins of the kingdom as regent when two of her two sons, Francois II and Charles IX, proved to be weak and erratic royals. She also engaged in another royal chess game with two of her daughters, using one to prevent a Spanish uprising and another to cement an alliance with the King of Navarre.

Catherine de Medici is often blamed for the massacre of thousands of *Huguenots* on St. Bartholomew's Day, which you'll read more about later in this chapter. There is some question as to whether she was actually responsible for plotting with France's Catholic leaders and ordering the massacre, designed to rid the country of dissenting religions, or was merely powerless to stop it. It took place on the same day as her daughter's marriage to Henry of Navarre, an event that many felt was deliberately planned to cover her complicity.

After Francois died in 1560 and Charles in 1574, Catherine's favorite son, Henry, ascended to the throne. He was a far more able leader than his older brothers had been, and Catherine stayed out of his affairs for the most part. No longer needed at court, she made several diplomatic trips on behalf of her son and devoted herself to cultural projects, including the expansion of the Louvre, the construction of the Hotel de Soissons, and the construction of the Tuileries and its splendid gardens.

Words for Women

Huguenots were French citizens who practiced the Protestant faith.

Jeanne d'Albret

The people who Catherine de Medici might have been trying to eliminate were the same folks that Jeanne d'Albret was working to support. Though she rarely gains much attention today, Jeanne d'Albret was one of the chief architects of the Reformation in France. Although frail and sickly through most of her life, she was strong of will and character—two qualities that carried her through her darkest times. As the highest-ranking Protestant in France, she did much to further the cause of the Huguenots.

Jeanne was born in 1528, the only child of Henry d'Albret and Marguerite of Navarre. D'Albret held the title of Vicomte of Bearn and reigned over the small kingdom of Bearn near the Spanish border.

A Woman's Place

Catherine de Medici also occupies the somewhat dubious role of being the first female smoker of record. She received the evil weed as a gift from Jean Nicot, France's ambassador to Portugal, who obtained it from Portuguese explorers when they returned from the New World.

He was also the King of Navarre, but primarily in name only as most of the country was in the hands of Ferdinand of Aragon, who had conquered its southern region in 1512.

Her mother, Marguerite, was the sister of Francis I, King of France—the father of Catherine de Medici's husband. Unlike Catherine, who fought against Protestantism, Marguerite was no fan of Catholicism and took every opportunity to speak out against the abuses she believed it fostered. While she was impressed by the theology advanced by Luther and Calvin, she never became a Protestant. She did, however, grant asylum in Bearn to Protestants fleeing persecution in France and asked her brother more than once to help keep them from harm.

Little is known about Jeanne's childhood. By all accounts, she had a privileged up-bringing as befitting a child of her social class. She was educated along Humanist lines, which emphasized the development of character and intellect through the study of classic texts. She was a quick learner and possessed a keen intellect.

Royal Chess Piece

Jeanne's family increased her involvement in the royal court when she turned nine. Henry, who was seeking to regain the territory he had lost in Navarre, wanted to arrange a marriage between Jeanne and Philip, the son of the King of Spain. However, Jeanne's uncle, the King of France, had other ideas. He wanted to use her for his own political gains, and he betrothed her to German's Duke of Cleaves.

Even though Jeanne's parents reluctantly agreed to the king's plans, Jeanne was solidly against it and made sure everyone around her knew how displeased she was. But her wishes, as was customary, were ignored. In June 1541, when she was 12, she was married to the duke in an elaborate ceremony. Even so, she had to be forcibly dragged to the altar by her collar.

The union between Jeanne and the Duke was short-lived. As France's alliance with Germany became unpopular, the marriage was no longer necessary. In 1545, Jeanne was able to leave the union she never wanted when her annulment was approved on the grounds that the marriage had never been consummated and that it had been made against her protestations.

Jeanne was again used as a political pawn in 1548. Her father still sought a marriage between her and the Spanish Prince Philip, but the new King of France, Henry II, had other ideas. He wanted to use her so he could consolidate north and south France, and he struck a deal to marry her to Antoine de Bourbon, Duc de Vendome. The two wed in 1549. Although Jeanne again had no input, she was happy with this marriage. Antoine was charming, gracious, and extremely easy on the eyes. Their marriage was happy and they had two children, Henry and Catherine.

Enter the Reformation

Calvinism began spreading through France in the mid 1530s. Jeanne found many of its philosophies to her liking, especially its emphasis on reforming the Church, and began attending sermons preached by Calvinist leaders. As it turned out, the new French court, led by Catherine de Medici on behalf of her minor son, Charles, seemed taken with the sect as well.

Jeanne publicly professed her belief in Calvinism on Christmas Day 1560. But her husband didn't share her convictions. Instead, he used religion for political gain. When the Huguenots seemed to be gaining favor, he was on their side. When the Catholics appeared to be in the lead, he would flip sides. From Antoine's perspective, there was a lot at stake. If he could remain on the good side of the French, there was a good chance that he and his heirs could rule France. If he could recover Spanish Navarre, the prize that had eluded his father-in-law, he could rule over it as well.

As long as the French royals remained sympathetic to the Huguenots, and the Spanish to the Catholics, he had to play both sides against the middle. But when Catherine de Medici switched her support to the Catholics in the face of a Spanish invasion, Antoine saw the writing on the wall. In order to curry favor with both the French and Spanish courts, he had to declare himself an adherent to Catholicism.

Words for Women

Calvinism is a form of Protestantism founded by the French Protestant reformer John Calvin (1509–1564). It emphasizes the doctrines of predestination and salvation solely by God's grace.

Betrayed!

Antoine waited until he and Jeanne were at court in Paris before he announced his loyalty to the Roman Catholic church. But Jeanne could not be dissuaded from practicing her new faith. As her conversion was guided by faith rather than politics, she saw no reason to renounce her beliefs.

In defiance of the Catholic Church and its followers, Jeanne held Protestant services in her private residence. When Antoine insisted that she attend Mass with him, she refused. Antoine retaliated by making her a prisoner in her home and took their son away from her. He also threatened divorce. By this time, Jeanne was suffering from tuberculosis, and the stress of the situation made things worse. Unable to put up much resistance when Catherine joined forces with Antoine to remove her from Paris, Jeanne returned to Bearn, leaving her son behind with Antoine.

Jeanne focused on her own kingdom when she reached Bearn. But a civil war had broken out while she was traveling there, and it threatened her country's safety as it was so close to Spain. She quickly fortified her army and waited for attack. Some months into the civil war, Antoine was wounded. Even though the two were still estranged, he asked to see Jeanne, but she was unable to reach him before he died from an infection caused by his wounds.

Now the ruling parties had to deal directly with Jeanne. While still separated from her son, she was able to arrange for Protestant tutors to educate him. Now in sole control of Bearn, she passed laws to protect the Calvinist preachers she had recruited to preach to her people. She suppressed Catholic services in some parts of her kingdom and began planning a Protestant Academy.

Another Marriage Proposal

While Jeanne worked to strengthen her rule and repelled the challenges constantly being mounted to it, she received a marriage proposal from Philip, the King of Spain—the same Philip her father had wanted her to marry. Now, Philip wanted her to wed one of his sons, but Jeanne still wasn't interested. Apart from the fact that she was tired of her husbands being determined for her by others, marriage would cause her to lose the land she had fought so hard to retain, and she would be forced to renounce her faith. Still, she felt she should reopen negotiations with Spain so she could gain complete control over Navarre. When Philip demanded that she ditch the Calvinists as part of their pact, she abruptly called the negotiations to an end.

Jeanne entered into a similar dance with Rome, which ordered her to reestablish Navarre's Catholic churches and return to the Catholic faith. Again, Jeanne refused. She was summoned before a papal audience in Rome and threatened with the loss of her land if she refused to appear. Jeanne decided to take her chances and let Spain and Rome stew over her. While they did, she continued to enact reforms in her countries. Her Protestant Academy became a reality. She also confiscated the Catholic Church's coffers and arranged for all the money it had collected from its followers to be distributed to the poor.

When another civil war broke out in 1568, Jeanne's life was threatened by Spanish and French Catholic troops. She and her son, who she was finally allowed to bring home, escaped to La Rochelle, a Protestant stronghold, and joined other French Protestants there. While in La Rochelle, she did everything she could to support the Huguenot cause. As the war continued, Jeanne supported it financially, supervising the care of thousands of refugees who came to La Rochelle.

The fighting finally came to an end in 1570 when the two factions offered their terms for peace and struck an accord. The Peace of St. Germain, signed by

Hear Me Roar

Although I am just a little princess, God has given me the government of this country so I may rule it according to his gospel and teach it his laws.

—Jeanne of Navarre

Charles IX in August 1570, granted the Huguenots most of what they were seeking: freedom of worship (except in Paris or near the court), full eligibility to public office, and the right to hold four cities under independent rule for two years to guarantee that the terms of the treaty would be upheld.

Peace between the Catholics and the Protestants was uneasy. The French were furious over the concessions that Charles had made. For his part, he was trying to gain his independence from his mother's iron hand and was considering a war with Spain to unify his people. Catherine offered an alternative: the marriage of her daughter Marguerite to Jeanne's son Henry. The wedding was set for the summer of 1572. Unfortunately, Jeanne didn't live to see the union take place. In June 1572, she collapsed on her way home from a shopping trip. Five days later she was dead.

Historians have long speculated whether Jeanne could have stopped what happened next. As previously mentioned, the wedding of Marguerite and Henry touched off a mass slaughter of Huguenots, including the movement's leaders. The final count of those killed during the Massacre of St. Bartholomew ranges from 5,000 to more than 30,000. Catherine forced Henry to return to Catholicism and virtually held him captive at court to make sure that he remained faithful. But Henry escaped from her court in 1576, after which he immediately returned to his mother's faith. He also rallied the weakened followers of the faith and restored his mother's legislation in the kingdom he inherited from her. After Charles IX and his son Henry III died, Henry of Navarre became Henry IV of France. Although he remained a Protestant for four years after becoming king, he had to return to Catholicism to unite France.

The Girl Who Would Be King: Christina of Sweden

One of history's more intriguing and enigmatic personalities, Christina not only refused to bend to what the court and society expected of her, but she even gave up her throne in favor of living the life she wanted to live.

The only child of King Gustavus II Aldolphus, Christina looked so much like a boy when she was born that the midwives who delivered her thought she was one. At birth, she later wrote, she was covered with hair from head to knee and had a strong, deep voice. Upon seeing her for the first time, the king voiced the hope that Christina would be like a son to him.

A Woman's Place

The emphasis on bearing male heirs was so strong in Christina's time that only King Gustavus Adolphus' sister had the courage to tell him he had a daughter after a midwife mistakenly pronounced Christina a boy.

The king did what he could to ensure that Christina would become exactly that. He educated her like a boy, a rarity at a time when women received an extremely narrow education designed to meet their "limited" needs and no more. Her father's influence most likely also made her a tomboy at an early age—even as a very young child, Christina far preferred her father's masculine gruffness to the softer, more womanly ways of her mother.

Sadly, Gustavus II Adolphus died when Christina was only six years old. As his only heir, she immediately became queen, but in name only due to her age. A group of regents managed the country and its affairs until she came of age.

A voracious learner, Christina devoted the majority of her time during the week to her studies, focusing on general lessons in the mornings and languages in the afternoon. Weekends were reserved for sports. Here, too, Christina showed a strong proclivity for masculine pursuits. She rode, fenced, and hunted. Her vigor for both intellectual and physical pursuits may have been overcompensation for her plain appearance—her complexion was bad, and she had a humped shoulder. They weren't the worst afflictions for boys, but they made the young queen an extremely odd duckling at a time when a woman's physical beauty was one of her greatest assets.

Rise to Power

Christina was both strong-willed and ambitious. She also had no intention of leaving her throne in the hands of her regents any longer than she had to. She began her involvement in affairs at state at the tender age of 12, received ambassadors at 15, and took over the reins of power from her regents in 1644 when she was 18.

It soon became clear that Christina also had no intention of sharing her throne with a husband. She later wrote that she would never allow a man to have authority over her or use her like a peasant in the field. Despite her looks, she had a good number of suitors, but she rejected them all. Love affairs were more to her liking. She had her fair share of them with both men and women, but reportedly found men far more interesting and intellectually engaging.

Christina's crowning in 1644 touched off a period of war and economic crisis for her country. Surrounded by dissention and revolt, she nonetheless managed to rule fairly effectively, extended the influence of her crown, and made an already powerful country into a leading empire of the time. She also protected the rights of her people by banning witch hunting and reforming Sweden's legal systems. Under her rule, Sweden's educational system also received a long-needed overhaul.

Dirty Girl

Her royal court was as much of a puzzle as Christina herself. A lover of wisdom and knowledge, she surrounded herself with the leading intellectuals of the time, including the French philosopher René Descartes. Yet her own appearance at court was hardly what you would expect of a queen. Contemporary reports describe her as peasant-like and unkempt, with wild hair and rough hands. She preferred male dress, which allowed her to do such decidedly unladylike things as straddle chairs when she sat.

Christina's clothing was often dirty, appearing as though she had come to court directly from hunting. So was her speech. For all of her great intellect, Christina talked as though she had just come from the streets, and not very good ones at that. She delighted in embarrassing the more refined ladies of her court with bawdy and off-color jokes, which she told loudly and often.

Her zeal for making Sweden a world power ended up costing Christina the throne. The battles she fought with other countries ate heavily into Sweden's coffers. To offset the expense, Christina sold land to nobles and raised taxes on the middle class. Voices of dissent soon arose. As they grew stronger, Christina decided to abdicate the throne. She had ruled only 10 years, yet she cited the burden of such authority as chief among her reasons for leaving. This was a hollow argument for many royal watchers, who believed instead that her abdication was more indicative of her unwillingness to marry and bear a royal heir.

On May 21, 1654, Christina's cousin Charles took her place on the throne as King Charles X Gustavus.

Once a Queen, Always a Queen?

Christina set off on a European tour soon after she abdicated. Among her many stops was Innsbruck, Austria, where she publicly declared her faith as a Catholic. The religion was banned in Sweden; the fact that she had secretly converted to it several years previous could also have influenced her decision to leave the throne. Next up was Rome, where she had Pope Alexander II bless her conversion.

She remained in Rome as somewhat of a quasi-member of the pope's court and established her residence at the Farnese Palace. She gave great parties, but many people didn't quite know what to make of this woman who expected to be treated like nobility yet walked, talked, and looked like a common peasant.

Christina grew tired of the tongue wagging at about the same time she realized that she really missed the power she had as queen. She decided to leave Rome and reclaim her noble status. The French statesman and cardinal Jules Mazarin promised her rule over Naples, but the throne there ended up going to someone else. Then, her cousin Charles died, and she returned to Sweden hoping to regain her crown. Her attempts here failed as well, as did her efforts to have Cardinal Decio Azzolino, her friend and lover, elected pope.

The former queen and the failed pope went on to have a storied love affair. (Remember, these are times when sex wasn't forbidden for the Catholic clergy, just discouraged.) They were together for some 25 years, long enough for Christina to get pudgy, which did nothing to improve her already dour countenance.

Near the end of her life, Christina became a recluse. Her riches gone, she died impoverished and alone in 1689.

The Least You Need to Know

➤ King Henry VIII's decision to divorce his wife and marry Anne Boleyn caused England's break from the Catholic Church and established Anglicanism as the national religion.

➤ Although not the son her father was hoping for, Elizabeth I proved to be equally effective as a ruler.

➤ Catherine de Medici worked to preserve the throne by serving as regent for her husband and two sons.

➤ Weary of fighting with people who disagreed with how she ran her country, Christina of Sweden abdicated her throne in 1654.

Employment

Like their status and their rights, the necessity for women to earn a living changed little throughout the centuries. Whether married or unmarried, they were expected to supplement their families' income. For the most part, they continued working at jobs related to their traditional household tasks—cleaning, cooking, clothes making, tending to children, and the like.

What they did varied, depending on where they lived, their social status, and their level of education. Regardless of the specific job, they were almost always paid less, and sometimes far less, than what their male counterparts received.

The courtly world of the Early Modern period offered new opportunities for some women to gain employment in areas that were once closed to them. So did the rise of Humanism, which you read about in Chapter 14, "Defending Our Rights," which created new generations of female scholars and then shut the door behind them. For others, the windows of opportunity remained closed.

Employment at the Court

The royal courts that developed during the fifteenth century and continued into the eighteenth century were larger and grander than ever before. It took a lot of people to keep the courts going in the manner prescribed by their rulers. In the past, these jobs had been the domain of patricians and aristocrats. Now, increased demand made them available to women and men of lower social status.

These court attendants, or courtiers, worked at a variety of jobs. They were singers and musicians, actors and dancers. They wrote ballads and love poems—and they received training in all of these areas if they lacked it.

Aristocratic families often arranged for daughters to be taught the ways of a courtier, either in their own homes or in the homes of other families with similar status. Some were sent to convents. But proper appearance and manners were really all it took for a courtier to gain entrance to a royal court, which meant that girls from less-privileged families also had a good shot at royal employment. After all, much of what a courtier was expected to do—serve their royals, make sure all their needs were met, arrange for their comfort and pleasure—were things that women were intimately familiar with and had been born and bred to do.

Women who needed a little fine-tuning in the ways of a courtier could turn to the definitive work on the subject—Baldassare Castiglione's *Book of the Courtier*. It told them all they needed to know about the desirable traits of the position, such as elegance, charm, beauty, discretion, and congeniality, and taught them the proper rules of behavior at court. Christine de Pisan's *Book of Three Virtues,* written in 1405, also went into great detail on how to serve the ladies of the court and was another popular guide for aspiring courtiers.

Most courtiers performed general services to the court. Some, however, displayed the right combination of comeliness, personality, and talent that took them to higher levels. Direct service to a member of the royal family was something that courtiers aspired to. Women and men had equal shots at such advancement. Talent and beauty, rather than gender, determined who would climb the court's ladder.

A Woman's Place

Anne Boleyn, the tragic second wife of King Henry VIII, met her future husband when her father arranged a courtier's position for her at the king's court.

For a woman, such advancement could even mean marriage to a king, or at least serving one as a courtesan rather than a courtier, which often wasn't such a bad deal as even that role could vastly improve both the woman's social status as well as her family's. If royal marriage wasn't in the offing, they had a number of other potential spouses of lesser status to consider. Courtier work was a great way to meet a good husband, and a number of courtiers did marry men they met at court.

Working as a courtier was by no means an easy job. Courtiers who served royals were expected to be at hand when their monarchs climbed out of bed, accompany them in all their daily activities, and put them to bed following the evening meal and entertainment. Their days didn't end when their monarchs went to bed, either, as there was still lots to do to prepare for the next day.

Courtiers in general service to the court often kept grueling schedules as well. It was common practice for them to be "on call" to the court at all times. If a king had a whim that needed pleasing at three in the morning, a courtier had to be there, ready to work, regardless of how tired she was or how hard she had labored the day before.

New Opportunities in Arts and Crafts

The demands of the royal court also created greater opportunities for craftspeople and artisans. Many of the professions in these areas were still controlled by guilds and would be until the late eighteenth century, which meant that women continued to find it difficult to get the training they needed to work at them. Some women got around guild strictures by getting male family members or friends to teach them. Or they'd study on their own, learning what they needed to know from the world around them.

This worked particularly well for artists, who used their nature studies to build their expertise in still life and portraiture painting. Developing special talent in such areas also helped female artists foil the guilds, as they hadn't yet expanded their control to artistic specialties.

A number of women used such techniques to build successful careers as court painters during the Renaissance and into the early modern period. Artemisia Gentileschi, who you'll read about in Chapter 17, "New Ground," was just one of them. The English court was fond of miniatures and hired several women to paint them, including Levina Bening Teerlinc, who executed several pieces for Henry VIII, and Susan Penelope Rosse, who painted a small portrait of the actress Nell Gwyn, the mistress of King Charles II. Women artists also sought and found patrons in the Spanish, French, and German courts.

A Woman's Place

The seventeenth-century Dutch painter Judith Leyster was one of just a handful of women ever admitted to one of Holland's most prestigious guilds, the Guild of St. Luke. One of her most famous works—*The Proposition*, painted in 1631—clearly shows the woman's viewpoint in its portrayal of a woman rejecting a man's advances.

Writing for Rulers

The lords and ladies of the court had an almost insatiable appetite for reading and delighted in being the first to get their hands on the latest best-seller. Many courtiers were also skilled writers and supplied their works to the courts, but they couldn't keep up with demand. Here, again, was the perfect opening for female authors to gain recognition for their work.

Christine de Pisan, whom you read about in Chapter 11, "Trailblazers," was one of the best-known of the early writers who worked for the court. Others included Marie de Gournay, a seventeenth-century French author who provided essays on education and public affairs to the court of King Henry IV and Marie de Medici; and Fanny Burney, an English novelist who worked out of an office in the home of England's king and queen. Queen Charlotte, the wife of King George III, gave her the honor in recognition of her talent.

Salon Society

Salons, which began in Italy during the fifteenth century, also provided women new arenas in which to present their creative work. These were grand private rooms originally used by nobility for events of a more intimate nature away from court. They became places where women and men could interact on equal footing without any fear of what others would say or think. They quickly grew into all the rage across Europe and were especially popular in France. While both men and women organized and held salons, the ones presided over by women became the most famous.

A Woman's Place

The salon in France was established by the Marquise de Rambouillet, who sought refuge from the wild scene at the French court in the private rooms she built in her home. When she took ill after giving birth to her seventh child, she invited the intellectuals and artists she had enjoyed at court into her home. She never recovered from her illness and remained bedridden for the rest of her life, so she kept on bringing the world to her side. Under her direction, the institution and traditions of the salon developed as a courteous and genteel arena for men and women of the intellectual and artistic worlds to converse freely.

Over time, salons became almost mini-courts where people who didn't meet the requirements for royal service for one reason or another—usually because they weren't quite aristocratic enough—could access the same social mobility that they sought at the courts. The salon hostesses, or salonieres, fought to attract the best and the brightest to their homes, and being invited to a salon often put a woman in good stead to meet people of higher social standing than her own.

Some of the women who came to the salons found sponsors for their work among the ladies who ran them. Other salonieres sought out talented but impoverished women who needed financial support. Still others used their salons as a basis for promoting their own work.

In the second half of the seventeenth century, salons proliferated. The most famous were those of the *precieuses*—women who refused to be dominated by men, turned their backs on marriage, and sought learning and conversation at the highest levels of contemporary thought. They challenged the belief that women had inferior intellects and contributed to the idea that the leisured lady was the arbiter of taste and civility.

Words for Women

Precieuses—literally, precious women—were salonieres who rose above their sexual desires and rejected physical love. They believed that their chastity reflected higher moral standards and gave them power over others. It also gave them the freedom to assume roles other than that of courtesan or wife.

In the eighteenth century, salons lost some of their social aspect. Now it was popular for salon hostesses to facilitate discussions between male philosophers, who often espoused Enlightenment ideas. These men questioned all the assumptions on which society was based—except those about the status of women. Women, because of their emotional and irrational nature, were considered far inferior to men.

The image of the ideal woman that formed during the *Enlightenment* would carry forward into the starched and structured behavior that characterized Victorian women of the nineteenth century.

Scientists and Scholars

Women have always had a special connection to the natural world, thanks to their earliest roles as gatherers. So it makes perfect sense that the female painters of the Early Modern period would find the education they sought in the world around them. It was also an ideal educational arena for women interested in the natural sciences.

Like artists, women who were drawn to such scholarly disciplines as botany and entomology found it extremely difficult to access formal education in

Words for Women

The **Enlightenment** was an eighteenth-century intellectual movement in Western Europe that emphasized reason and science in philosophy and in the study of human culture and the natural world.

these areas. Young women of learned families had the best shot at a formal education as they were, if not encouraged, then certainly allowed to study at the same level as their male colleagues. Some even devoted their lives to scholarly pursuits.

A Woman's Place

A seventeenth-century Italian woman named Elena Cornaro Piscopia was the first woman to be granted a doctorate of philosophy. It was a great accomplishment, even if received under unusual circumstances. A brilliant scholar, Elena made no secret of her preference of studying to marriage and even took a vow of chastity to insure that she'd be able to devote her efforts entirely to learning. Her father, realizing he couldn't budge his daughter from her resolve, decided to capitalize on her intelligence by arranging for her to be tutored by the best instructors available in their home city of Padua. Once she had attained the requisite knowledge, he then lobbied the University of Padua to grant her the doctorate.

For the most part, however, attending colleges or universities was still off limits to most women. So, they taught themselves. Away from the strictures of institutionalized learning, they had true academic freedom to develop their own theories, conduct tests and experiments to prove or disprove them, and publish the results.

One of the best-known naturalists of the Early Modern period was the seventeenth-century German entomologist Maria Sibylla Merian, who developed a love for nature at an early age when she accompanied her father, a still-life artist, on his trips to the fields to gather specimens for his work.

A gifted artist in her own right, Merian combined her love for bugs and flowers into a flourishing career as an entomological and botanical researcher and illustrator. She published two noted works, *Neue Blumenbuch* (*New Flower Book*), a three-volume catalog of flower engravings; and *Metamorphosis Insectorum Surinamsium*, a finely researched study on the insects of Suriname, which she visited in 1699 at the age of 52.

The eighteenth-century courtier Emilie du Châtelet, who you'll read more about in the next chapter, was also one of the foremost mathematicians and physicists of the day. Her courtier status helped her gain access to intellectual forums she otherwise wouldn't have been able to enter. She had some formal education thanks to her good friend, the Duke de Richelieu, who both encouraged her and hired tutors to teach her at home. But Emilie was on her own after that. When not at court, she studied and conducted experiments around the clock at the country estate that she shared with Voltaire, the noted French philosopher.

Other women scientists of note during the Early Modern period include the following:

➤ The French astronomer Jeanne Dumee, who published a treatise summarizing the arguments in favor of Copernian theory.

➤ Elisabetha Hevelius, a Polish astronomer who helped her husband run the Danzig observatory and edited a star catalog that he wrote.

➤ The seventeenth-century Italian mathematician Maria Agnesi, who defended almost two hundred mathematical theories before a crowd of spectators and published *Propositiones Philosophicae,* a collection of essays on science and philosophy. She also published a treatise on calculus, dedicating it to Austrian Empress Maria Theresa.

Astronomy seems to have been a particular passion of female scientists of this period, with women pursuing studies of the stars in many European countries. Madame de la Sabliere, a French *saloniere,* conducted her salon specifically as a gathering place for scholars with interests similar to hers. Maria Kirch, a German astronomer, discovered a comet in 1702 while working with her husband as his astronomer assistant. Because she was a woman, her discovery couldn't be named after her.

Work Among the Masses

Women of the lower classes—still the largest social group in Europe—had little hope of attaining any of the accomplishments of the women already described in this chapter. For them, the working life meant drudgery and little relief from it, just as it always had. Held back by their social class and their limited education, they were in especially dire straits when growing industrialization began limiting the jobs they could do.

Cottage industries, where rural women and children did piecework at home, making lace, gloves, or shoes, allowed women the chance to earn money while still considering themselves farmers' wives. However, as factories appeared in England during the eighteenth century, piecework jobs dwindled, although some smaller operations still employed women to do these jobs at home. Such

A Woman's Place

By 1800, 10 to 15 percent of the population of Europe had moved from the country to towns and cities.

inventions as the spinning jenny, which spun thread onto six spools at once instead of just one, were initially small enough to fit in cottages, which meant women could continue their traditional jobs as spinsters. The mule, a larger and heavier version of the jenny, was almost impossible for women to operate. Men could operate them, and did.

Many working-class women continued to seek employment as domestics both in the country and in the city. Young women often moved to the city to earn money for a dowry, and then return to their villages. Domestic positions were plentiful—every family who could afford one wanted a maid, and men were abandoning domestic service for better jobs in other areas. The men who stayed in domestic service, however, were highly prized by their employers and received the best positions and the highest wages. For women who worked in service, there was a hierarchy of positions. A lady's maid or companion was at the top, followed by the cook, the housemaids, and then the kitchen scrubs. Knowing how desperate women were for work, employers often exploited them, making them work at night or giving them long day shifts. The wages paid were extremely low. Employers justified the practice by rationalizing that single women didn't need much money since they only had themselves to support. Married women could depend on their husband's support. They didn't need to be paid well, either. Both rationales, of course, were sheer folly, but they formed the basis for wage discrimination that continues today.

A Woman's Place

Women spinners in the French city of Troyes staged a mass protest against the use of spinning jennys in 1791. They successfully blocked the installation of these machines in city factories.

In the late eighteenth century, factory work became an option for women tired of domestic labor, but these jobs were exceedingly hard on them. Still, a number of women took them and paid the consequences. Poor health was common among women factory workers. Many lost their lives due to unsafe working conditions and diseases such as tuberculosis.

Taking to the Stage

An interesting employment option developed in the sixteenth century that not only provided jobs for women of lower social classes but also gave them the opportunity to climb social ladders. Jobs in the performing arts—the theater, opera, and ballet—had always been the domain of the lower classes as they were considered too lowly for aristocrats. Even members of the middle classes eschewed them for jobs in the crafts and trades.

Men traditionally worked as performers, even taking female roles on stage, but as their opportunities for employment in other fields grew, acting, singing, and dancing became acceptable work for women, especially if they came from theatrical or musical families. Poor young women—especially if they had looks and talent—found the doors of the theaters and opera houses wide open to them.

French and Italian women began appearing on the stage as early as the sixteenth century. Women in England and Germany followed them during the seventeenth century.

Talent transcended social class on the stage. Great celebrity could come—and did—to women of even the poorest of backgrounds who could sing or act. Even women for whom the spotlight shone less brightly found steady employment on the stage. Many also found husbands and married into higher classes than their own.

Work in the Colonies

As mentioned in Chapter 14, the first women colonists had nearly equal footing with men when it came to their rights and privileges. They also had employment opportunities that exceeded those in the Old World. It didn't matter who did the work as long as it got done in the earliest days of the colonies. As the colonies developed and the population grew, there was a greater division of labor between the sexes and a stricter adherence to gender roles, but women still had greater access to employment in many areas.

A number of female colonists were landowners, receiving their holdings through inheritance or directly through land grants, and they ran their farms or plantations themselves. If they didn't own their own land, they could work for other families, either in farm-related roles (although not in the field), or as domestics.

Women often managed the businesses of their husbands, especially if they worked in occupations such as whaling or fishing that took them away from home for long periods of time. Some wives even accompanied their husbands on their voyages, either doing "women's work," like cooking or mending sails, or serving as navigators.

Many colonial women worked with their families or husbands, but not all did. A fair number of them established businesses on their own, working as apothecaries, barbers, blacksmiths, and printers, among other occupations, often learning their skills from their fathers or husbands. Others worked as innkeepers or tavern-keepers.

American women would continue to work in these professions and others as the colonies developed. But change was on the way, both in the colonies

Going for the Vote

Eliza Lucas Pinckney began managing her father's plantations in the Carolinas when she was just 17. She experimented with new crops that became extremely important to colonial economy, including indigo, which yielded seeds used to make blue dye.

and in Europe. In the next century, another revolution would take place that would change everything, from the jobs that men and women did to their roles in society.

The Least You Need to Know

➤ Royal patronage provided opportunities for some artistically talented women and increased social status for other women who attended court as courtiers.

➤ Since they couldn't study at colleges and universities, Early Modern women often were self-educated and drew their knowledge and inspiration from the world around them.

➤ Salons, hosted by women, provided a forum for intellectual discussions.

➤ Women played an essential role in the growth and development of the American colonies.

Oroonoko by Aphra Behn

Chapter 17

New Ground

In This Chapter

➤ Breaking ground with a brush

➤ Living a spy's life

➤ Challenging the Church

➤ Questioning the status of women

Much of what we know about the women who lived during the Early Modern period is limited to accounts of the lives of the noble and the rich. Very little is known about how common people lived as no one saw much reason to pay attention to them or document the details of their existence.

What makes the women in this chapter remarkable is that they weren't noble, yet we still know a great deal about them. In some cases, they were notorious or involved in notorious events—the trial of the man who raped the artist Artemisia Gentileschi for example, still exists intact. Several left bodies of work through which biographies can be constructed. Still others made singular contributions to the world around them that earned them a place in the history books even if they weren't noble.

Painting with a Mighty Brush: Artemisia Gentileschi

Men dominated the European art world when Artemisia Gentileschi dared to enter it. Nevertheless, she rose above gender prejudice and some early adversity to prove that a woman's lesser status didn't translate into lesser talent.

Born in Rome in 1593, Artemisia came by her talent naturally. She was the only daughter of the noted realist artist Orazio Gentileschi, who encouraged his daughter's talent at a young age by training her himself and by introducing her to other talented artists, including the noted Milanese artist Michaelangelo Merisi da Caravaggio. She greatly admired Caravaggio's dramatic use of chiaroscuro, or strong contrasts of light and dark, and she used similar techniques in the works she created.

Orazio Gentileschi painted murals with another artist, Agostino Tassi. He asked Tassi to teach Artemsia the technical skills necessary to paint landscapes. While doing so, Tassi raped the 18-year-old girl and continued to force her into having sex by telling her they'd get married. When Orazio found out about the illicit relationship, he had Tassi arrested for rape and sued him for injury and damage. A celebrated court trial followed, during which Artemisia's testimony was all but thrown out—remember, she was a woman and women didn't have much standing in many courts when it came to rape cases. The judge even had her examined by midwives to determine whether she had lost her virginity prior to Tassi's alleged attack. After a long trial, Tassi was convicted and sentenced to prison, but was released after eight months when the charges against him were dismissed.

A Woman's Place

Interestingly, and perhaps due to her rape by Tassi, Gentileschi never painted landscapes. When she needed landscape backgrounds in her portraits, she hired other artists to render them. She also never drew or painted independent images of the nude male body.

The early scandal ruined Artemisia's reputation. She tried to repair it by marrying Pietro Antonio di Vincenzo Stiattesi, a Florentine artist, which worked to a certain extent. In some circles, however, her honor was always suspect, and there really wasn't much she could do about it. Artemisia didn't let wagging tongues hold her back, however.

She and Stiattesi settled in Florence, where she gave birth to her daughter Prudentia, named after Artemisia's mother who had died when she was young. She continued painting while working at the Academy of Design with Stiattesi and became a member of the institution in 1616, which was a remarkable honor for a woman of her day. In Florence, she gained the support and patronage of Grand Duke Cosimo Medici, which probably influenced her nomination to the Academy. She painted a number of works for him before his death in 1621. After he died, she returned to Rome.

Artemisia received numerous commissions over the years, sometimes in concert with her father. Records reflect that she was the head of her household in Rome, although it's not clear what happened to her husband. They obviously separated, although it's not known when or if they were ever divorced.

A Woman's Place

Artemisia Gentileschi's best-known masterpiece, *Judith Slaying Holofernes*, was painted in Rome at the time of the rape trial against Agostino Tassi. Although the painting's composition was similar to another painting of the same subject executed by the noted Milanese artist Michaelangelo Merisi da Caravaggio, Artesimia's work adds elements of violence that the other doesn't have, suggesting that Artemisia was settling a personal score when she painted it. According to some analyses of the work, there is a resemblance to Tassi in the decapitated head of Holofernes in the painting, which would confirm Artemisia's desire to wreak some revenge through her work.

The talented painter loved to work on a grand scale and turned out a number of large paintings based on Bible stories and Greek legends. She was the first woman to paint these subjects. She especially enjoyed creating works that featured the powerful women of ancient times. One of her best-known works depicts the ancient Jewish heroine Judith after she beheaded the enemy leader Holofernes. In this work, as in her others featuring women, the action is portrayed from the woman's point of view—a first for the art world.

In her later years, Artemisia traveled to England to work for a new patron, King Charles I. She was in residence at the English court from 1638 to 1641 as one of many artists called to work for the king, a renowned patron of the arts. Some records reflect that she went to England to assist her father, Orazio, in a massive project to paint murals on the ceilings of the Queen's house in Greenwich. When civil war broke out in England in 1641, Artemisia returned to Naples, where she lived until her death.

Aphra Behn, First Professional Writer

Aphra Behn loved a good story. She also lived a fair number of them as the first Englishwoman to make a living as a professional writer.

Born Aphra Amis in 1640 in Kent, her parents took her to Suriname at an early age. Further details of her early life are sketchy, but at some point she married a Mr. Behn (his first name is lost to history), a Dutchman who took her back to London in 1665. It was bad timing on his part as it was the year of the Great Plague. Mr. Behn died, leaving Aphra broke.

Luckily for Aphra, England was at war with the Dutch. Having grown up in *Suriname,* she spoke the language fluently. Desperate for work, she sought an audience with the English King Charles II. When granted one, she told him about her background and her ability to speak the enemy's language and asked him for an espionage job.

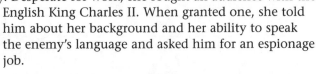

Words for Women

Suriname was a Dutch protectorate on the coast of South America, north of Brazil. At one point, it was known as Dutch Guiana. It gained its independence from the Dutch in 1975.

Charles agreed to hire her and sent her to Holland. There, Aphra successfully uncovered the Dutch plot to sail up the Thames and bomb the English fleet. For some reason, the king decided not to believe her. He also decided not to pay her.

Stranded and broke, but hoping she could convince the king to pay her what he owed, Aphra borrowed the funds to cover her trip back to London. Unfortunately, she met the same resistance when she arrived at home. Not only did the king continue to stall; he also put her in debtor's prison.

Aphra used her time in prison wisely. Instead of hatching devious plots to get her money from the king, she started writing a play, which she produced soon after her release in 1670. Believing the production would have a better chance of success if people thought a man wrote it, she produced it anonymously. The risqué little piece was a success. When she finally felt comfortable enough to claim it as her own, people didn't believe her.

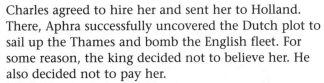

A Woman's Place

Aphra Behn used the stage to get the last laugh in her battle with Charles II over the money he owed her. After abandoning her efforts to collect the debt, she skewered him in *The Rover,* one of her more famous plays. Produced in 1688, it featured the madcap adventures of a woman bearing a very strong resemblance to Nell Gwyn, Charles's mistress.

Aphra had a wry and sardonic outlook on life, which was keenly reflected in her writing. It's also what made her plays popular with both men and women. At first audiences were a little surprised and even shocked that a woman could write as she did, but they soon roared with laughter over the witty and bawdy scenes in her plays.

During the course of her career, Aphra Behn wrote 20 plays and 14 novels. One of them, *Oroonoko,* about the fate of a "noble savage," introduced her readers to the horrors of slavery and was translated into French and

German. Some of her plays, such as *The Forced Marriage,* had somewhat feminist overtones that may have escaped her audiences.

As one of England's first ladies of letters, Aphra Behn was buried at Westminster Abbey. The fact that she was a woman, however, kept her from her rightful place in the Poet's Corner. She was instead laid to rest among the women of the stage in the actresses' section.

Midwife: Louise Bourgeois

When it came to delivering her babies, Marie de Medici, the wife of the French King Henry IV, trusted only one person to attend her. In a time when royalty often chose male physicians to assist royal births, Queen Marie instead selected Louise Bourgeois, a French midwife.

In doing so, she picked a pro. Bourgeois was France's leading midwife, who supervised or delivered some 2,000 babies during her career. By 1610 she had also assisted in delivering six of Marie's babies, including Louis, the heir to the throne.

Bourgeois was somewhat of a rarity. Although prevented from practicing as a physician, her knowledge of obstetrics and gynecology was indisputable and her reputation was right up there with the top physicians and surgeons of the time.

Bourgeois decided to share her knowledge by writing *Several Observations on Sterility, Miscarriage, Fertility, Childbirth and Illnesses of Women and Newborn Infants,* which was published in 1609. This comprehensive text on obstetrics and gynecology became essential reading for anyone working in these areas and was translated into German and Dutch.

A Woman's Place

Louise Bourgeois was noted for her ability to revive babies from apparent stillbirth. Her techniques for doing so included rubbing the infant's body to stimulate breathing or bathing it in warm water and wine. She would also take wine into her mouth, warm it, and pass it into the baby's.

Explorer's Interpreter: La Malinche

When the Spanish explorer Hernando Cortez came to the New World in 1519, he was presented with 20 slave girls. One of them would help Cortez find his way around the uncharted territory and help him conquer it

La Malinche, also called Marina, Dona Marina, or Malintzin, was the daughter of Mexican nobility. Born in the village of Viluta, Mexico, in the early 1500s, she received a good education and learned how to speak several languages. While a young girl, she was either captured or sold into slavery during a period of war, which ended her privileged life and relegated her to one of misery and hardship.

Cortez had come to the New World with two goals: to conquer the land and seize its riches for Spain, and to convert its indigenous population to Christianity. When he met La Malinche, whom a tribal chief had sent along with the other slaves and some gold as a gift to Cortez, he realized she could help him meet his goals. Her ability to speak Nahuatl (Aztec) and Mayan, in particular, made her extremely valuable. When she quickly learned Castilian Spanish, she was an obvious choice for an interpreter.

A Woman's Place

The baby born to La Malinche and Cortez was the first mestizo and the beginning of an ethnic group of the same name. People of this mixed Spanish and Indian heritage populate most of Mexico today.

Since she was a slave, La Malinche had little choice in the matter. She joined Cortez's group and accompanied him on all his journeys. Although Cortez initially questioned her loyalty, he realized she was on his side when she told him about the Aztecs' plans to attack him and his troops. Cortez launched a preemptory strike and killed most of the Aztec warriors. She also helped Cortez assemble an army of Mexicans to fight the Aztecs.

Many Mexicans today revile La Malinche because they feel she was a traitor and instrumental in Spain conquering the Aztec Empire. However, others argue that in acting as an interpreter, La Malinche may have saved thousands of Indian lives. She also became Cortez's mistress and bore him a son. He was faithful to her (though not his wife in Spain) and arranged for her to marry a Castilian knight.

First Lady of Mexican Letters: Sor (Sister) Juana Ines de la Cruz

Although born poor and illegitimate, Juana Ines de la Cruz would become a favorite of the Mexican court, a renowned writer, and a defender of her sex. Born in 1648 in the Mexican countryside, Juana was from a good family, even though her mother was illiterate. She never met her father. As a toddler, her grandfather let her explore his large library. Juana fell in love with the books and learned to read—something her mother couldn't do—when she was three.

A Woman's Place

Juana's passion for learning bordered on the obsessive. When she tackled a new subject, she set a time limit for her studies by whacking off her hair. When it reached the length it had been before she started hitting the books, she was either done with that particular subject or she'd cut it all off again.

Clearly a prodigy, Juana soon eclipsed the resources of her grandfather's library. At just six years old, she came up with a plan to go to Mexico City, disguised as a boy, so she could continue her studies. Her mother at first said no, but let her go two years later—dressed as a girl.

Now living with relatives, Juana studied with even greater fervor than before. By her early teens, she had mastered mathematics, history, religion, poetry, and a host of foreign languages. She claimed it only took her 20 lessons to learn Latin.

Sometime during this period, Juana was introduced to the Marquesa de Mancera, the wife of the new viceroy of Mexico. Taken with Juana's somewhat sad situation and her intelligence, de Mancera invited the young girl to join her court as a lady-in-waiting.

Juana spent four years at the viceroy's court. There is some evidence that she may have been courted while there, but Juana showed no interest. Preferring a scholarly life, she decided to leave the court at about the same time a new viceroy was appointed to become a nun.

The new viceroy and his wife, however, asked her to stay on at court. Juana did so as there was something more than friendship brewing between her and the viceroy's wife. She contributed to the court's entertainment by writing ballads for the troubadours and love poems for the courtiers. Some of her lustiest and best-known writing is dedicated to Maria, the viceroy's wife, making it clear that they were more than friends.

Juana devoted her time to reading and writing when not at court. Her works were both religious and secular and include a number of personal essays, religious exercises, plays, and poems.

A Woman's Place

Like her ancient predecessor Sappho, Sor Juana was often referred to as the Tenth Muse.

Through the generosity of her royal benefactors, Sor Juana became far wealthier than the average nun. By 1690, she had amassed a library of some 4,000 books, possibly the largest in the Americas. She also had an extensive collection of musical and scientific instruments as well as an expensive assortment of fine jewelry.

Sor Juana was popular at court but she also had a fair share of critics who chastised her for her secular writings and her love of learning, considered unacceptable for a woman. When she was under the protection of the court, nothing much could hurt her. But when a new viceroy and his wife replaced Maria and her husband, she became vulnerable to attack.

Hear Me Roar

Frivolity is not exclusively feminine, intelligence is not men's privilege.

—Sor Juana

Behavior Unbecoming

Near the end of her life, Juana incurred the wrath of the Church when she wrote a critique of a famous sermon. The piece came to the attention of the Bishop of Puebla, who decided to publish it under the pseudonym Sister Filotea de la Cruz. He also added a preface in which he both praised Juana's scholarship and criticized her for not devoting herself to more sacred matters.

The Bishop hoped that publishing Juana's letter would prompt her to retract it. Instead, she responded by publishing *Repuesta a Sor Filotea* (*Reply to Sister Filotea*). In it, she claimed the right of all women to attain an education similar to what she had received. Such an education, she said, would give them the basis for forming rational opinions and speaking their minds.

Juana now had gone too far. Her confessor, who had encouraged her to write down her thoughts in the first place, pleaded with her to stop writing. The Bishop of Puebla turned against her. Without the support of her confessor or the bishop, or that of her royal benefactors, Juana was at the mercy of the archbishop of Mexico, who had more than once voiced his disapproval over a woman who spoke out when she should remain silent.

After two years of harassment by the archbishop and other high-ranking church officials, Juana renounced her secular life and reconciled with the church. She quit her studies and disposed of her library and her collections. She died soon after while nursing her fellow nuns during an epidemic.

Going for the Vote

In 1676, a Puritan woman named Mary Rowlandson was taken from her home during an Indian attack on Lancaster, Massachusetts. Six years later, her account of her 83-day captivity was published in Boston to help other Puritans understand the providence of God and to encourage religious meditation. A new, totally American literary form, her captivity narrative was a best-seller in Boston and London. Historians estimate that between 1675 and 1763, 1,641 men, women, and children were taken captive by Indians. This continued as Europeans moved westward across the continent, and many published accounts of their ordeals.

Emilie du Châtelet

The lovely and lively Emilie du Châtelet defied the mores of the time and proved that women could be beautiful and smart. Possessed of a keen intellect, she cunningly used her political connections to create her ideal—a life of luxury and learning.

Emilie was the daughter of the Baron de Breteuil, who served as head of protocol under Louis XIV. Thanks to her father's status, she received a privileged education, including instruction in languages and mathematics, which she loved.

Emilie was 16 when she made her debut at the court of Louis XV in 1722. The king loved her youthful ways and she soon became a fixture there. Several years later, she married the Marquis du Châtelet, whom she had met at court. They had two sons and a daughter together.

The marquis was an army officer and was frequently away on governmental business. As was the custom of the time, Emilie didn't hesitate to take lovers to keep from being lonely. She had a number of them, but her most noted one was the renowned playwright Voltaire, with whom she enjoyed a 16-year relationship. They even shared a house in the country together, where they studied, wrote, and entertained—all with the tacit understanding of the Marquis du Châtelet (who, one could surmise, was filling his time with affairs of his own).

Emilie du Châtelet expressed her love for all good things in *Traite sur le bonheur* (*A Treatise on Happiness*), published in 1740. In it, she acknowledged that a woman's life wasn't as free as a man's. Accept it, she wrote, and focus on things in which happiness could be found, such as friends, family, good food, and nice clothes. Happiness could also be found by setting goals and working toward them, she wrote, and by pursuing an education.

In addition to her own writing, Emilie is noted for translating Isaac Newton's *Principia Mathematica* into French. The translation was published in 1756, after her death. Her love of mathematics remained strong throughout her life, and she helped support a number of scholars in that arena, including the German philosopher Liebniz.

A Woman's Place

Before she was presented at court, Emile du Châtelet received detailed instruction on appropriate court behavior, including eight acceptable ways for eating a boiled egg.

Feminist Pioneer: Mary Wollstonecraft

If there were such a thing as a shot heard around the world at the beginning of the women's rights movement, it would have been fired by Mary Wollstonecraft.

Wollstonecraft played a pivotal role in both the European and American women's rights movements. Her desire to work for the betterment of women started at an early age. She grew up watching her mother regularly submit herself to drunken abuse at the hands of her farmer father. Committed to escaping a similar fate, she left home at a young age to be a companion to a wealthy woman. After her mother died in 1782, Mary went to live with a friend, Fanny Blood, and supported herself as a seamstress.

Several years later, Mary, Fanny, and Mary's sister, Eliza, opened a school for girls in London. They ran the school together until Fanny married. Mary then traveled to Ireland, where she worked as a governess, but was dismissed when the children confessed that they liked her more than their mother.

Mary returned to London and the friends she had there, including the publisher Joseph Johnson, for whom she worked as a book reviewer. Under his tutelage, she wrote a children's book, *Original Stories from Real Life,* which was published in 1788. She also wrote a monthly column in one of Johnson's magazines where she explored a number of issues of the day, often focusing on those that concerned women.

Over time, Mary's magazine ponderings jelled into some fairly radical ideas for the time. In *A Vindication of the Rights of Woman,* she challenged virtually all of society's conventions, arguing for equal rights for women in education, in the work force, in the courts, and in marriage.

Hear Me Roar

Do you not act a tyrant's part when you force all women by denying them civil and political rights to remain immured in their families, groping in the dark? It is time to effect a revolution in female manners, time to restore women to their lost dignity and to make them labour by reforming themselves to reform the world.

—Mary Wollstonecraft, *A Vindication of the Rights of Woman*

Excited by the prospects for reform presented by the French Revolution, Mary traveled to Paris in 1792 for a firsthand look at what was going on. While there, she worked on the book that chronicled her impressions, *An Historical and Moral View of the Origin and Progress of the French Revolution.* Despite her earlier protestations against anything even closely approximating marriage, she also fell in love with an American, Gilbert Imlay. The two had a daughter together, and Imlay even had Wollstonecraft do some work for him, but he eventually deserted her.

After Imlay's departure, Mary returned to London and went back to work for Johnson. It was in one of Johnson's salons that she met the philosopher William

Godwin, whom she married just days before their daughter Mary was born in 1797. Sadly, Mary Wollstonecraft died shortly after the birth and was robbed of the opportunity to see her daughter—Mary Godwin Shelley—gain a great name for herself as the author of *Frankenstein*.

Revolutionary Warrior: Deborah Sampson

Inspired more by a love of adventure than love of country, Deborah Sampson nevertheless took up arms as a soldier in the American Revolution.

The daughter of early American settlers, Deborah was forced to become an indentured servant when her father, a farmer, abandoned his wife and six children and went to sea. She worked for a family in Middleborough, Massachusetts, for 10 years and earned her independence by age 18.

Now a free woman, Deborah began working as a teacher. She enjoyed it, but she also dreamed of living a fuller life than she had to date. The Revolutionary War was in full swing at the time, which gave Sampson an idea: Why not enlist in the army?

It wasn't a bad idea, but Deborah first had to overcome a big problem. Women weren't allowed to serve in the military. Bigger and stronger than most women, Deborah realized it wouldn't be that difficult to disguise her identity by wearing men's clothing. She adopted a pseudonym, Robert Shurtleff, and enlisted in a Massachusetts-based regiment in May 1782.

War turned out to be far from the glamorous life that Deborah had envisioned. Although disheartened, she honored her obligation and fought in a number of battles throughout the Northeast. When she was wounded in the leg, she removed the gunshot from her leg herself rather than risk exposing her true identity. But her leg never healed properly, and her sex was finally revealed when she was hospitalized for a wound-related infection in 1783. Despite her deception, she was given an honorable discharge in recognition of her stellar service record.

Hear Me Roar

If men were to contend for their freedom and to be allowed to judge for themselves respecting their own happiness, be it not inconsistent and unjust to subjugate women, even though you firmly believe that you are acting in the manner best calculated to promote their happiness.

—Mary Wollstonecraft, *A Vindication of the Rights of Woman*

After recovering from the infection, Deborah returned to Massachusetts, where she married a farmer named Benjamin Gannett. They had a family together and she returned to teaching. When stories about her service as a soldier began to surface, she added professional lecturer to her list of accomplishments. By all accounts, she enjoyed talking about her experiences and delighted in appearing in her uniform. Both the United States and her home state of Massachusetts honored her service by granting her military pensions.

The Least You Need to Know

➤ The art world of the sixteenth century was a boy's club more than anything else, but Artemisia Gentileschi was talented enough to crack it.

➤ Renowned for her bawdy plays, Aphra Behn still reigns as one of Britain's most noted female playwrights.

➤ The midwife Louise Bourgeois wrote one of the most celebrated gynecological texts of the Early Modern period.

➤ Her perspective honed by her mother's repeated beatings at the hands of her father, Mary Wollstonecraft would go on to challenge virtually every aspect of how women were treated by society.

Mary Tudor

Chapter 18

Reign of Terror

In This Chapter

➤ Catholic queens vs. Protestant queens

➤ Off with her head: Mary, Queen of Scots

➤ Living a life of crime

➤ A courtier with real class

There were a number of tough and feisty women throughout history, but the ones you'll meet in this chapter really take the cake. Legend has it that one of them even encouraged her subjects to eat that cake, reflecting her callous disregard of their plight.

As you'll see, they hesitated at nothing and pulled out all the stops to get what they wanted. Given their exalted positions, or, in some cases, their amazing capacity for cunning and deception, there weren't many people who would or could stop them.

Mary Tudor

When Catherine of Aragon commissioned the Spanish humanist Juan Luis Vives to write the *Instruction of a Christian Woman,* it was to guide the education of her daughter, the future Mary I of England. Mary may have received the genteel education that Vives envisioned, but it didn't make much of a lady out of her.

Born in 1516 to the first wife of Henry VIII, Mary was raised as a Catholic. Her upbringing in the faith would color her future actions as queen of a Protestant country, made so by her father.

A Woman's Place

There is much interconnectedness between the people in the first part of this chapter. Here's a quick genealogical rundown (in order of their rule) to help eliminate some confusion. Everything begins with the death of King Henry VIII in 1547.

➤ Edward, who held the title of Edward VI, was the son of Henry's third wife, Jane Seymour. A minor, he was too young to rule the country; his uncle, the earl of Hertford, was appointed lord protector and assumed the government. In 1553, Edward assigned the crown, in keeping with his father's wishes, to Lady Jane Grey. Edward died later that same year.

➤ Lady Jane Grey, mentioned briefly here, was the granddaughter of Henry VIII's sister Mary. She was in line to the throne thanks to Henry's will, which left the crown to Mary's side of the family if none of his own children had heirs. But she had no desire for the crown, which went instead to Mary Tudor after some political haggling. Lady Jane and her husband were executed in 1554 following a rebellion caused by Mary Tudor's marriage to Philip of Spain.

➤ Mary Tudor, or Mary I, was the daughter of Catherine of Aragon and Henry VIII. Catherine of Aragon was Henry's first wife, whom he divorced to marry Anne Boleyn. Mary ruled from 1553 to 1558.

➤ Elizabeth, who would gain the throne in 1558 as Elizabeth I following Mary Tudor's death, was the daughter of Anne Boleyn, Henry's second wife.

➤ Mary Stuart, or Mary, Queen of Scots, was the daughter of James IV of Scotland, one of Henry VIII's brothers. A Catholic, she felt her claim to the throne was stronger than Elizabeth's because the Catholic Church had never recognized Henry VIII's divorce from Catherine of Aragon, thus making Elizabeth illegitimate. She proclaimed herself Queen of England and Scotland in 1559 after her husband, Francis II, ascended to the French throne.

Mary wasn't first in line for the throne—that honor was reserved for her half brother, Edward, the son of Henry's third wife, Jane Seymour. When Edward died, Mary ascended to the throne after failed attempts to unseat her in favor of her cousin, Lady Jane Grey.

Mary I, an ardent Catholic, only ruled for five years, but it was a half decade full of extreme religious strife. While she was queen, England reestablished its relationship with Rome, Parliament repealed a law that would have made Protestantism England's state religion and reinstated laws that banned heresy and any statements against the Catholic Church. She herself called for the burning of some 300 Protestants at the stake in a show of force designed to eradicate the religion from England once and for all.

Among the noted church leaders who lost their lives through Mary's actions were Thomas Cranmer, Hugh Latimer, and Nicholas Ridley, all well-known Protestant clergymen. During her crusade on behalf of the Catholic Church, she also briefly imprisoned her half sister Elizabeth (the future queen) in the Tower of London. Her ruthlessness earned her the sobriquet "Bloody Mary."

Mary was married to Philip II of Spain, a partnership that couldn't have found less favor with the English people. Not only did they distrust Philip because he, too, was Catholic, but they also saw Spain as their greatest enemy. Immensely unpopular because of her marriage, Mary lost even more favor with her subjects when she heeded her husband's request to join him in a war against France. France won the war, and Mary lost Calais, the last of England's holdings in France.

Words for Women

Dropsy is an abnormal accumulation of fluid in body cavities or tissues.

The year in which Mary lost Calais—1558—proved to be a bad one in other ways for the bloodthirsty queen. Believing for a time that she was pregnant, she was instead diagnosed with having *dropsy*. She died later that year without producing an heir.

Mary, Queen of Scots

A real thorn in Elizabeth I's side, Mary Stuart only ended her challenge to the English throne when Queen Elizabeth signed the order for her execution in 1587. Another Catholic, Mary Stuart caused uproars in Scotland and England similar to those of her cousin, Mary Tudor, in the name of her faith.

The daughter of King James V of Scotland and Marie de Lorraine, his French wife, Mary Stuart was just six days old when she ascended to the throne of Scotland after her father's death. She was nine months old at her coronation, an event she reportedly cried through.

Marie de Lorraine sent her young daughter Mary to live with the boy she would eventually marry—Francois, the dauphin of France, and his family when she was just five. England was at war with Scotland, and Marie wanted to give her daughter a more stable upbringing than she might have had at home. The two were married when Mary was 16 and Francois was 15.

After Mary Tudor's death in 1558, Elizabeth gained the throne. A year later, Mary Stuart assumed the title of Queen of England and Scotland when her husband, Francis II, became King of France. She believed she had a stronger claim to the throne than Elizabeth did, and she had plenty of support for her position: Catholics living in England had never recognized Henry VIII's divorce from Catherine of Aragon, Mary Tudor's mother. Nor had they recognized Henry's subsequent marriage to Anne Boleyn, Elizabeth's mother. As far as they were concerned, Mary Stuart was the rightful heir to the throne. Elizabeth was a bastard and unfit to rule. However, the crown was Mary Stuart's in name only.

Mary Stuart became Queen of France in her own right in 1559 when her father-in-law died. Just 17 years old, she held the position for only 7 months when her husband, who had always been in poor health, also died. Since she had shown more aptitude for playing games than ruling up to that point, her mother-in-law, Catherine de Medici, took over as regent (see Chapter 15, "Early Modern Rulers," for more information). Mary, unwilling to share the throne, returned to Scotland in 1561, a country she barely remembered.

She was now the Queen of Scotland, having taken the throne from her illegitimate half-brother, James Stuart, who had ruled since her mother's death a year earlier. James was a Protestant and had successfully convinced the Scottish Parliament to abolish the Catholic Church. This made it difficult for Mary Stuart to gain any support in her own country. But she still had support in England, and she decided to use it to her advantage in Scotland.

In an attempt to further solidify her claim on the English throne, she refused to sign a treaty between the two countries until it was modified to name her as Elizabeth's successor. In 1565, she married her cousin Henry Stuart (also Lord Darnley), also a Catholic and also a potential claimant to Elizabeth's throne. She named him king and declared Catholicism as Scotland's national religion.

Mary Stuart's actions won her no support from her followers, who had been quite happy with the status quo. Her nobles plotted several insurrections, finally forcing her and her infant son from court. Henry had died, possibly at the hand of Mary's new lover, James Hepburn, the Earl of Bothwell. The two had married in May 1567, which further enraged her nobles and left her with no political support.

With few options left, she gave her throne to her son, who became James VI of Scotland. After that act, she was thrown into prison, from which she escaped and began organizing troops to overthrow the government. But the Scots, who really wanted her gone, overpowered her with larger troops of their own. Defeated, Mary

Stuart fled to England, hoping that Elizabeth would protect her and help her regain her crown.

But Elizabeth was still angry over Mary Stuart's earlier attempts to take the throne, and she wasted no time in jailing her as a suspect in Henry Stuart's death. Mary spent 18 long years in prison, during which time her Catholic supporters in England tried several more times to install her as queen. This further irritated Elizabeth as she suspected that Mary Stuart was behind such efforts. In 1586, Elizabeth called for Mary Stuart to be tried for treason. She was convicted of the crime, and Elizabeth had her beheaded.

A Woman's Place

According to accounts of Mary Stuart's execution, it took three whacks with an axe to behead the tough Scotswoman.

Mary Frith, Moll Cutpurse

A notorious criminal at the time of the English Civil War, Mary Frith proved to be a versatile one as well.

Born to a cobbler and his wife in 1584, Mary made a tidy living for herself by picking pockets, telling fortunes, forging various legal documents, and receiving stolen goods. She even sold the goods she received to their rightful owners from a pawnshop on Fleet Street.

Mary was a cunning thief, light on her feet and fast of finger. She evaded the authorities by changing her identity often, rotating men's and women's wardrobes. Her ingenuity kept her out of prison throughout most of her long career. She was jailed only once.

Catherine the Great

Sophia Augusta Frederika may have faced limited prospects as a German princess, but she didn't let something as minor as circumstance stop her from becoming the ruler of one of the greatest countries in the world.

The future Catherine the Great of Russia was born in 1729 in Stettin, Germany, the daughter of the Prince of Anhalt-Zerbst and Princess Johanna of Holstein-Gottorp, a duchy located in north-central Germany. She received a good education that covered subjects that would put her in good stead for marrying someone with greater social standing than she herself had, which had been her goal from an early age. Thanks to her mother, her early ambitions would be realized. Sophia would have a clear shot at a throne, and a good one at that.

When Sophia reached a suitable age, her mother contacted the Russian court on her behalf. The Empress Elizabeth, the formidable daughter of Peter the Great, seized upon the prospect of finding a good match for her nephew, the Grand Duke Peter, who was next in line for the throne. She commanded Sophia's presence at the Russian court.

Sophia and her mother left for the Russian court in January 1744. They arrived in Moscow in time for Peter's birthday on February 10. When Sophia met her potential husband, she was alarmed at his apparent frailty. As it turned out, he was emotionally unbalanced and underdeveloped physically. He liked to play childish games, and he hated Russia, which wasn't his country of birth (his aunt, Catherine, had brought him there from Germany after the other male heirs to the throne died, making young Peter Ulrich the heir to the throne).

Prior to her wedding, Sophia started to learn Russian and study the Orthodox religion, efforts that greatly pleased the Empress. On July 28, 1744, Sophia and Peter were betrothed, and Sophia became the Grand Duchess Ekaterina Alexeyevna. The name Ekaterina, or Catherine, was chosen for her by the Empress, in honor of her mother.

Hear Me Roar

The title of queen, even when I was a child, flattered my ears.

—Catherine the Great

A Woman's Place

The descendants of Peter the Great famously failed to produce male offspring, which established the tradition of female regents and rulers in Russia.

The wedding between Catherine and Peter took place in August 1745. Unfortunately for Catherine, she didn't get much in the way of a husband—she knew the young duke wasn't very bright, but what little he had in the way of looks had been robbed of him when he contracted smallpox in the year prior to their marriage. And, he had started drinking, which made his behavior coarse and crude. According to some sources, the marriage was never consummated. In others, a surgical procedure performed somewhat later allowed Peter to have normal marital relationships. For now, however, Catherine was childless, and the Empress blamed her for it. Accounts vary here as well, with some having Elizabeth arranging for a young lover for Catherine, who twice impregnated her, but she miscarried. Some sources suggest that Catherine found her own suitor. In others, the aforementioned surgical procedure allowed Peter to impregnate Catherine. In any case, she did have a son, Paul, in 1754, who was immediately taken away from her and delivered into Elizabeth's care. Both Catherine and Peter embarked on extramarital affairs after the birth of their son, Elizabeth with a young Russian lieutenant, Gregory Orlov, and Peter with a woman named Elizabeth Vorontsova, the niece of Russia's vice chancellor.

When Elizabeth died on Christmas day 1761, Catherine's husband ascended to the throne as Peter III. As ineffective a ruler as he was a husband, he immediately alienated his fellow Russians with his pro-German views and his hatred of all things Russian. Catherine, whose earlier efforts to become as Russian as she could be had endeared her to the people, soon realized that she could gain control of the throne and become empress of Russia.

In 1762, with the help of the Russian army, her lover, Gregory Orlov, and his brothers, Catherine arranged a royal coup. It was successful, and Catherine, at age 33, was proclaimed empress in June of that year. Peter, her husband, was imprisoned and assassinated without her knowing about it. If she had known, she probably would have stopped it, as she didn't dislike Peter. If anything, she felt sorry for him. But the word was that she did nothing to stop the execution, which made her seem exceptionally bloodthirsty even in the eyes of the people who adored her.

Hear Me Roar

Nothing in my opinion is more difficult to resist than what gives us pleasure. All arguments to the contrary are prudery.

—Catherine the Great

Catherine ruled Russia for 34 years, dying of a stroke in November 1796. She was a strict ruler but also a great one. Almost single-handedly, she made the sleepy country into a great power.

She completed the work begun by her husband's grandfather, Peter the Great, who had sought to centralize the country's various regions into one power. She expanded Russia's influence with foreign countries and promoted its cultural assets.

Catherine also improved Russia's agricultural production by developing new crops that would grow better and introducing modern methods for breeding sheep and cattle. She encouraged broader use of the country's natural resources by establishing mines and factories to process furs, long a part of Russia's wealth. Manufacturing increased significantly under her rule as did the number of factories, increasing from 984 to 3,161.

Education was also on her agenda. Russia had few schools at the time, so Catherine had much to do. She converted a convent in St. Petersburg into the Smolny Institute, a boarding school for girls. She also issued a royal decree in 1786 requiring the establishment of elementary and secondary schools. Since Russia also had few qualified teachers, she stopped there.

Unfortunately, Catherine's reforms did little to improve the plight of the serfs, Russia's lower class. Her blind eye toward social injustice led to a national uprising that lasted for two years, from 1773 to 1775, and planted the seeds for the Russian Revolution that came a little more than a century later.

Following the uprising, Catherine took up with Gregory Potemkin, a military officer some 10 years her junior. He would become her greatest love and closest advisor, although their affair only lasted two years.

Marie Antoinette, Louis XVI's Queen

The daughter of the German Emperor Francis I and Maria Theresa of Austria, Marie Antoinette goes down in history as the woman who fueled the fire that became the French Revolution.

An air-headed, silly thing from the get-go, Marie Antoinette had one destiny as far as her mother was concerned: She was going to be the Queen of France. But Maria Theresa must have assumed her daughter was either brighter than she was or would learn what she needed to know about being a queen by osmosis. When Marie was presented to the French court at age 15, her lack of knowledge made her a laughing stock. She even insulted the king's mistress, Madame du Barry, which was a supreme faux pas.

Even so, the French dauphin found her very attractive, and he chose her for his wife. They married in 1770. Four years later, he became King Louis XVI, and she became queen.

Although Marie was far from the only reason behind the fall of the French monarchy, she definitely contributed to it. She was silly and frivolous at court and a tremendous flirt, which distracted her husband from his duties. She loved to shop and gamble and had her husband's ministers fired when they tried to stem her spending. Over time, she took a good chunk out of the French treasury for her shopping sprees.

At the outbreak of the French Revolution in 1789, Marie Antoinette showed that she was made of more than fluff. When Louis proved to be a poor match for the revolutionaries, she stepped in and tried to rally support from other countries, including Austria, which was ruled by her brother, Leopold II. However, her efforts were less than successful. Fearing for their lives, Marie and Louis tried to escape from Paris in 1791, but were stopped by the revolutionaries. The entire royal family was sent to prison. Louis XVI died on the guillotine on January 21, 1793. It was Marie's turn eight months later.

Hear Me Roar

Let them eat cake.

—Marie Antoinette, supposedly in response to the French people's cries for food at the beginning of the French Revolution

A Woman's Place

The oft-repeated cake-eating story was nothing more than a fable cooked up to incite even more hatred for the unpopular queen. Marie supposedly asked an official why the Parisians were so angry. When told they had no bread, she reportedly said, "Then let them eat cake."

Madame de Pompadour, Louis XV's Mistress

Of all the young women who went to court to become courtiers (and perhaps win a king), none was more famous than Madame de Pompadour. Although she would never marry her lover, the French King Louis XV, and, in fact, was eventually discarded by him in favor of a younger consort, she, nonetheless, enjoyed many of the rights and privileges that such a marriage would have afforded her.

Born Jeanne-Antoinette Poisson in 1721, the future courtesan was nine years old when a mystic told her she would find favor with a king when she grew up. Soon, a number of events unfolded that paved her way to that destiny.

Jeanne-Antoinette's father, Francois Poisson, was a successful businessman but not always a scrupulous one. His fraudulent ways caught up with him in a big way in 1725 when he was sentenced to a long prison term following a black market scandal. While he was away, Jeanne-Antoinette's mother took a lover. Charles le Normant de Tournehem was a tax collector with good connections and a steady income. He lavished Jeanne-Antoinette and her mother with expensive gifts and made sure that the young girl received an education befitting her class. He also introduced her to men of wealth and influence, including his nephew, Charles le Normant d'Etioles, whom Jeanne-Antoinette married. The two were frequent guests at France's most fashionable salons. The witty and intelligent Jeanne-Antoinette gained a fast friend in Voltaire (remember him as Emilie du Châtelet's lover?) and other distinguished salon-goers.

A Woman's Place

In an amazing show of extravagance, Mme. de Pompadour had one of her gardens designed just to delight her sense of smell. Each day the gardeners exchanged the plants to insure their freshness and purity of their scents.

A Woman's Place

King Louis XV's discontent with his queen stemmed from her rebuttals of his advances. It would be hard to blame her for doing so. The dutiful Maria bore 10 children in the first 12 years of her marriage, which did little to fire her continued ardor in the boudoir. Literally worn out from performing her royal duty, she used religious piety as an excuse for abstaining from sex with the king on saints' days. She eventually refused all sexual contact with him.

Jeanne-Antoinette met her king soon after. King Louis XV was famously unhappy with his marriage to Maria Leszczyanska, the daughter of the exiled King of Poland, and had had a number of affairs before Jeanne-Antoinette came into his life. He quickly dumped his latest mistress for her and in 1745 gave her the title Marquise de Pompadour. He also bought her an estate to live on and arranged to have her marriage dissolved.

Jeanne-Antoinette wasn't King Louis's last mistress, but he depended on her friendship and counsel even after he went on to someone else. In the position of confidant and advisor, she acquired great political power and was instrumental in establishing closer ties between Austria and France. She also founded the famous royal porcelain factory at Sevres and furthered the careers of her favorite fellow courtiers.

The Least You Need to Know

➤ The strife between Protestants and Catholics fueled more than one battle over the throne.

➤ Catherine the Great readily gave up her German identity in her quest for the throne.

➤ Marie Antoinette's foolishness as queen helped launch the French Revolution.

➤ After she lost her position as king's mistress. Mme. de Pompadour acquired greater political power than she had as a royal consort.

Part 4

The Nineteenth Century

The women of the early nineteenth century didn't know it, but the winds of change were definitely blowing their way. The calls for "a new order and a new day" that women such as Mary Wollstonecraft had penned at the end of the eighteenth century had not gone unheard. In fact, they found fertile ground prepared by revolutions in America and France during the previous century.

While women had fought in both revolutions, they soon realized that their efforts were in vain when it came to improving their own lives. They also realized that freedom and liberty were concepts that seemingly only applied to white men of certain social status.

During the nineteenth century, women began working together as never before to fight against social injustice. As they did, they also began fighting for their own rights and freedoms.

Chapter 19

Life During the Victorian Era

In This Chapter

➤ Home as sanctuary

➤ The rise of the middle class

➤ Bloomers and crinolines

➤ Social consciousness

Devoted wife, skilled housekeeper, upholder of beauty and grace within the home—this is the traditional image of the Victorian woman. Like all stereotypes, it describes certain aspects of life during the nineteenth century for certain women. Like all stereotypes, it falls short of reflecting what life was really like for women of this period.

The Victorian era is often extolled as a golden age during which men and women happily toiled away in their separate spheres. Husbands went to work while wives stayed home and managed the house and family. Men were the leaders; women, the followers. Men were active and strong; women were passive and weak. The public domain was his; the private life of the home was hers. Men were physically and intellectually superior; women had the upper hand when it came to morality.

A great deal of this was true, but history also shows that there was a lot more to women during this period. While it's definitely true that women were defined by their relationships to men—daughter, wife, mother—many women began expanding their

A Woman's Place

Some scholars estimate that as few as 10 percent of married women in the nineteenth century augmented their household income by working outside the home.

Hear Me Roar

Long hours are to be beguiled after the lamps are lighted and the family gathered in the pretty, glowing light. Games, plays and frolics of all kinds are welcome and home—talks that instruct even while they entertain.

—Augusta Salibury Prescott, in *Godey's Lady's Book*, March 1890

thinking and their actions beyond these prescribed roles. As they did, they found they could have identities and accomplishments apart from being daughters, wives, and mothers.

Most women of the nineteenth century stayed home and took care of their households and families as was expected of them, but this isn't where life ended for all of them. By the end of the century, the lives of many women had expanded far beyond their parlors.

Leisurely Living

Life circumstances changed drastically for many women during the nineteenth century. The affluence created by the Industrial Revolution created a wider gap between rich and poor. Now there was a large and prosperous middle class comprised of the men who worked at the new jobs created by the Industrial Revolution. These men made enough money to support their families without assistance from their wives, so their wives stayed home. Having a supposedly "idle" wife quickly became an important social marker for middle-class men as it illustrated their success in the business world.

The household, always a key aspect of a woman's life, had gained even more importance by the end of the eighteenth century. Now it was truly the center of the universe for many women. The Victorians idolized the home as a sanctuary and refuge, where a weary breadwinner could gratefully retire at the end of the day to the embrace of his "better half." And it was up to that better half to make sure her breadwinner was completely happy with his home and everything in it.

The vast majority of married women, if they weren't slaves, didn't work outside the home (single young lower- and middle-class women did until they got married so they wouldn't be a financial burden on their families). Instead, they became mistresses of their domain, modeling their activities and behavior on the advice they gleaned from new periodicals like *Godey's Lady's Book*. As you'll read about later in this chapter and in Chapter 20, "The Fight for Rights," having more leisure time meant they could pursue other activities for virtually the first time in their lives as well.

As a whole, members of the middle class enjoyed a lifestyle that, for the most part, didn't exist before the nineteenth century. It wasn't quite as fancy and lavish as that enjoyed by the more privileged upper class, but it had many of the same trappings, such as time for leisure activities and the ability to hire others to do housework and other dreary chores.

More than ever before, the middle class had time on their hands, and many of the leisure-time pursuits of the Victorian era took advantage of that time. Reading became an extremely popular pastime, as did sketching and painting. Letter-writing and conversing became arts.

New Rooms

The homes the ladies of leisure presided over were changing drastically as well. The poorest families, and especially the urban poor, were still crammed into one-room dwellings. But as their wealth grew, the homes of middle-class families, especially those living in cities, grew as well. Some homes were even large enough that rooms were designated for specific purposes.

Beds were now confined to the bedroom rather than being scattered all over the house. Food was served and consumed in the dining room. People washed up and took care of their personal needs in the bathroom. By the end of the century these rooms were equipped with new hygienic equipment such as toilets and hot and cold running water made possible by electric water pumps and heaters.

Kitchens and foodways changed a lot in the nineteenth century. By mid-century, cast-iron cookstoves were popular, replacing the open hearth. White flour was cheaper and more available than ever before in the United States. In towns and cities, there was a greater variety of foods available. Fewer people grew their own food; canals and trains brought food to populous areas. Nonlocal items such as oranges and bananas traveled by clipper ships from warm climates.

Cheaply manufactured household utensils, including egg beaters, apple parers, and pots and pans with special uses, were readily available, filled the middle-class kitchen, and set the standards for those aspiring to middle-class life. The result was that meals became more elaborate, having several courses and exotic ingredients. Rather than lessening the burden on women, modernizing the kitchen and the industrialization of America increased women's work. Cookbooks and ladies magazines raised the level of expectation that women had to meet.

During receiving hours, another Victorian convention, guests were greeted and entertained in the front room or parlor, which, logically, was near the front door. When not entertaining guests, families entertained themselves in the family living room by playing games, reading aloud, and telling stories. Since women set the standard for how the home was run, it was also up to them to coordinate these leisure-time activities.

Godey's, one of the leading women's magazines of the day, even gave women tips on how to join their families in these pursuits when their daily tasks weren't complete. If still working on mending or sewing, for example, they could bring the work into the living room and "name long stretches of sewing after various countries, and discuss them as the work goes on ... Perhaps if interest is sufficiently aroused, someone will read aloud on the subject."

May I Call on You?

The Victorians followed a rigid moral code that strictly dictated their behavior. How one used calling cards, for example, differed depending on the age, sex, and status of the caller as well as the status of the individual or family being called upon. Questions regarding exactly how cards should be worded and presented were almost a standard feature of the etiquette column in *Godey's*. A faux pas in this area could set tongues wagging for weeks.

For many middle- and upper-class women, especially during the first half of the century, calling on others was almost the only contact they had with the outside world outside of going to the market. The overwhelming emphasis on domesticity isolated them from their communities and limited their opportunities to be anything more than housekeepers and mothers. It also robbed them of more of their rights.

As you'll read more about in Chapter 20, men were so intent on preserving the world outside the home as their domain that they passed protective legislation that gave women even less control over their property and their children. For many middle-class women, their newfound leisure and better quality of life offset any discomfort they may have felt over losing such rights. But they rallied on behalf of poor women, widows, and unmarried mothers who were in the same position (as far as their rights went) as they were.

Dressed to the Nines

As you have read, households became larger and grander as the century progressed—so did women's clothes. How a woman dressed indicated the wealth and status of her family, if she were single, and of her husband, if she were married.

While not indicative of fashion throughout the nineteenth century, the crinoline, a special underskirt that kept overskirts stiff and wide, became the symbol of the Victorian wife. At first, crinolines were starched and lined with horsehair, but they later were made of hoops that consisted of compressed horsehair and padded frames. Eventually, the horsehair padding was replaced with steel springs, or hoops, that substantially reduced the number of underskirts necessary to create the desired look.

Crinolines were considered the height of Victorian elegance. As they grew more popular, they also increased in width. Bows, puffs, frills, and laces were added to the overskirts that decorated them. They made women's waists appear miniscule, but corsets were also used to make the waist almost disappear. Corsets seriously constricted breathing and digestion, contributing to the idea that women were physically frail. Before long, the amount of decoration added to ladies' dresses also served to distinguish members of various social classes.

By the middle of the nineteenth century, crinolines were abandoned in favor of the bustle, a horsehair cushion held in place horizontally by laces or bands and suspended like a cage between the skirt and the underskirt in the back. When the bustle went out of fashion, skirts became so narrow that they hampered the movement of the wearer. Women who wore these hobble skirts walked in a series of little hops as if they were sparrows. It was impossible to sit in them as well.

Crinolines reappeared in a smaller version called the crinolette toward the end of the nineteenth century. Bustles made one last pass as well. But fashions that restricted how women moved were on the way out by the end of the nineteenth century. Women now had the time to take up sports such as tennis, bicycling, swimming, and fencing, and they needed clothing that freed up their arms and legs and allowed them to breathe.

A Woman's Place

Nineteenth-century feminists Elizabeth Stanton and Susan B. Anthony advocated the wearing of bloomers, an invention of English actress Fannie Kemble. Kemble took a manner of dress favored by Turkish men—a short skirt over baggy trousers—and adapted it for her own use. The style came to be called bloomers after Amelia Bloomer, the publisher and editor of a well-known women's rights newspaper called the *Lily*, wrote about them several times and praised them as a sensible alternative to the restrictive fashions of the time. However, the style met with so much derision that most women gave them up. Feminists quit wearing them as they feared that doing so would diminish their effectiveness as suffragists and women's rights activists.

Long hair—the longer it was, the better—was the fashion during the nineteenth century. It was an important aspect of a woman's feminine image, and women took great pride in their tresses. Although hair was always gathered onto the head, often into topknots or cascades of curls, it could reach the floor when let down.

Once again, *Godey's* and other popular women's periodicals served as the arbiter of style when it came to hair care, advising no more than a monthly dunking except in very warm weather. Rinsing the scalp with a sponge soaked in tepid water was enough, according to the magazine, to keep both scalp and hair clean. One popular shampooing routine of the time began with rubbing two whipped eggs (thought to nourish the scalp and promote hair growth) into the roots of the hair. After they dried for about an hour, they were rinsed out with a mixture of warm water and borax.

By now, finally, a daily bath was encouraged to preserve health, youth, and beauty. Warm baths were prescribed for those with strong constitutions; tepid baths for weaker women and children. Adding bran or starch to the bath was recommended if skin was rough. For coarse skin, gelatin was the answer. Scenting the bath with such herbs as hyssop, mint, rosemary, sage, or thyme was recommended to combat perspiration and odor. Bathing in borax, eau de cologne, tincture of benzoin, or lime juice were other remedies for women with these problems.

In the earlier decades of the century, bathrooms were still unknown in many areas and uncommon virtually anywhere. As water closets and flush toilets also were rare, most households used "privy-pails" to gather personal waste. In developing towns and cities, homes for the new middle-class were often built on elevated sites. Sewage from these homes would flow down to lower areas where laboring populations often lived.

Sanitation wasn't much better in areas where housing was all built on roughly the same level. Sewer systems often had drains made of stone, and they leaked. Most towns lacked paved streets, which meant that people might walk in sewage for weeks after a heavy rain. It would be the end of the century before modern sanitation systems were designed and built, largely thanks to the pioneering research of the noted home economist Ellen Richards (you'll read about her in Chapter 23, "New Frontiers").

Such diseases as cholera were still endemic during the nineteenth century due to poor sewer systems and contaminated water supplies. Deficiency diseases, such as scurvy and rickets, caused by the lack of essential nutrients in food, were rampant. People suffered from chronic food poisoning caused by minerals unknowingly introduced into food and water by bottle stoppers, water pipes, wall paint, or equipment used to process food and beverages. The deliberate adulteration of food—such as using alum to whiten flour—was common and virtually unrestricted until 1860.

School Days

In general, women became more educated during the nineteenth century, although "more" in this case is definitely a relative term. At the beginning of the century, girls were still relegated to a "feminine" education in such areas as music, art, poetry, dance, and embroidery that gave them the skills they needed to run an efficient household and taught them how to instill the appropriate morals in their children. Higher education was still off limits at the beginning of the nineteenth century, but change was on the way.

Women began campaigning in earnest for equal access to education at all levels in the early nineteenth century. At the same time, a handful of pioneering women were working to give them that access. They included the following:

A Woman's Place

The emphasis on preparing women to be vanguards of morality for their children paved the way for teaching as a profession. It remained one of the few professions—nursing was another one—considered acceptable for women to pursue well into the next century.

➤ Rosa Philippine Duchesne, a French nun, who arrived in New Orleans in 1818 with four colleagues and proceeded to open boarding schools and day schools for girls in frontier towns. Duchesne saw no color boundaries: Several of the schools she established were for African-American and Native American girls.

➤ Emma Willard, who in 1821 opened Troy Female Seminary, the first publicly funded girls' school to offer a full curriculum.

➤ Mary Lyon, who founded Mount Holyoke Seminary in 1837. From its beginning, Mount Holyoke, which was the first seminary for female teachers in the United States, offered a curriculum similar to those found in men's colleges and academic standards to match.

➤ Prudence Crandall, who opened the Canterbury Female Boarding School in 1831. She closed the school after the public went up in arms when she accepted an African-American girl as a student. Encouraged by abolitionists and African-American families, she reopened the school in 1833 as an educational institution for "young ladies and little misses of color."

As these schools and others were established, the literacy rate for women began to increase and the gap between the education offered to women and men narrowed. By 1850, roughly half of the women in the United States could read and write.

Institutes of higher education slowly and, in some cases, very grudgingly, began accepting female students. The University of Zurich was the first European university to enroll women students, doing so in 1865. The University of Paris followed suit the next year. Other Swiss universities began accepting women in the late 1870s. Many women who studied at them were Russians pursuing medical degrees, which they weren't allowed to do at home.

The University of London graduated its first women in 1878. Other English universities, such as Oxford and Cambridge, accepted women students but didn't grant them degrees (and wouldn't do so until 1948).

Oberlin College, which opened in 1833 in Oberlin, Ohio, was the first institute of higher education in the United States to admit both women and blacks. Although most female students opted to take classes in the college's "Female Department," designed to prepare them for lives as wives and mothers, not all did. In 1840, Georgia Female College was the first college to grant full Bachelor's degrees to women.

A Woman's Place

At the time Oberlin College opened its doors, Brazil was the only other place in the world where women could receive a college degree. As the century progressed, co-educational colleges and universities, especially the land grant colleges of the American West, provided education for women, but in a traditional mode. In 1900, of the 61,000 women in co-educational institutions, 43,000 were training to be teachers and 2,000 were studying home economics. The rest pursued other studies such as economics, geology, botany, astronomy, medicine, and engineering.

Women's colleges, mostly in the northeastern United States, created vibrant female communities where teachers and students formed close, nurturing bonds based on intellectual pursuits.

Erasing Society's Ills and Evils

Three factors—the general increase in women's educational levels, greater leisure time, and women's perceived roles as the upholders of morality—came together to cause a virtual explosion of civic activity by women during the nineteenth century. Since what they were doing wasn't perceived as work but instead a logical extension and reflection of their superior moral character, these efforts were not only permitted but also often encouraged.

By the end of the nineteenth century, women had created hundreds, if not thousands of voluntary associations, ranging from temperance societies to settlement houses. There was hardly an issue that women didn't see as their duty to reform or a social evil they didn't try to erase. Among the issues women went up in arms over were …

➤ **Temperance.** Drinking was on the rise during the early nineteenth century, and two relatively defenseless populations—women and children—were often the victims of drunken behavior. Such organizations as the American Society for the Promotion of Temperance, established in 1826; the American Temperance Union, established in 1836; and the Women's Christian Temperance Union, founded in 1873, crusaded against the "evil brew" and were successful in getting temperance legislation passed in about half the states.

➤ **Abolition.** The leading pro-abolition organization in the United States—the American Anti-Slavery Society—was a guy's-only group, so female abolitionists formed their own organizations. By 1837, more than half of the entire membership in abolition groups was female. The abolishment slavery was the first political issue to unite large numbers of American women. Their work in this arena would also fuel their efforts in the women's rights arena.

➤ **Working conditions.** Although middle- and upper-class women weren't directly affected by the conditions that working and lower-class women suffered in factories and mines, women of all classes came together to call for safer working conditions, higher wages, and shorter workdays.

➤ **The poor and less-fortunate.** Women whose heartstrings throbbed at the sight of the disenfranchised started women's clubs, settlement houses, and other charitable organizations dedicated to improving the plight of the needy and of immigrants.

The work these women conducted during the nineteenth century on behalf of the less-fortunate and to cure society's ills resulted in a great deal of change. It also changed the women themselves. As they came together to form societies, build settlement houses, and rally support for various causes, they also developed new organizational skills as well as increased levels of self-esteem, self-worth, and independence. No longer were their identities based solely on their roles as wives and mothers. Their successes showed them that they were capable of doing more and gave them the courage to keep moving forward on the one issue that had the potential to create change beyond belief—the right to vote.

The Least You Need to Know

➤ The home was the center of the universe for Victorian families.

➤ Nineteenth-century women were seen as morally superior to men while inferior in physical and mental strength.

➤ Women's access to education increased significantly during the nineteenth century.

➤ Work conducted on behalf of the poor and less fortunate gave nineteenth-century middle-class women greater feelings of self-worth and independence.

Chapter 20

Susan B. Anthony

The Fight for Rights

In This Chapter

➤ The beginning of the fight for women's rights

➤ Declaring women's sentiments

➤ Suffrage around the world

➤ Suffrage state by state

The concept of the good and dutiful wife may have prevailed during the nineteenth century, but there were plenty of women who, quite frankly, thought the notion was a lot of bunk. Tired of putting up with situations and circumstances they hadn't created, they started campaigning for change.

Women hadn't gained much from the revolutions in America and Europe, but they now knew that reform on a grand scale was possible. They also knew that they had to be the ones to work for it. Such seminal statements of democracy and freedom as the Declaration of Independence and the Constitution had reaffirmed the lesser status of women. Clearly, men were going to skirt the issue for a long time to come. It was up to women to fight for their freedom, their justice, and for their full status as human beings.

The nineteenth century stands apart from other eras in women's history as the period during which the first real cracks began appearing in the structures and assumptions that had governed women's rights and roles for eons.

The next two centuries would bring about staggering changes for women in virtually all areas of their lives.

Tea and Revolution

The organizers of the anti-slavery convention held in London in 1840 had unknowingly sown the seeds of change for another reform movement when they banned Elizabeth Cady Stanton and Lucretia Mott from their seats on the main floor. The irony of the situation was incredible to them both. As women attending the world's first conference to address the oppressive institution of slavery, they had been subjected to similar oppression. It made their blood boil, and they decided to do something about it.

A Woman's Place

The similarities between slaves as property and women as property formed a close connection between the anti-slavery movement and the women's movement from the beginning. A number of women determined to attack the social ills of the day supported both. Lucretia Mott, in fact, was one of the foremost leaders of the American abolitionist movement.

On July 19, 1848, Stanton and Mott gathered some of their friends for afternoon tea. The group ended up talking about the irony of living in a new democracy while their rights and freedoms were as restricted as they had been in the Old World. Stanton said she felt the new republic would benefit from women taking more active roles. Her friends agreed with her. What's more, they decided to hold a convention to gather together other like-minded women.

They weren't the first group of women to have a conversation like this, but they were the first to develop a specific plan of action. Several days after their afternoon tea, Stanton, Mott, and their friends had picked a date for their Women's Rights Convention, found a suitable location, the Wesleyan Methodist Church in Seneca Falls, and placed a small ad announcing the event in the *Seneca County Courier*. They called it "a convention to discuss the social, civil, and religious condition and rights of women."

Declaring Women's Rights

While preparing for the convention, Stanton drew up a document that would clarify the group's purpose and enumerate the issues they were protesting. Her template for her "Declaration of Sentiments" was nothing less than the greatest symbol of American liberty, the Declaration of Independence.

How Stanton began the Declaration of Sentiments was a direct mirror of how the Declaration of Independence began, but with one small (and very important) twist. In her version, all men, and women, were created equal. The highly impassioned statements that followed made no mistake about the current tenor of women's sentiments about their roles in society.

Stanton then went into great detail about the legal grievances that women were subjected to, stating that ...

➤ Women were not allowed to vote.

➤ Married women were legally dead in the eyes of the law.

➤ Women had to submit to laws when they had no input in how they were formed.

➤ Husbands had legal power over and responsibility for women to the extent that men could imprison or beat women without fear of being punished themselves.

➤ Divorce and child custody laws favored men and gave no rights to women.

➤ Most occupations were closed to women, and when women did work, they received only a fraction of what men earned.

➤ Women had to pay property taxes although they had no representation in the levying of them.

Hear Me Roar

The history of mankind is a history of repeated injuries and usurpations on the part of man toward woman, having in direct object the establishment of an absolute tyranny over her. To prove this, let facts be submitted to a candid world.

—Elizabeth Cady Stanton, from the opening to her Declaration of Sentiments

Stanton listed 18 grievances in all. The message they contained was loud and clear: Women were living under a code of laws and beliefs that made them totally dependent on men and were being robbed of their self-confidence and self-respect because of it. She then called for women to "receive immediate admission to all the rights and privileges which belong to them as citizens of these United States," and detailed to the letter what these rights and privileges should be in a list of 12 resolutions, including one calling for the right to vote.

With only a few changes, the 200 women who attended the Seneca Falls convention endorsed the Declaration of Sentiments and its resolutions. The only one that didn't pass unanimously was the call for women to receive the vote. It was inconceivable to many, even to Mott, Stanton's dear friend, that women would ever be given that right. Furthermore, they feared that demanding the vote at the time was simply too radical a move and would not garner the support they needed to carry the movement forward.

The resolution was the subject of heated debate during the two-day convention, but it did pass, in large part thanks to the support of the black abolitionist Frederick

Douglass, who argued that women, like slaves, were entitled to the same rights as the white male citizenry of the United States enjoyed. It was the first public demand by women for *suffrage*. At the end of the second conference—those who attended Seneca Falls reconvened about two weeks later in Rochester, New York—68 women and 32 men put their signatures on the Declaration. (Yes, men attended the convention, although few accounts mention them being there. In fact, the Seneca Falls convention was chaired by James Mott, Lucretia Mott's husband.)

Misconceptions, Misrepresentations, and Ridicule

Stanton had concluded the Declaration of Sentiments by stating that she and the others who supported it were anticipating "no small amount of misconception, misrepresentations, and ridicule." That was putting it mildly. When word got out about what had happened in Seneca Falls, attacks flew from all quarters.

Words for Women

Suffrage comes from the Latin *suffragium,* meaning "vote."

The press—of course, overwhelmingly controlled by men—was particularly vicious. Newspapers ran editorials dripping with vitriol over the audacity of the women to demand the vote. To ridicule the women further, a number of papers published the entire Declaration of Sentiment along with the names of those who had signed it. Some of the signers were embarrassed by the attention and withdrew their signatures. Others were pressured to do so by their families. Most, however, stood firm.

Many men also had a lot to say in opposition of the convention and those who had organized and attended it. What the attendees at Seneca Falls hadn't anticipated, however, was the resistance mounted by other women. While they knew everyone didn't see things the way they did, they were largely unprepared for the attacks they got from their own sex.

Clearly, the injustices that inflamed some women weren't even issues for others. Many women, even while they campaigned for other reforms, still believed in the superiority of man and the natural position of women as inferior to man.

The Movement Spreads

Inspired by the Seneca Falls conference, women in other parts of the United States held similar events. Women's Rights Conventions were convened on a regular basis from 1850 until the beginning of the Civil War. They drew large crowds—some even turned people away due to lack of space—which further confirmed that large numbers of women were concerned about their rights and ready to do something about it.

A Woman's Place

Elizabeth Cady Stanton and Susan B. Anthony met soon after Seneca Falls. As two of the leading theorists of the women's rights movement, they formed a friendship and a political partnership that lasted for 50 years and helped the women's movement advance its agenda into the next century. Along with other leaders of the movement, they stumped for women's rights all over the United States, Canada, and Europe, holding rallies and giving speeches. They also wrote numerous articles in feminist journals. Neither Stanton nor Anthony lived long enough to see American women get the vote, but their efforts made it possible for suffrage to move forward into the twentieth century and gain enough support to become a reality.

The United States was by no means the only country where women were coming together to campaign for reform. In England, much to the chagrin of Queen Victoria, who believed that giving women greater rights would cause them to lose their femininity, women began organizing around the middle of the century.

The English Women's Rights Movement

One of the earliest voices of reform in England was Caroline Norton, who, although she believed in the natural superiority of man, decided to take on existing laws when her barrister husband accused her of adultery, refused to let her see her children, and denied her any means of support. To add insult to injury, when she finally did make some money on her own, he took it away from her. All of this was perfectly legal under English law.

Another was Harriet Hardy Taylor Mill, who published an essay advocating women's suffrage in 1851. She reported on the Seneca Falls convention and others that were taking place in the United States and called for full legal and political citizenship for Englishwomen. She also called for equal opportunities in higher education, new laws that would allow women to keep their own wages, and laws that would protect them from male violence.

A Woman's Place

Harriet Mill's' second husband, the English philosopher John Stuart Mill, took up his wife's work when she grew too ill to carry on by writing *The Subjugation of Women*, which he published in 1869, eleven years after his wife's death. In it, he gave full credit to Harriet's influence on his ideas, saying that the ones that were most striking and profound belonged to his wife.

Education reform was an area in which the English feminists scored some early hits. In 1848, Queen's College was established so that women could have access to college-level lectures. Bedford College did the same in 1849. Barbara Leigh Smith, later Barbara Bodichon, who would become a leader of England's women's movement, attended Bedford and then opened her own school.

The battle to give married women more rights drew high levels of support as so many women had been victimized by the existing laws that barely recognized them at all. By 1856, a group of women including Smith, Bessie Raynor Parkes—Smith's childhood friend who had published a book on women's education—and the well-known writers Mary Howitt and Anna Jameson, successfully gathered 26,000 names on a petition they planned to present to Parliament. Unfortunately, their efforts were in large part a failure. Parliament did pass slightly more liberal divorce laws in 1857 that allowed legal separation and divorce in cases of cruelty or adultery. But women gained no additional control over their own property or money.

The group's defeat galvanized the women into turning their efforts into a real movement. During the 1860s, they lobbied for legislation allowing married women greater control over their earnings (including the right to keep them after separation or divorce), which they won in 1878. A similar effort on property rights, allowing women independent ownership of their own property, passed in 1882. The British feminists also successfully founded women's colleges at the major universities and even convinced college authorities to allow female students to attend some classes at men's schools.

Smith and Parkes were among the women who campaigned for John Stuart Mill when he made a bid for Parliament in 1865. When he won, one of the first issues he brought forward was women's suffrage.

Women's Rights Down Under

They were halfway around the world from the site of all the action, but such isolation didn't keep women in Australia from organizing their own women's movement. Even though women were a scarce resource in the land down under, and would continue to be for decades, they were subjected to many of the same inequities and inequalities women in the rest of the world faced. In Australia, as in other countries, a woman's role as homemaker and housekeeper was of prime importance. Things like education or job training ran a very distant second.

By the late nineteenth century, Australia's women's movement, lead by such reformers as Caroline Chisholm, was making its voice heard on such issues as education and the rights and status of women. Here, the movement's agenda merged with temperance issues and came under the aegis of the Women's Christian Temperance Union, which began in 1885. The WCTU worked hard to advance women's suffrage issues even while railing against the evils of alcohol. What might seem like a strange combination proved to be a winner in Australia, however. Australian women won full voting rights by 1908, way before women in Europe and the United States got them.

Going for the Vote

It was in New Zealand, of all places, where the first breakthrough toward women getting the right to the vote took place, thanks in large part to the efforts of two women: Mary Muller and Katharine Sheppard. Muller, a British woman who immigrated to New Zealand in 1850, championed the vote in her new country by talking to lawmakers and submitting anonymous articles to various publications, including the *Nelson Examiner,* New Zealand's most influential newspaper. Sheppard, an organizer for New Zealand's branch of the WCTU (Women's Christian Temperance Union) who continued Muller's efforts after Muller's husband put the kabosh on her work, organized several petition drives directed at New Zealand's parliament. After several years of political maneuvering, the parliament passed the bill making New Zealand women the first nationally franchised female voters in 1893.

Women's Rights in Italy

Italy had struggled for many years to become a unified country. Women had aided that effort, but the fight for unification left little room for taking up other causes.

When the country's first civil code was drawn up, it failed to give women the vote. It also upheld long-standing traditions by giving husbands legal authority over their wives. Italian women were understandably aggrieved. Some responded by writing about it.

In 1864, Anna Manna Mozzoni published a book criticizing the prevailing view that women's lives should focus solely on home and family. Other women published political journals, the first of which appeared in 1872. Although the little booklets would come and go with great frequency, women found them an ideal way to voice their opinions and reach others with similar views. By the end of the nineteenth century, a women's movement began to emerge in Italy. At first, women of all classes were united in their fight for suffrage. Later on, support for women's rights in Italy ran along class lines. What had started as a unified voice for change ended up separating into movements that reflected their members' political orientation and social class. The lack of unification didn't do Italy's women's movement much good. It wasn't until Benito Mussolini's Fascist regime toppled that women regained the freedoms they had lost under his control. They finally won the right to vote in 1946.

Women's Rights in Japan

The women's movement in Japan began to stir near the end of the nineteenth century but didn't really gain steam until the twentieth. As in Australia, the Women's Christian Temperance Union took up the issue of suffrage and advanced it with their temperance agenda. They also worked against prostitution and concubinage. In the 1880s, women working in textile plants struck for better conditions

Going for the Vote

Suffrage—gaining the right to vote—became the linchpin for women's movements around the world. It was the door to all the other reforms that meant so much to women. It would also prove to be the most elusive. In the United States, it would take 72 years for women to get the vote due to the staunch opposition against it.

In the United States, both suffrage and the women's rights movement in general had suffered a setback due to the Civil War. Many people who might have lent their support to women's issues in other times now saw them as secondary in importance to ending slavery.

After the Civil War's end, women's rights continued to remain on the back burner as politicians felt the needs of the freed slaves took priority. Some women's rights activists agreed with this agenda, which caused a split in the women's movement. The hard-line suffragists who put women's vote above anything else followed Elizabeth Cady Stanton and Susan B. Anthony into the National Woman Suffrage Association, organized in May 1869.

More moderate suffragists started the American Woman Suffrage Association. Unlike Stanton and Anthony's group, the AWSA, headed by Lucy Stone, allowed male members and adopted a state-by-state strategy for getting the vote instead of a national campaign. The rift between the two factions continued for almost 20 years before they reunited in 1890 in the National American Woman Suffrage Association, or NAWSA, with Stanton as its first president.

England's women's movement was suffering the same division among its members. The movement split from 1884 to 1897 along political lines—some members wanted to build an alliance with England's Liberal Party, others wanted to remain independent of any political affiliation. In 1897, the various groups that had formed during the split united as the National Union of Women's Suffrage Societies. Its main focus was on getting the vote.

But the English women's movement also wouldn't stay united for long. By the early twentieth century, it again divided into two rival factions: The Women's Social and Political Union, led by Emmeline Pankhurst, and the National Union of Women's Suffrage Societies, led by Millicent Garrett Fawcett. Although the two groups followed different agendas, mostly defined by the personalities of their leaders, they both worked toward winning the vote.

Suffrage State by State

In the United States, pushing for the vote at the national level was the original emphasis of the suffrage movement and was the initiative supported by Stanton and Anthony. This didn't preclude efforts at the state level, which many women mounted in addition to their national agendas.

State-based suffrage initiatives often included testing the laws at that level by attempting to vote. In 1872, 16 women, led by Anthony, went to the polls. Anthony was arrested for her efforts and convicted at a trial without a jury by a judge who had decided what he would do before he heard a scrap of evidence. She was fined but no serious attempt was ever made to collect it for fear that she would appeal the decision.

That same year, Virginia Minor, an officer in the National Woman Suffrage Association, sued Reese Happersett, the registrar of voters in St. Louis, Missouri, for not allowing her to register to vote. The case went all the way to the U.S. Supreme Court, which ruled in 1874 that being a citizen of the United States didn't automatically give one the right to vote.

After this defeat, suffragists shifted their tactics and worked to change state constitutions, a strategy that had succeeded in Idaho, Colorado and Wyoming, which was the first state to give women the vote, doing so in 1869.

It also worked in Utah, which gave women the vote in 1870, but not in the way you might think. In the heavily Mormon state, men voted for the enfranchisement of women so that women would support polygamy. When the federal government made multiple-spouse relationships illegal during the 1880s, Utah women lost their voting rights, but they were restored when Mormon leaders agreed to ban polygamy, which paved the way for Utah's admittance to the union in 1895.

The state-by-state effort may not have been the approach that the founders of the women's movement would have liked, but it proved more effective than national efforts had been. Prior to the passage of the Nineteenth Amendment in 1919, 11 other states gave women full voting rights. Fourteen more gave women limited suffrage.

The Least You Need to Know

➤ The women's rights movement in the United States is considered to have started with the Seneca Falls Women's Rights Convention.

➤ Suffrage, or the right to vote, was the only issue that didn't receive complete support at Seneca Falls.

➤ Securing the vote turned into the top issue for the women's movement in the United States and abroad.

➤ Following an unsuccessful constitutional challenge in the Supreme Court, suffragists focused their efforts on gaining the vote through changing state constitutions.

Chapter 21

Women at War and Politics

In This Chapter

➤ The woman known as "Mrs. Satan"

➤ Giving voice to the plight of women

➤ The last empress

➤ Fighting for India's freedom

The monarchy, which had formed the basis of European rule for generations, was on the wane during the nineteenth century. Many of the dynastic families had merged their interests, either as a result of war or in attempts to stave it off. There were far fewer ruling families by the turn of the twentieth century and fewer ruling queens. As you'll see in this chapter, several of the ones who were left were toppled from control as well.

A new world order was being created, one that would give more people greater rights and authority than before. Power and influence were no longer reserved for nobility. In the years to come, women (and men) would have new opportunities to influence public opinion, reform old and outdated legal systems, and even lead their countries into battle.

Victoria Woodhull

Along with her sister Tennessee, Victoria Woodhull defied Victorian conventions by tilting at the windmills of proper female place and deportment. Her decidedly eccentric approach to life undermined her actions to a certain extent, but there's no denying that she got people thinking and shocked their sensibilities, which was pretty much what she set out to do.

The seventh daughter of 10 children born to Buck and Roxanna Claflin of Ohio, Victoria spent her early years as an itinerant traveling across the country with her family in a medicine show. The Victorians were mad for people who exhibited *paranormal* talents, such as fortune telling and contacting the dead. Victoria and Tennessee put together an act that showcased their supposed talents as spiritualists, and they became the hit of the show. Victoria left the show at age 15 when she married Canning Woodhull. The two had a son and a daughter, but the marriage was short-lived thanks to Woodhull's alcoholism. Victoria rejoined the family circus immediately after divorcing him.

Words for Women

Paranormal refers to events or phenomena that can't be explained or understood in scientific terms.

Hear Me Roar

All talk of women's rights is moonshine. Women have every right. They have only to exercise them.

—Victoria Woodhull

In 1868, Victoria claimed that she had seen a vision of the ancient Greek orator Demosthenes, who had encouraged her to move to New York. Victoria and Tennessee, accompanied by Victoria's lover (and later husband), the Civil War veteran Colonel James Harvey Blood, made the move, which turned out to be a propitious one. The sisters were able to wrangle an introduction to the famous industrialist Cornelius Vanderbilt, who had recently lost his wife.

Vanderbilt was looking for someone who could enter the spirit world and establish contact with his beloved wife. Victoria and Tennessee couldn't have had a more ideal way to elbow their way into New York society if they had conjured it up themselves. They, of course, gave Vanderbilt exactly what he was looking for. He, in turn, helped them launch an immensely successful real estate venture. The sisters then turned their attention to Wall Street, and, again with Vanderbilt's help, opened Woodhull, Claflin and Co., the first stock brokerage owned and operated by women.

Their business went so well that the two sisters were able to step away from actively managing it in a very short time. Victoria turned her attention to an acquaintance, Stephen Paul Andrews, who was supposedly a philosopher and linguist. In reality, he was a fervent abolitionist with *anarchic* tendencies.

He found a fast friend in Victoria, whose beliefs often landed her on the flip side of convention. Before long, the two were vocal proponents of free love, legalized prostitution, and a whole host of other reforms that matched Victoria's growing conviction that marriage was simply a way to keep women subordinate to men. While their beliefs were definitely extreme, the people who took the time to examine their basis saw that Woodhull and Andrews were also supporting women's rights.

Intent on publicizing her views on women's rights, which were so radical that the suffrage groups eschewed any connection to her, Woodhull organized her own political party and urged Congress to legalize women's suffrage under the Fourteenth Amendment.

Words for Women

Anarchic refers to the complete absence of government and law created by anarchy.

In 1872 she announced her candidacy for the presidency of the United States. With a radical platform espousing (among other things) free love, taxation reforms, legalized prostitution, shorter skirts, and the right to birth control, she had little expectation of success, but she knew she could bring her beliefs before a wide audience and hopefully gain some support for them.

To insure that her platform reached as broad an audience as possible, she published the *Woodhull and Claflin's Weekly*. At first it only presented Woodhull's presidential agenda. But Woodhull soon expanded it to include exposés of various ills. It was also the first periodical to print Karl Marx's *Communist Manifesto*, thanks to Andrews' involvement.

Yeah, RIGHT.

Woodhull's campaign ended in a scandal that rocked the nation. About a year before the election, Woodhull's first husband appeared out of nowhere and moved in with her and Blood. Tongues wagged, especially when rumors started circulating that Woodhull might still be married to husband number one. The controversy moved into the public arena when Woodhull turned the tables and suggested that the relationship between the Reverend Henry Ward Beecher (Harriet Beecher Stowe's brother) and Elizabeth Tilton, the wife of editor Theodore Tilton, undergo the same scrutiny.

A Woman's Place

Victoria Woodhull was known to many people (especially her detractors) as "Mrs. Satan," a sobriquet that especially suited her reputation as a spiritualist. No one ever knew if she could really contact the dead, but even the thought that she could aroused old suspicions of witchery and evil.

Woodhull might have made it through to the election if she had contained her argument to a verbal vendetta. Instead, she revived *Woodhull and Claflin's Weekly,* which had suspended publication, and printed the gory details in a final special edition.

This proved to be a huge mistake as she was then arrested for disseminating obscene material through the mail in violation of the *Comstock Law*. When election day rolled around, she was in jail.

Woodhull was eventually acquitted under the guarantee of free speech accorded her in the First Amendment. Following her acquittal, she left the country with her sister Tennessee and settled in England. Successfully having left their prior lives behind them, they both settled down, married, and gained a certain level of respectability that had eluded them in their native country.

Words for Women

The **Comstock Law** was named after Anthony Comstock, its chief proponent and a New York morals crusader of the late nineteenth century. Passed in 1873, this federal law prohibited sending obscene material through the United States mail.

The Good Queen Victoria

She ascended to the throne at age 18 and vowed that she would "be good." Over the course of her 63-year reign, she upheld her vow more often than not while forever changing the role of the British monarchy.

As the granddaughter of King George III, Victoria was fifth in the line of succession when she was born. A series of untimely deaths in her family elevated her status to heiress at a fairly young age. Because of this, she was groomed for her future role before she was accustomed to the idea that she would be a queen. It was a rigorous upbringing for a little girl, and she would always regret her stolen childhood.

Victoria was by no means a confident queen at first, and many worried that she would follow the British monarchy's tradition of ruling at arm's length. But her husband, Prince Albert, whom she married in 1840, encouraged her to do more. Victoria gradually came into her own as queen and asserted her authority in many areas. She demanded that Parliament follow her orders instead of acting on its own. From about 1850 on, she directly shaped England's political agenda, including the country's foreign and domestic policies and the reorganization of its colonial authority over countries like India.

Although Victoria had intended her husband to take a backseat role to her authority, she truly loved Albert and barely bristled when he gradually worked his way into public affairs. When he died in 1861 of typhoid fever at 42, Victoria was heartbroken. She really never recovered from the loss and substantially cut back on her public functions from that point forward, although she retained her authority over her prime ministers. She went into deep mourning and adopted the severe clothing that she would wear for the rest of her life in her dead husband's memory.

When Victoria finally emerged from mourning in her 70s, she found companionship and comfort in John Brown, one of her servants. Their relationship caused much speculation, most of it exaggerated.

Victoria was beloved by her subjects throughout the course of her 63-year reign, the longest in England's history. She recast the role of the monarchy and helped it regain its prestige and power as other European families were losing theirs. Her austere and matriarchal authority over her family and her country remains a model that the British sovereigns continue to follow to this day. By the time she died at age 81, her influence had spread to other royal families through her children and numerous grandchidren, who married into virtually every royal family in Europe.

Taytu Betul

The African country of Ethiopia has a strong tradition of female rulers who wield great power. When Taytu Betul ascended to the throne in 1883, it was clear that she would continue the traditions of those who had come before her.

Born of a princely family near the city of Gondar, Taytu was married twice before she became the wife of King Menelik II. The political ups and downs that befell her previous husbands gave her vast knowledge of Ethiopian politics, making her the ideal wife for the somewhat naïve king. In 1889, two days after Menelik's coronation as emperor, Taytu, which in Amharic means "the sun," was crowned Empress. Her official title became "Light of Ethiopia."

A Woman's Place

The fight for women's rights began during Victoria's rule. Like many rulers of her time, she opposed it, fearing that giving women more rights, including the ability to vote, would erode the God-ordained relationship of men to women—men superior, women inferior. She called on her advisors to help her check "this mad, wicked folly of women's rights."

More educated than the average woman of her day, Taytu could read and write Amharic. She was also familiar with Christian Orthodox doctrine, thanks to her step-father's association with a monastery. She could play the begena, a royal lyre believed to be related to the biblical King David's harp, and was adept at Ethiopian chess, a form of the game closely related to that played in the Middle East during medieval times.

Strong-minded and forceful, Taytu wielded great influence over her husband. Among other things, she convinced him to move Ethiopia's capital to a more pleasant location and climate. She saw her role as Menelik's protector, believing him too trusting of the various foreigners trying to gain influence in Ethiopia.

Taytu's fears over her husband's ability to repel foreign influence were vindicated when a dispute arose between Italy and Ethiopia regarding each country's authorities. According to Ethiopia's version of the Treaty of Wechale, King Menelik could avail himself of Italy's support when dealing with European powers, but wasn't required to. The Italian version stated that it was mandatory for him to do so. The dispute was all the Italians needed to claim a protectorate over all of Ethiopia. Menelik refused to honor their claim.

In 1896 it became clear that the Italians could no longer be kept at bay. With Taytu's encouragement, Menelik declared war. Taytu was an active participant in the two-year battle that ensued, and even brought 3,000 of her own troops to the battlefield. Ethiopia's eventual victory was a turning point in African history and caused the downfall of the Italian government.

Queen Taytu was a great businesswoman, renowned for her generosity and her acumen. She easily managed her vast estates while maintaining a full schedule of responsibilities at court. Among her business ventures was Addis Ababa's first important hotel, which bears her name to this day.

During the last years of Menelik's reign, as his health deteriorated, Taytu effectively became the ruler of Ethiopia. Having no children of her own, she attempted to build an alternative power base by promoting her relatives and arranging dynastic marriages. But her efforts weren't very successful, and she was eventually barred from matters of state. When Menelik died, she left the capital and established a simple home in Entoto, where she spent her remaining years in prayer and quiet contemplation.

Elizabeth Cady Stanton

The daughter of a judge in Johnstown, New York, who honored his faith as a Quaker by making sure his daughter understood what injustice was at an early age, Elizabeth Cady Stanton would become one of the foremost leaders of the women's movement in the United States.

A Woman's Place

Elizabeth Cady Stanton reflected her feminist leanings at an early age when she insisted that the word "obey" be removed from her marriage vows. She also insisted on keeping her family name and used it in conjunction with her husband's name for the rest of her life.

Elizabeth had learned her lessons well from her father by the time she entered Emma Willard's Troy Female Seminary. There, she met other like-minded women and began developing her beliefs on abolition and suffrage. In 1840 she tied the knot with Henry Brewster Stanton, an abolitionist attorney. The two spent part of their honeymoon in London at the world's first anti-slavery convention. Enraged over being banned from the main hall, Elizabeth found a kindred spirit in Lucretia Mott, who had also been banned.

The two joined forces in protest and became fast friends as well as the founders, along with Susan B. Anthony, of the American women's movement. Mott and Cady Stanton were the prime movers of the 1848 Seneca Falls Women's Rights Convention, which launched the movement in America. There, Cady

Stanton revised the United States Declaration of Independence to include women. Pointing out the injustices women faced, she called for the establishment of women's rights along the lines that men enjoyed, including the following:

➤ Equal pay for equal work

➤ Equal access to education

➤ The freedom to train for and enter all professions

➤ The right to own property

➤ The right of guardianship over one's own children

➤ The right to vote

Cady Stanton and her husband had seven children, but her responsibilities as a mother didn't keep her from her work of advancing the women's rights agenda. An energetic speaker and writer, she frequently addressed the New York State legislature on family law issues, contributed to the *Woman's Journal,* founded the newspaper *Revolution* with Susan B. Anthony in 1868, co-authored *The History of Woman Suffrage* with Anthony, and served as president of the National Woman Suffrage Association for 20 years. In 1890, Cady Stanton became president of the National American Woman Suffrage Association, a merger between her NWSA and the American Woman Suffrage Association led by Lucy Stone.

One of the suffrage movement's most forceful and eloquent speakers, Cady Stanton's fervent beliefs and her ability to articulate them did much to advance the women's rights agenda in its earliest days and set a strong foundation for continuing the movement's work into the next century.

Lydia Kamekeha Liliuokalani

As the last reigning monarch of the Hawaiian Islands, Lydia Kamekeha Liliuokalani lost her throne when Hawaii became part of the United States. Although the politics of the time worked against her rule, Liliuokalani was well liked and she clearly believed in preserving her people's history and legacy.

Liliuokalani, called Lydia as a child, was born into the family of a high Hawaiian chief. Her parents were court counselors to King Kamehameha III, who held the throne from 1825 to 1854. Her parents' status at court gave Lydia better access to an education than she would have otherwise received. She attended the Royal School, which was run by American missionaries, and received quality instruction there.

Lydia's brother Kalakaua ascended to the throne in 1874. When her younger brother died, she was next in line to the crown, which she attained in 1891 following Kalakaua's death. During his reign, Americans had seized a fair amount of control over the country's legislature and had managed to replace the king's Hawaiian cabinet with an all-American one. The goal was to weaken the monarchy and put Americans

217

in control of the country's economy, and the Americans were winning. They were even able to pass a constitution that granted voting rights to foreign residents but denied them to most Hawaiians. Lydia's first goal as queen was to restore the power and authority of the crown and use both to preserve the islands for her people.

Lydia's plans met with severe resistance as soon as she made them public. When she tried to establish a new constitution and replace the American cabinet with Hawaiian representatives, a group of prominent American businessmen living in Hawaii asked the U.S. government to step in. American military troops occupied the government buildings in Honolulu and removed Lydia from the throne in 1893. After she was deposed, the Americans organized a new government and petitioned Washington for annexation. Lydia tried to regain control, only to be placed under house arrest. Hawaii was annexed by the United States in 1898 and became a U.S. territory in 1900.

After losing the throne, Lydia continued to live in Honolulu. She had studied music at an early age and now had the time to pursue her love of traditional Hawaiian music and culture. She became a noted composer and went on to write more than 160 poetic melodies and chants, including one of the four Hawaiian national anthems. Her best-known work, which exemplifies her skill in blending ancient Hawaiian and Western musical traditions, is the romantic ballad "Aloha Oe" ("Farewell to Thee").

Queen Min of Korea

Foreign countries have fought over Korea for centuries, and the Koreans haven't much cared for it at all. In the late nineteenth century, Japan was the world power knocking heaviest on Korea's doors, much to the displeasure of the country's population and of one of its rulers. Her actions to oust foreign influence from her beloved homeland made Queen Min into a national icon after her death.

It was actually Queen Min's husband, King Kojong, who allowed the foreign infiltration in the first place. Kojong was weak, impressionable, and far too easily swayed by the Japanese who were using him to push Korea toward becoming a colony of Japan. Internal revolts erupted as he tried to do as the Japanese wished while still retaining control over the country.

Sensing that Korea would become a part of Japan if her husband continued to kowtow to the Japanese, Min decided to ask Russia and China for help while she wrested control away from King Kojong.

When Japanese officials caught wind of her plans, they decided she was far too capable of rallying the support she needed. She was an obstacle in need of removal, and they proceeded to do exactly that.

In 1895 the Japanese minister sent troops into Kyongbok Palace, Queen Min's home. They ransacked the building and stabbed her to death in front of her son, the crown prince. Following her death, Korean leaders were pressured into signing a treaty with Japan and into promising to open Korea's doors to foreign trade.

Queen Min didn't accomplish her goals for her country, but her efforts on behalf of her people endeared her to them. Her grave at Kyongbok Palace, which went unmarked for many years, is today often festooned with flowers left in her honor.

Old Buddha (Dowager Empress Ts'u His) or Tz'u-hsi

Another powerful Asian ruler, Dowager Empress Ts'u His, called "The Old Buddha," ruled China during the last century of the Manchu dynasty. When she died, the Chinese monarchy disappeared for good.

One of several children born to a minor mandarin named Hui-cheng, Ts'u His's royal heritage (her family was Manchurian, which made them part of the Manchu dynasty) made her eligible to be an imperial concubine. In 1851 she went to the Forbidden City in Peking to join the court of Emperor Hsien-feng. Although she lacked any formal education or training, she had taught herself to read and write and was a gifted painter. Five years later, she gave the Emperor his only surviving male child, which elevated her to concubine of the second rank.

However, she didn't maintain favored status for long. When the Emperor died a somewhat mysterious death in 1861, Ts'u His was sent away from court. Even still, she was able to have her son, Tung Chih, declared crown prince. She was appointed co-regent with the Emperor's widow. Although the men of the court paid little attention to Ts'u His's role behind the scenes, she actually wielded a great amount of authority, which she refused to relinquish when Tung Chih came of age.

Tung Chih died in 1875, and Ts'u His had her sister's son, Kuang Hsu, appointed emperor in his place. Still unable to give up control over her country, she ruled in his name as well until 1889. She took a hiatus from public life for a time after this and built herself a magnificent summer palace outside of Peking.

It wasn't long before Ts'u His returned to politics, this time in opposition to Kuang Hsu's plans to bring China into the modern world. His reforms weren't winning him any friends among other government leaders. Ts'u His joined them in a coup in 1898 that bounced her nephew from the throne and placed her on it.

Ts'u His ruled with an iron hand and upheld the China's traditions until the Boxer Rebellion of 1900. Forced to flee from Peking in disguise to escape the wrath of the Chinese masses, she saw their living conditions for the first time and realized that she had to do something about them. In 1901 she proved that an old dog could learn new tricks. In her late 60s, Ts'u His instituted the reforms she had earlier rebelled against. In January 1902 conditions finally allowed her return to Peking. She brought the Emperor and the Empress, whom she had deposed, with her.

219

After dispatching an exploratory committee to Europe to investigate modern forms of government, Ts'u His announced that China's monarchy would have a constitution. But the country was in a recession thanks to years of war and oppression, and she received very little support for this governmental reform.

The Emperor Kuang Hsu and the dowager Empress Ts'u His died within a day of each other on November 14 and 15, 1908. The uncanny timing of their deaths led to speculation (never confirmed) that the old empress had her nephew murdered as they were both dying so he couldn't tell tales. The Chinese monarchy ended three years later.

A Woman's Place

During her reform years, Ts'u His abolished foot binding and modernized China's educational system. She established a Ministry of Commerce to help the country build its trade relations and nationalized China's customs services, which had been controlled by Europeans. She also abolished torture and the most severe forms of execution, and she suppressed opium farming. She also brought electricity to her country.

Lakshmi Bai

An early force in India's struggle for independence from British rule, Lakshmi Bai is often referred to as India's Joan of Arc for her valor on behalf of her country.

Bai was born into a high-caste family in the northern Indian principality of Jhansi. The family was wealthy, and she was taught to read and write along with her brothers. In her spare time, she rode horseback and played with weapons—two pursuits that would serve her well as an adult.

At age 14, Bai married Gangadhar Rao, the maharaja of Jhansi. He was older and more sophisticated, and Bai, now the Rani of Jhansi, felt oppressed by him and her new role as a queen. When she asked for permission to resume her riding as a break from her duties, he denied her request. She went around him and did it anyway.

Gangadhar Rao died four years later. The principality was in jeopardy as the royal couple's only son had died soon after birth. As was the custom, Rao had adopted one of his young relatives as his heir, but the British refused to recognize the young man as the next maharajah. They instead mobilized forces to attack the principality and bring it under British rule.

Bai was furious over this development and wasted little time in telling the British that she and her husband had done fine on their own as rulers and that their small province would do better under her control than theirs. The British, of course, ignored her. Not only that, they insisted that Jhansi had been mismanaged all along and that she was now responsible for enormous debts incurred by her late husband.

Bai retaliated by recruiting a large army to repel the British forces when they came, which she knew would be any day. In 1858, she led her troops in defense of the principality and its capital city. After a difficult siege, however, Jhansi fell to the British.

Bai left the city under the cover of darkness and led an attack against the nearby fortress of Gwalior, which she managed to seize. But Gwalior would be her last battle. Legend has it that she was holding the reins of her horse in her mouth to free her hands for sword-fighting when the British attacked her from behind and toppled her to the ground. Jhansi came under the complete control of the British following her death.

The Least You Need to Know

➤ The Victorian Age takes its name from the dominance of Britain and the length of Queen Victoria's peaceful and prosperous reign.

➤ Two very different women acted as spokeswomen for women's rights in the United States. Victoria Woodhull, radical and colorful, put women's issues on a presidential platform. As one of the founders of the women's rights movement in America, Elizabeth Cady Stanton became one of the movement's most eloquent and forceful speakers.

➤ Although ultimately unsuccessful, rulers like Queen Min, Taytu Batul and Lydia Kamekeha Liliuokalani endeared themselves to their subjects by trying to save their countries from foreign invaders.

➤ Lakshmi Bai is often called India's Joan of Arc for her sacrifices on behalf of her country's freedom.

Chapter 22

Women at Work

In This Chapter

➤ A changing economy

➤ Working in the mills

➤ Teaching teachers

➤ New voices in literature

Of all the changes that took place during the nineteenth century—and there were many—none would be as profound as the ones brought about by the development of industrialization. As turning points go, it was one of the greatest. It changed the Western world from a rural and agricultural society to an overwhelmingly urban and industrial one. The shift from agriculture to manufacturing caused the first significant reconfiguration of the world's economy and social structures since the development of agrarian societies in the ancient world. Now that's change!

Industrialization left no aspect of daily life unchanged. It revolutionized the production of goods and increased people's standard of living. At the same time, its rapid growth in cities caused overcrowding, unsanitary conditions, and truly horrendous working conditions.

The Industrial Revolution also had a profound impact on the work that women did during the nineteenth century. Although women began staying home in large numbers during this period, the ones who ventured out into the workforce found tremendous changes awaiting them. Some were good; others were very bad.

For the laboring classes, conditions that were poor to begin with grew worse in many cases. Women of higher classes, on the other hand, had greater access to education and to professions that had been closed to them before.

Farewell Farm and Field

For the first time since nomadic tribes had settled down to farm and raise animals, agriculture no longer drove the economy in the Western world. While agriculture would continue to remain an important segment of the economy, new industries made possible by industrialization rapidly eclipsed it.

Industrialization took away a number of the jobs that poor and working class women were accustomed to doing. Single women who worked at a number of jobs on family farms found that they were no longer needed when those farms were consolidated into commercial operations that provided the raw materials used in manufacturing. Married women, who often took in piecework so they could stay at home with their children, also lost those jobs as manufacturing expanded, centralized, and moved into cities.

Piecework was brought into the factories, and the women who did it had the choice of following it there or finding other jobs. Because their odds of finding gainful employment in another area of work were practically nil, they were off to the cities and the factories.

A Woman's Place

The household had been the central economic unit for centuries until the Industrial Revolution. Historically, manufacturing was done in homes by women who supplied their own families and traded or sold the excess for other goods, services, or cash. Not only did the growth of centralized manufacturing put an end to most piecework done in the home, but it also sent many men who previously had worked with their families at home out into the new world of the working class.

In addition, women no longer had to make everything they needed. Rather than grinding their own grain, they could buy flour. They could buy soap and candles, pots and pans, and cloth—all mass-produced.

Hello Factories

One of the major innovations of the *Industrial Revolution* was the modern factory, created by the introduction of power-driven machinery in the textile industries of England and Scotland.

Words for Women

Although the basic elements of the **Industrial Revolution** can be traced back to commercial development in Europe hundreds of years before, the term Industrial Revolution commonly refers to the period during the 1700s and 1800s when large manufacturing establishments, powered by coal or steam, began to mass produce products, and the social changes that following as a result of such development during this period.

The textile business was the linchpin of the new economy. In the United States, cotton was king, comprising an estimated sixty percent of all export goods by the middle of the century. In the south, where the economy retained much of its agricultural basis, poor black women and men harvested cotton (we talk about their particular plight later in this chapter).

In the North, and especially New England, white women and later, immigrant men, women, and children, spun and wove the cotton into cloth on such machines as steam-powered looms that could churn out fabric faster than ever before.

It took scores of people to operate the massive machinery of the industrial era. Running the machines that turned out textiles remained a woman's domain as it had throughout history. Men, for the most part, weren't interested as they saw the work as being beneath them. Working with cloth had always been women's work. Even in the new area of mechanization, they still saw it as being such. But men were hired to supervise the women workers.

Wanted: Young White Female Workers

Mill owners didn't much care who ran the machines that they were building huge factories to house. But having women comprise the majority of their workforce was almost too good to be true. Not only were women willing to work long hours for far less pay than their male counterparts, many had been displaced from their former jobs and would do anything to find gainful employment. By 1870, 10 percent of the workers in American factories were women.

Young women came to the mills in droves and found plenty of jobs waiting for them. As the few men who worked in textile factories yielded to the lure of the West and headed for the frontier, women took those jobs, too. Although their contribution was never acknowledged in their time, these women played a key role in developing America's new economy.

A Woman's Place

Even when they worked the same jobs and the same hours, the pay scale for women working in factories was often half what men earned. Still, mill work was comparatively lucrative; the wages of a factory girl were higher than those in other female occupations. In 1847, Horace Mann reported that female teachers only made one sixth to one seventh of what mill workers earned. Mill women made $2.50 to $3.20 a week, while seamstresses made $1.00 a week.

The practice of hiring young unmarried women for mill work began in 1813 when Francis Cabot Lowell's Boston Manufacturing Company built the first textile mill in Waltham, Massachusetts. Young farm women were an abundant and cheap source of labor. Men weren't interested in the work for the most part. The importance of agriculture for the nation and the opportunity to own one's own land kept many of them on the farms. Adventurous men migrated westward. The choice of a female workforce was facilitated by certain societal assumptions, too: Carding, weaving, and spinning were traditional occupations for women. In the work ethic of the new republic, all citizens were to be productive. Moreover, busy female hands would be kept from vice and mischief. Daughters who could send home wages to their farm families were blessings. But in exploiting these young women, the mill owners unwittingly liberated them.

Big Brother Is Watching

Lowell built several more mills in what would eventually become Lowell, Massachusetts. He hired young girls at all of them. These new mills centralized a number of steps under one roof for the first time, making textile production even more efficient than before. Lowell went one step further to insure the highest levels of efficiency: He built dormitories to house his workers.

Offering such housing was supposedly an employment benefit. The mill owners tried to provide an environment that would appear appropriate and safe to the families of the female workers worried about their virtue. The company, through the boardinghouses and the women who ran them, acted as substitute parents. But providing housing also let Lowell keep a tight rein on his employees. Workers who wanted to live in the dormitories had to uphold a strict set of rules in addition to consenting to being watched during virtually every waking hour. Women working for the Lowell mills had to tell their supervisors where they were living and let them know when they moved. They couldn't smoke, drink, or engage in any other behavior deemed improper by mill management. They were severely reprimanded and even punished if they weren't in their dorm rooms by the 10 P.M. curfew. Other regulations included mandatory church attendance and pox vaccinations.

A Woman's Place

Women spent less than two years on average working in the New England mills. Most left to marry. Others sought and found positions as teachers or domestics.

Other textile factories in New England used the Lowell dormitories as a model for their own employee housing. Over time, living in dormitories or company boardinghouses became a requirement of employment. The same strict rules applied to the boardinghouses, whose keepers could lose their right to take in borders if the rules of the mills weren't enforced or they neglected to report infractions to mill management.

Such severe regimentation gave mill workers little or no freedom, but they rarely complained about it. Their employment options were limited, and they were expected to work until they were married so they wouldn't be burdens on their families. Despite the severe strictures of the Lowell mill system, the women who sought employment in them saw such work as a means of improving their lots in life.

Having money to spend was powerfully liberating. The women who worked in the mills were paid in cash monthly. After paying for their board, they had enough money to send home or spend on such personal items as gifts, books, writing paper, ribbons, and hats.

Factors other than wages also encouraged a sense of self-esteem and liberation. The factory system rewarded seniority, as older more experienced hands taught the newcomers. Proud of their skills and their product, not defined as someone's daughter or someone's sister, they stood on their own courage and merit. These women gained knowledge of other people and ways of doing things, developed organizational skills, made lifelong friendships, and even published a newspaper, *The Lowell Offering*.

Through talking and sharing, they developed a strong sense of female community and identity.

Educational opportunities were another liberating factor. In Lowell, there was a debating club and the Lyceum offered a series of 25 lectures for 50 cents. Lecturers included John Quincy Addams and Ralph Waldo Emerson. Night school courses were offered, and the Lowell Library, founded in 1825, lent out books. Of course, some women were too exhausted to take advantage of these offerings, but many others did.

Cruel and Inhumane

As conditions worsened due to the economic reversals of 1837 and 1848, the Lowell factory workers were more than vocal on numerous occasions. They were subjected to appalling working conditions. Shifts typically lasted for 12 hours with little or no time off for lunch hours or dinner breaks. The long hours, often spent standing, and lack of food made many women chronically weak or ill. The noise that the looms made was deafening, the machinery made the factory stifling and hot, and dusty lint was in the air to be breathed in all day. Wages were reduced, and the workload increased as the influx of immigrant labor devalued mill work. As you read in Chapter 20, "The Fight for Rights," these conditions brought about protests, strikes, and walkouts. Although women won concessions in some areas—most notably the length of the workday—calls for higher wages and safer working conditions repeatedly failed.

A Woman's Place

In 1846 an estimated 8,000 of the 20,000 servants in New York City were born in Ireland. Two thousand hailed from Germany. The majority of the rest were members of other ethnic minorities.

Immigrants were also drawn to mill work as they saw it as better than what they had left behind. As tough as this work could be, it was definitely a step above the other jobs open to immigrant workers. In urban areas, newcomers to the United States who mistakenly thought they had left such drudgery behind when they came to the land of freedom and opportunity almost always took available jobs as laundresses, domestic servants, and seamstresses.

The immigrants who toiled in these positions were often severely exploited by their employers, who treated them poorly and paid them next to nothing. Long hours of sewing or washing clothes could earn an immigrant as little as $2 a week.

Slave Labor

The invention of the cotton gin in 1793 expanded the cotton industry in the South and fueled the need for more fieldworkers. Since black men were often taken from the fields and promoted into skilled positions necessary to the running of other parts of the plantation, most of the slaves working in the fields were women. While Emancipation released them from slavery, their employment options beyond the field after the Civil War were tantamount to slavery.

White women, believing that former slaves had the appropriate temperament for domestic work (and would appreciate such jobs), regularly sought out free black women as servants both before and after the Civil War. For the most part, black women lacked the training that would secure them better jobs, so they had few options beyond domestic service. White employers were well aware of the situation, and they often mercilessly exploited their black employees, subjecting them to sub-human working conditions, long hours, and little pay—conditions blacks thought they had left behind when slavery was abolished. Many black women who took jobs as cooks or maids, whether they were married or not, were separated from their families and forced to live with their employers.

Industrialization in Europe

In Europe, where the Industrial Revolution began, workplace conditions for single and married women of the laboring classes were similar to those in America. Unlike in America, however, young women in Europe far preferred jobs as domestics to factory positions. Regardless of the specific arena of employment, worker exploitation was high. Women were often forced to work the worst shifts and were paid very little for doing so. Again, few had the requisite training they needed to pursue better positions. Nor did such positions exist in any great number.

Employment opportunities for young working women in Europe were generally limited to jobs as domestics, in factories, or as street peddlers. Some women worked as prostitutes either as their only jobs or to supplement income from other positions. As the middle class became wealthier and men moved on to other work, domestic service jobs for women became even more plentiful. Still, their tenure in such positions was often short due to poor working conditions and equally poor treatment by employers. Servants often weren't included in laws that were written to protect other workers. In France, for example, there were no restrictions on the number of hours servants worked, no guarantee of a weekly day off, and no retirement or insurance benefits. Servants also could be fired for virtually any reason.

Over time, more women chose to work in the mills. The majority of them were young and unmarried, and they planned to work only until they could find suitable men to marry. These jobs paid better than others open to them, but their wages still remained lower than men's. The best-paying jobs were often beyond their reach as they lacked special training or skills. Should they try to advance into such positions, the men they worked with almost always blocked their progress. They had no interest in seeing their jobs lose status and pay, which happened in virtually all the professions that women entered.

Better education was clearly an important element in gaining better employment—in fact, the lack of education was now seen as the greatest obstacle women had to hurdle if they wanted to earn more than the bare minimum they needed to survive.

Recognizing that the new jobs created by industrialization required a more educated workforce, most European countries provided some form of free primary education for girls and boys by the end of the nineteenth century. Girls were taught to read, write, and do simple arithmetic. Anything beyond this was believed unnecessary and the efforts to provide it controversial.

Hey Teach!

The growing emphasis on elementary education also drove the need for more teachers. Although women had always taught their own children in one way or another, teaching as a profession wasn't open to them until they could attain the necessary education themselves. The establishment of teaching seminaries and academies during the nineteenth century provided the instruction they needed to instruct the wage earners and parents of tomorrow.

Women experienced few barriers when they entered teaching, as many men were no longer interested in it. As had happened in other professions when women entered them, teaching no longer paid as well or commanded the status it once had.

None of this deterred women from becoming educators. Even if salaries and status weren't as high as when men commanded the profession, they were still far better than what women could earn doing virtually anything else. In Europe, teaching was the leading occupation for women above the working-class level until World War I. By 1870, more than half the 200,000 primary- and secondary-school teaching jobs were held by women.

Going Higher

As you read in Chapter 19, "Life During the Victorian Era," higher education remained almost entirely off limits to women until the nineteenth century. As these institutions began admitting female students, they also opened the doors to professions that had been off limits as well.

While their numbers were miniscule, women began attaining the education necessary for practicing in such male-dominated professions as medicine and the law. They faced extreme opposition and ridicule from both classmates and instructors as they did so. But their persistence, and their success, proved that they were just as able as their male counterparts were of studying at higher levels and entering male-dominated professions.

Some women even revolutionized those professions. Marie Curie's groundbreaking research in radioactivity resulted in numerous discoveries and created a new medical specialty. The psychoanalyst Karen Horney, who as Karen Danielson earned a medical degree from the University of Berlin in 1911, took on Sigmund Freud's theories that women were merely dysfunctional versions of men by suggesting that men may actually envy women's abilities to bear children and breast feed.

A Woman's Place

Greater access to higher education allowed some women to attain medical degrees in the nineteenth century, but their numbers were still miniscule. Women were still seen as a threat to the male-dominated profession, which meant that most women doctors either had to limit their practices to treating women only or to patients who couldn't afford male physicians or lived too far away from them.

When the Civil War first broke out in the United States, neither side commissioned female physicians even though medical personnel were sorely needed. Evidently, a few women managed to break through the ranks and served as doctors. Mary Edwards Walker, who received a Congressional Medal of Honor for her service, finally received a commission from the Union Army in 1864, three years after she applied for it. Her tenure was brief—she was sent to the front in Tennessee and captured as a spy. Other women who went to the front as nurses met with similar fate when their job titles were changed to spy or scout.

Men had been extremely loath to give women access to higher education. The official stance was that women were already getting out of hand and would be impossible to control if they were better educated. The real concern was that women would prove just as able as men were to work in a number of occupations. Men sensed that well-educated women could give them a real run for their money. They weren't ready for the challenge, and they did what they could do to quash it.

But the doors had been opened, and they would never close again. As women became better educated, they broke the barriers in many male-dominated occupations.

Writing a Woman's Life

While there have always been women writers, and even a few journalists, greater numbers of women than ever before began putting their creative juices to work in these arenas during the nineteenth century. They wrote novels and supplied stories both to the general audience and to the growing genre of ladies' publications.

Writing had always been an acceptable way for a middle-class woman to earn money because she could do it in the privacy of her own home (not in the male, public sphere) and could meet her domestic responsibilities at the same time. During the nineteenth century, which had its share of depressions and panics, more women than ever turned to writing to help support their families. Single women, too, felt the need to earn money to support themselves.

Godey's Lady's Book (discussed in Chapter 19) was one of at least a hundred such periodicals that sprang up during the nineteenth century to meet a more literate population's growing demand for reading materials. Another was the *Ladies Home Journal,* launched in 1883 by publisher Cyrus Curtis after the women's supplement to his farming journal, edited by his wife, proved to be more popular than the journal itself. He dropped the publication's agricultural content, gave it a new name, and made his wife, Louisa Knapp Curtis, its first editor.

Conversely, the women who wrote for these periodicals and others promoted women's dependency on men and the glories of being a housewife. Supposedly, they put their own feelings aside in the interest of earning a living. They also wrote what they knew could get published.

When it came to writing books, women authors could and did unleash more of their own opinions and beliefs. Many wrote novels with domestic themes that reflected their own experiences and the problems they faced in everyday life. Most were set in the household—the primary women's arena of the time. But instead of describing the home in the idealistic prose of the Victorian era, many women told it like it really was.

A Woman's Place

Men were also challenged on the literary front by such talented female authors as Jane Austen, Mary Shelley, the Brontë sisters, Louisa May Alcott, Elizabeth Barrett Browning, and others who proved that women could hold their own as serious authors as well.

Popular female novelists such as Mary Virginia Terhune, Catharine Maria Sedgwick, and Lydia Sigourney wrote about women being held captive in their homes by the moral and social standards of the day. The husband was the villain in these books, which probably explains why male authors of the day took every opportunity to deride the novels for their content and characterize their authors as hacks.

While there's no question that many of these "domestic novels" were far from great literature, they sold like crazy. Male authors might have been appalled at their content and shocked at the decidedly unfeminine opinions expressed in many novels, but the fact that women's novels outsold theirs most likely bothered them more.

Women would continue to push the edges of the employment envelope into the next century, and men would continue to bristle about it. Their argument that women's inferior intellectual and physical capacities precluded them from most employment became increasingly less effective as women continued to prove them wrong.

The Least You Need to Know

➤ Industrialization revolutionized the workplace for both women and men.

➤ In the nineteenth century, thousands of women who worked in the mills, earning money and living independently of their families, returned to their homes changed by the experience.

➤ Expanded access to education allowed women to enter professions that were closed to them in the past.

➤ Novels written by women during the nineteenth century often took on feminist tones and portrayed men as villains for imprisoning their wives in their homes.

Chapter 23

New Frontiers

In This Chapter

➤ Setting a course to the stars

➤ Creating a science out of homemaking

➤ Fighting for the right to practice law

➤ Going undercover to expose corruption

They may not have come crashing down, but many of the traditional barriers that women encountered in the professions definitely started to lift during the nineteenth century. Successful careers in fields that had traditionally been off-limits, like medicine and the law, were still difficult to accomplish and the women who pursued them generally met with extreme resistance from their male counterparts. But even these professions couldn't keep women out for long.

As a whole, the female population was becoming better educated. Some women took full advantage of greater educational opportunities afforded to them, worked until they were married, and then stayed at home. Others launched successful careers as scientists, mathematicians, physicians, and journalists, and worked at them in various ways throughout their lives regardless of their marital status and their responsibilities at home. Things were changing, and more middle-class women were working than ever before. Many women remained single; some were widowed (by the Civil War, for example); and some married women were forced to work to help support their families in volatile economic times.

Probing the Stars and Planets

Maria Mitchell was helping her father gather data for the U.S. Coastal Survey at their Nantucket home in 1847 when she spotted what she thought was a new comet. It passed muster as being exactly that, and Mitchell's career and reputation as a first-rate astronomer was assured.

Mitchell's love for the stars was clearly influenced by her father's celestial passion. He had little formal education but a great deal of intellectual curiosity, which he also passed along to his daughter. While she did attend school, a subject as exotic as astronomy was far beyond the resources of the town's tiny educational institution.

Hear Me Roar

I was born of only ordinary capacity but of extraordinary persistence.

—Maria Mitchell

A Woman's Place

As was typical of the time, even a brilliant scientist and instructor like Maria Mitchell was paid about half the salary that a male professor received. Women working as professors today are still likely to be paid less than their male counterparts and are less likely to receive tenure.

After graduation, she took a job as a librarian and continued teaching herself. She even taught herself to read French and German so that she could study scientific texts in those languages.

Mitchell became a celebrity when she found the comet that would bear her name. A year later, she was the first woman to be elected to the American Academy of Arts and Sciences. She also received a gold medal from the king of Denmark in recognition of her discovery. But the sudden renown made her uncomfortable. She retreated to the safety of her library, where she continued to work until 1861.

Matthew Vassar, the founder of Vassar College, had other plans for the famous but shy astronomer. He wanted her on the faculty of his new institution, knowing that her status and reputation would bring it instant prestige and respect. He made Mitchell an offer she almost couldn't refuse: Come to Vassar and explore the heavens in your very own observatory with your very own 12-inch telescope, at the time the third largest in the United States. It proved a powerful lure for Mitchell, and she accepted, albeit reluctantly.

Mitchell overcame her inherent shyness to become one of Vassar's most renowned and beloved instructors. She taught her research principles to some of the brightest young women of the country and delighted in having a role in shaping their futures. She also gave numerous lectures calling for greater recognition for women scientists.

In 1875 Mitchell founded the Association for the Advancement of Women, which worked to advance equal opportunity in the workplace. She was also the first woman elected to the American Philosophical Society, which honored her accomplishments by granting her membership in 1869.

Making a Science out of Housework

Domestic science was a fairly common class for girls to take in the nineteenth century as it underscored the standard beliefs that a woman's place was in the home and that she should have perfect mastery over all areas in it. Thanks to Ellen Swallow Richards, domestic science—renamed home economics—would also become a recognized scientific discipline.

Richards was inspired to pursue the life of a scientist by Maria Mitchell, with whom she studied at Vassar. Following her education there, she went on to the Massachusetts Institute of Technology, where she graduated in 1873 with a Bachelor of science and Master of arts in chemistry. She was the first woman to receive a chemistry degree from MIT.

Richards first worked in sanitary chemistry as it related to air, water, and food quality. In a study of municipal water and sanitation systems, she proved that faulty or inappropriately sited sewage systems could contaminate water supplies and result in disease. She exposed adulterations in various foods in a report she submitted to the Massachusetts state legislature in 1879. The state passed its first food and drug act a few years later, giving full credit for the act to Richards' research.

While working as an instructor at MIT, she explored her theory that science and technology could even lighten the burdens of housekeeping. In so doing, she defined the scientific principles of home economics. She presented these principles at the first conference on home economics, which she organized in 1899 at Lake Placid, New York. She also became the first president of the American Home Economics Association in 1908.

A Woman's Place

Ellen Richards' application of science to the home resulted in a number of innovations in kitchen design and construction, which were showcased in the Rumford Kitchen, a model kitchen she designed as part of the state of Massachusetts's exhibit at the Chicago World's Fair in 1893. Her futuristic kitchen proved to be one of the most popular exhibits at the fair. To help offset some of the expenses of the exhibit, the food cooked in the Rumford Kitchen for exhibition purposes was later sold to fair attendees.

Richards' scientific explorations sometimes led her down paths that even she didn't anticipate. When working to develop a noncombustible oil for a client, she instead discovered dry cleaning after noticing that a piece of wool that she had dunked in some naphtha came up sparkling clean.

Elizabeth Blackwell

The first woman to graduate from a medical school in the United States gained her entry to that institution by way of a cruel joke. Intent on becoming a doctor after a dying friend lamented the lack of compassion shown her by male physicians, Blackwell applied to school after school and was rejected by all because she was a woman. She was thrilled when her perseverance paid off in a letter of acceptance from Geneva Medical College in New York. Her high hopes were dashed, however, when she arrived on campus and discovered that her merits had nothing to do with her acceptance. The faculty and students thought they were the victims of a practical joke perpetrated by a rival medical school, and they decided to play it out to the end to see what would happen.

Once on campus, Blackwell decided to make the best of things. She studied hard and did her best to ignore the jokes and slurs made at her expense. She was polite to everyone she came into contact with and always showed the proper amount of deference to her professors. By the time she graduated, she had won the grudging respect of her peers and professors.

A Woman's Place

Elizabeth Blackwell was not the only member of her family to pursue a medical career. Her younger sister Emily followed in her footsteps and received her medical degree from Western Reserve University in 1854. Emily also helped her sister establish the Women's Medical College of the New York Infirmary.

After she graduated in 1849, Blackwell continued her medical studies in Europe where her acceptance was mixed. She could only be accepted as a student midwife in Paris, but received full privileges to study at St. Bartholomew's Hospital in London. When she returned to New York, she encountered still more opposition to her dream of practicing medicine, ranging from being ignored by her colleagues to being barred from hospitals and dispensaries. She regularly received hate mail and found it difficult to rent consultation rooms.

Despite these difficulties, Blackwell established the New York Infirmary for Women and Children in 1857. Recalling all too well her problems in getting accepted to medical school, she also started the Women's Medical College of the New York Infirmary in 1868. She then returned to England—the country of her birth—for good in 1858, where she served as a mentor to aspiring physicians Elizabeth Garrett and Sophia Jex-Blake, among others. Honored by inclusion in the

British Medical Register in 1859, she spent the remainder of her career as a professor of gynecology at a hospital in London.

A fervent believer in preventative medicine, Blackwell was one of the first physicians to promote regular medical checkups as a way to catch health concerns before they became large problems. She also was an early advocate of hand-washing and other personal hygiene techniques to help prevent infectious diseases from developing and spreading.

The Lady with the Lamp: Florence Nightingale

Fascinated from an early age with healing the sick, Florence Nightingale's work as a battlefield nurse helped erase the notion that nursing wasn't a respectable profession for women.

Nightingale, who was born in 1820, was the second daughter of Frances Smith and William Edward Nightingale. Her parents were wealthy British socialites who took a two-year tour of Europe for their honeymoon. Both Florence and her older sister, Parthenope, were born during their parents' travels. Florence was named after the city of her birth.

As a member of the English upper class, Nightingale was expected to make a good marriage and lead a comfortable and sheltered life. But she wanted more. In 1837, when she was 17, she gained some idea of what her future held. While in the gardens of one of the Nightingale family homes, she believed she heard God's voice calling her to service. But she had no idea what such service would be.

Like many women of the Victorian era, Nightingale developed an interest in the social issues of the day. She began visiting the sick in local villages, which led to her desire to study nursing, much to her parents' dismay. Nursing wasn't considered a suitable profession for women, and especially not women of Florence's social class and education.

In an attempt to distract their daughter from her ambitions, Nightingale's parents sent her on a tour of Europe with some family friends. They traveled to Italy, Greece, and Egypt, with Nightingale visiting hospitals and clinics wherever she could. They returned through Germany in July 1850, where Nightingale visited the Institute of Protestant Deaconesses, a hospital and school for nursing, in Kaiserswerth, near Dusseldorf.

After a year of arguing with her parents, Nightingale was allowed to return to Kaiserswerth and study medicine and surgery at the Institute. The three months of instruction at the Institute was the only formal training Nightingale ever had. She entered the Institute in 1850 at age 30, 13 years after she had heard the voice in the garden urging her to do good works. Sometime during this period she turned down a marriage proposal, fearing that domestic life would conflict with her professional goals.

Changing the Face of Military Hospitals

After Nightingale graduated from Kaiserswerth, she was named superintendent of London's Establishment for Gentlewomen during Illness in 1853. A year later, Britain, France, and Turkey declared war on Russia. The Crimean War broke out soon after. While the Allies were scoring victories on the battlefield, their facilities and methods for treating the wounded were roundly criticized. Nightingale, whose expertise in public health and hospitals had come to the attention of the British government, was asked to take a party of 38 female nurses to the front in Constantinople and oversee their integration into military hospitals.

A Woman's Place

Although her own health was compromised by an illness she contracted during the Crimean War, Florence Nightingale worked around the clock to bring comfort and support to soldiers under her care. They called her "the lady with the lamp" in recognition of her compassion and zeal.

At first, the doctors didn't want the nurses there and ignored them when they offered to help. But the ongoing flood of casualties from the field overrode the doctors' opposition to their unwanted co-workers. Soon everyone was laboring around the clock.

As part of her work during the Crimean War, Nightingale also established blood banks in Scutari and Balaklava and established emergency nursing techniques in the field that drastically reduced the military mortality rate.

A National Hero

Reports of Nightingale's efforts on the behalf of the Crimean War soldiers reached home before she did. Although she loathed the attention, she was welcomed as a hero when she returned to England in 1856. In recognition of her accomplishments, a public fund drive was launched to raise money for a nursing school at London's Saint Thomas's Hospital. The public contributed some £50,000 in her name to establish the Nightingale Training School in 1860.

Hear Me Roar

A Lady with a Lamp shall stand
In the great history of the land,
A noble type of good
Heroic womanhood.

—Henry Wadsworth Longfellow, in "Santa Filomena," a poem he wrote in 1858 dedicated to Florence Nightingale

Meanwhile, Nightingale took a hotel room in London, from which she campaigned for the establishment of a royal commission to investigate the health of the British army. Although she was now bedridden due to an illness she had contracted while serving in the Crimean War, Nightingale became a leading expert on public health and was called to consult on health issues in England, India, Europe, and America. She published more than 200 books, pamphlets, and reports on health care and nursing. Her book *Notes on Nursing,* written in 1859, became a standard reference for women seeking advice on nursing their families.

Nightingale spent the latter part of her life as an invalid and rarely left her bed. She was never seen in public, preferring instead to correspond by letter with her many acquaintances and colleagues. She received the Order of Merit, one of Britain's top honors, from King Edward VII in November 1907, becoming the first woman ever to be so honored. She died in 1910.

Opening Legal Doors: Belva Lockwood

Belva Lockwood fought long and hard to gain the right to practice law after the role of primary breadwinner for her family fell on her shoulders. Her efforts paid off in her becoming the first woman to plead a case before the U.S. Supreme Court.

A Woman's Place

The legal establishment grudgingly allowed women into law schools during the nineteenth century but expressed its displeasure of female attorneys by making it difficult to impossible for many of them to actually practice. Arabella Mansfield became the first woman to be admitted to practice in the United States in 1869, but she preferred teaching to the battles she anticipated in court. Myra Bradwell, who published the *Chicago Legal News* with her lawyer husband, was initially refused permission to practice in Illinois, which didn't admit women to the bar until 1872.

Lockwood applied to a number of schools before being accepted at the National University Law School in New Hampshire in 1869. Although she passed her final exams, the school withheld her degree. Only when President Ulysses S. Grant, who was also the school's ex-officio president, interceded on her behalf did she finally receive her diploma. She won her first case a few days later.

Necessity dictated Lockwood's gaining the right to appear before the Supreme Court. She was living and practicing in Washington, D.C., where the federal courts take the role of state courts in legal proceedings. When one of her cases came before the federal court of claims, she was denied permission to plead it because the system didn't allow women to practice law. She petitioned the Supreme Court for such privileges, but the court refused to hear her case. In 1877 Lockwood appealed to some members of Congress who she felt would be sympathetic to her cause. Thanks to several pro-suffrage senators, legislation was passed in 1879 permitting female attorneys to practice before the Supreme Court. Lockwood was the first to exercise her right to do so.

A fervent feminist, Lockwood often used her clout as an attorney to advance women's issues. She fought for equality and the vote, and even ran for president in 1884. Unlike Victoria Woodhull's earlier attempt, Lockwood's candidacy was legitimate and her efforts taken seriously. More than 4,000 male voters—all of them men since women still couldn't vote—were sufficiently impressed by her talent and beliefs to cast their votes on her behalf.

Going for the Vote

Lockwood's pioneering efforts helped set the stage for other female attorneys, including Marie Popelin, the first woman to obtain a doctor of law degree in Belgium. Unfortunately, the Brussels Court of Appeal refused to let her take the lawyer's oath, stating that custom forbade women to work in the profession. It wasn't until 1922 that Marcelle Renson and Paule Lamy became the first Belgian women to take the lawyer's oath.

Going for the Glow: Marie Curie

The most famous of all women scientists, Manya Sklodowska is better known as Marie Curie. As one of the most brilliant scientific minds of her day, she laid the foundation for nuclear medicine and research through her landmark discoveries of radium and polonium.

The daughter of a mathematics and physics teacher, Marie was born and educated in Warsaw. By age 16 she had already completed her secondary education at the Russian Lycee and receive a gold medal in recognition of her talent. Although she was clearly destined to continue her studies, the family had no money to support her. Instead, she worked as a governess to finance her sister Bronia's medical studies in Paris. Once Bronia was done, Marie would receive similar assistance.

In 1891 Marie arrived in Paris to study at the Sorbonne. She was so poor that she virtually lived on bread and butter while studying far into the night in her student's garret. Her world consisted of little else besides school and study, and she developed an almost super-human capacity for hard and long work as a result.

Marie married Pierre Curie, a physics professor at the Sorbonne, in 1895. The two worked together until his accidental death in 1906 (weakened by exposure to radiation, Pierre fell in front of a horse-drawn carriage and was killed), and were responsible for the discovery of polonium, radium, and what they called "excited radioactivity."

Curie was awarded a Doctorate of Science for her role in the discovery of radium; she and Pierre both received a medal from the British Royal Society for the discovery. Their discovery of radioactivity earned them the Nobel Prize for Physics. Curie was the first woman to be so honored.

A Woman's Place

Marie Curie also invented the first portable x-ray machine, which helped physicians make diagnoses in the field during World War I. Renault cars were fitted with the small devices and driven onto the battlefield. Curie even drove one herself, often bringing her daughter Irène along with her. Inspired by her famous parents, Irène also became a physicist and married one as well. The two were awarded the Nobel Prize in Chemistry in 1935. Sadly, Irène also suffered medical problems caused by her earlier exposure to radioactive substances and died of leukemia in 1956.

After Pierre's death, Curie became the first female instructor at the Sorbonne when she succeeded to his professorship there. She also won a second Nobel Prize, this time in Chemistry for the isolation of pure radium.

The affects of radioactivity were just beginning to be understood during the course of Marie Curie's research. We now know that excessive exposure can cause cancer and death, but in Curie's day the only negative effects seemed to be scarring of skin that came into direct contact with the radioactive elements. Curie's hands were extremely scarred when she was diagnosed with leukemia caused by the excessive accumulation of radium in her body. She died of the disease in 1934.

Nellie Bly

Elizabeth Cochrane hadn't anticipated getting a job offer as a result of her letter to the editor of the *Pittsburgh Dispatch*. In fact, she took him to task for printing an editorial opposing women's suffrage and affirming the home as the only valid arena for women's work. But editor George Madden was so impressed with her letter that he offered the 21-year-old a job. She accepted it.

Writing under the byline Nellie Bly, the fledgling reporter decided to hit the streets and search out stories that exposed the underside of society. She investigated slums, factories, the problems of working girls—anything that was controversial for the times. She quickly developed a devoted readership, and the *Dispatch* decided to give them more of their favorite journalist by sending Bly to Mexico in 1886 so she could dig for the same stories there. Her pieces on corruption in the Mexican government so irritated Mexican officials that she was summarily booted out of the country with the strong suggestion that she never return.

A Woman's Place

Elizabeth Cochrane was one of many women who reported on the world around her during the nineteenth century. Others included British journalist Lady Florence Dixie, the first woman war correspondent to cover the Boer War; Amy Leslie, who became the *Chicago Daily News'* first female drama critic in 1890; and Mary E. Clemmer Ames, who wrote a weekly column, "Women's Letter from Washington," for the *New York City Independent*.

Bly decided to leave her old job behind and try her luck in New York. She successfully landed a position on the city's most innovative and popular paper, Joseph Pulitzer's *New York World*. She persuaded Pulitzer to let her continue her exposés by posing as a mental patient so she could investigate the goings on in a mental hospital on Blackwell (now Roosevelt) Island in New York. Her horrific accounts of the brutal conditions in the hospital launched a full-scale investigation into the hospital's practice and resulted in long-overdue reform.

Bly's most famous adventure was her around-the-world trip that mirrored the one that Phineas Fogg took in Jules Verne's novel *Around the World in Eighty Days*. Pulitzer thought it would be great fun to see if Bly could beat Fogg's fictional record, which she handily did, making the entire trip in 72 days, 6 hours, and 11 minutes. The public loved the stories she sent back from the exotic stops that she made along the way. When she returned, she was given a hero's welcome.

Bly was also the first woman to cover the skirmishes on the Eastern Front during World War I. It would be her last assignment. Journalism had turned yellow in her absence, and she wanted nothing to do with it. Rather than compromise her principles, she retired.

Antoinette Brown Blackwell

The first American woman to be ordained by a Protestant denomination, Antoinette Brown Blackwell fought against the biblically based belief that women's voices shouldn't be heard in church, and won.

Somewhat of a prodigy when it came to the pulpit, Blackwell's home church in her community of Henrietta, New York, made her a full member of the congregation when she was only nine years old. No one took her seriously when she would announce her intention to enter the ministry. Since she knew she'd meet opposition from any school she applied to, she decided to pursue a nondegree course of study at Oberlin College in Ohio, which also had a school of theology. When she completed her studies in the first course, she met with college officials and told them of her plans.

Blackwell had the Oberlin officials caught between a rock and a hard spot. The college was proud of its tradition of accepting men and women openly and without restrictions. While she wasn't prohibited from pursuing her divinity studies, the faculty and students made it very clear that they didn't welcome a woman in their midst.

A Woman's Place

Most women found it nearly impossible to open the doors of the ministry of established religion throughout the nineteenth century. Those who wished to fulfill their religious callings often succeeded by working outside of conventional boundaries. Mary Baker Eddy founded the Church of Christ, Scientist (Christian Science) in 1879 after she received a miraculous healing at the hands of one Phineas Quimby of the back pain that had plagued her for years. With her minister husband William, whom she had convinced to leave the Methodist Church, Catherine Booth started the Salvation Army in 1878 as an outreach ministry focusing on the problems of the poor. Mary de Chappotin de Neuville, a Frenchwoman, founded the Franciscan Missionaries of Mary in India in 1877. Elizabeth Ann Seton, founder of the Sisters of Charity of St. Joseph, was made the first American saint in 1975 in recognition for her work with the underprivileged during the early 1800s.

Blackwell completed her studies in 1850, but Oberlin officials refused to give her a degree in theology. She was also refused her minister's license. Undaunted, she took her message on the road and delivered sermons wherever she was invited to do so. After several years of working as an itinerant preacher, the South Butler, New York Congregational Church offered her a position as a minister. She was ordained on September 15, 1853.

Blackwell spent only one year at South Butler before asking to be released from her duties so she could affiliate herself with a more progressive church. While there, she met her future husband, Charles Samuel Blackwell, who happened to be Elizabeth Blackwell's brother. The two had seven children together.

Although she would never deliver sermons on a regular basis again, Blackwell remained relatively active in church and called on her theological training to write several books of philosophy. She became one of the few women elected to the American Association for the Advancement of Science, receiving that honor in 1881. She also helped to ordain several other female ministers and worked on behalf of women's rights.

The Least You Need to Know

➤ The brilliant astronomer Maria Mitchell helped launch the careers of a generation of female scientists.

➤ Elizabeth Blackwell opened a medical school so women could access the education she had such a tough time getting for herself.

➤ Although the elements she discovered eventually caused her death, Marie Curie's work in radioactivity gave new dimensions to medical research and practice.

➤ Nellie Bly's fearless probes into the underbelly of society formed the basis for the practice of investigative journalism.

Chapter 24

Rabble-Rousers and Reformers

In This Chapter

➤ Campaigning for education

➤ Speaking out against slavery

➤ Establishing the first American settlement house

➤ Working for women's rights

After years of playing second fiddle to men, nineteenth-century women entered the public arena in unprecedented numbers. They could have stayed home, and frankly, their husbands probably would have preferred that they had. But these women, especially those who belonged to the middle class, felt the pull of injustice. And they had more time to do something about it than ever before.

In the early nineteenth century, middle-class Americans held ideas about women that excluded them from the public arenas of politics and business by assigning them to a domestic sphere separate from the public one in which men operated. This cult of true womanhood portrayed women as morally superior and self-sacrificing. To escape these gender conventions, women justified moving into the public sphere as reformers by claiming that they were raising society up from sin and degradation. They cleaned up society as they cleaned their homes, cared for children, educated the next generation, and acted as the moral compass for their men.

The efforts of the pioneering reformers in this chapter and many others like them helped shape the face of the women's rights movement to come and set the stage for other reforms that would take place in the late nineteenth and early twentieth centuries.

Educational Reformer: Emma Willard

There was nothing even approximating advanced education for women in the United States until Emma Willard came along. Believing that women were as capable as men at mastering a higher education, she set out to establish institutions that would offer it. Her pioneering work on behalf of education reform resulted in the first publicly funded school for women that offered more than basic instruction.

Born Emma Hart, the ninth of 10 children on a farm in Berlin, Connecticut, Willard was encouraged in her studies by her father, Samuel, who delighted in discussing current events and philosophy with his smart daughter. By age 13, Willard had taught herself geometry, a subject far beyond the curriculum offered in the one-room schoolhouse she attended. She enrolled in the Berlin Academy two years later. Two years after that, she was back at the village school, this time as a teacher.

Willard then took a position as the head of a women's school in Middlebury, Vermont. While there, she met and married John Willard, with whom she had one son. When John encountered financial problems in his business, Emma had to take on additional work. Knowing her best success lay in an educational venture of some sort, she opened the Middlebury Female Seminary in their home. Although it offered a curriculum similar to men's colleges, she called it a seminary to avoid problems with college officials.

A Woman's Place

Mary Lyon, the founder of Mount Holyoke College in South Hadley, Massachusetts, is just one of many individuals who sought Willard's advice on establishing and funding institutions of higher education for women.

Emma's seminary was a success. To spread the concept, she decided to ask for the same public funding that men's schools received. She wrote her *Plan for Improving Female Education* while still living in Connecticut, but it met with a lukewarm reception. Several of her students suggested that neighboring New York might be more open to the idea. In large part due to their encouragement, the Willards moved their seminary to Waterford, New York. Emma then submitted *An Address to the Public, Particularly to the Members of the Legislature of New York, Proposing a Plan for Improving Female Education* to the state legislature in 1819. Unfortunately, the New York state legislature, too, refused to entertain her idea.

The city of Troy, New York, was interested, especially if the Willards would agree to move their school there. With the promise of $4,000 in start-up funds, the

Willards relocated and opened the Troy Female Seminary in September 1821. The seminary was the first American educational institution to treat women as though they had minds. Instead of offering classes in the "female arts"—embroidery, reading the classics, conversational French, and the like—it offered a full range of subjects with academic standards as rigorous as those found in the top schools for men. It attracted mostly girls from wealthy families, which made it financially successful in a very short time and also allowed Willard to offer scholarships for needy students.

The institution Willard established changed its name in her honor to the Emma Willard School in 1895. It not only turned out women with far better educations than they ever could have received before, but it also served as a template for other pioneering institutions of women's education.

Sojourner's Truth

Her slave name was Isabella. Her last name changed every time she was sold to another family. But the future African-American preacher and social reformer left her identity crisis behind when she renamed herself Sojourner Truth at age 46 and set out on her mission to fight against slavery and for women's rights.

Born a slave in upstate New York near the end of the eighteenth century, Truth was sold several times—the first time when she was only nine years old—which gave her a multitude of last names. Eventually, she was sold to the Dumont family, with whom she lived for some 20 years. During this time, she was married to another slave named Tom, with whom she had five children. As was the custom of the time, however, several of her children were sold away from her.

New York abolished slavery in 1827. Accounts vary, but Sojourner either was set free or ran away from the Dumonts soon after. She went to New York with two of her children and sought work as a domestic. Deeply religious since childhood, she also joined a spiritual community there. At the age of 46, she renamed herself Sojourner Truth and set off on a religious mission.

Sojourner traveled to New England on foot, preaching and singing along the way. There, she joined with others who were against slavery and began meeting the leading abolitionists of the day. She was tall and commanding, with a beautiful deep voice. The abolitionists knew she'd be a powerful speaker and wasted little time putting

Yeah, RIGHT.

A Woman's Place

Sojourner Truth was one of a number of women who traveled across the United States and abroad during the nineteenth century in the name of reform. Others included author Elizabeth Oakes Prince Smith, who wrote *A Woman and Her Needs* and gave lectures on "The Woman Question"; and Sarah Parker Remond, an African American who spoke on slavery issues in England, Ireland, and Scotland.

her before audiences so she could tell her story. Although she could neither read nor write, she had an excellent memory—in fact, she had memorized most of the Bible, which she often quoted at length—and a true gift for oration. Her supporters were right—Sojourner mesmerized her audiences with stories about her experiences as a slave. She became a sought-after speaker at abolitionist and women's rights meetings. She also dictated an autobiography, *The Narrative of Sojourner Truth,* which she sold to pay her way.

A Woman's Place

Another slave who wrote her autobiography was Harriet Jacobs, author of *Incidents in the Life of a Slave Girl* (1861), which addressed the issue of the sexual abuse of slave women by their masters—including the retaliation of jealous mistresses and slave children who were the sons and daughters of their owners. Jacobs was able to save her children from slavery by sending them north. She hid in her grandmother's attic for seven years before she was able to escape and find a sympathetic northern woman who employed her, helped her avoid capture, and eventually bought her freedom.

Sojourner continued speaking out against slavery after the Civil War began and took her story to Washington, D.C., where she met with Abraham Lincoln. After the war, she helped ex-slaves reestablish themselves by finding them places to live and employment.

After the Civil War, Sojourner Truth also protested the exclusion of women from the Fourteenth Amendment, which gave the vote to black men only. She was one of a number of women's rights activists who tested the amendment by trying to vote in the 1872 presidential election. Her efforts, as well as those of the white suffragists, failed. But she continued her work on behalf of African Americans and women until her death at 86. More than a thousand people attended her funeral. Fellow suffragette Lucy Stone delivered the eulogy, honoring her persistence in "moving friend and foe alike."

Hear Me Roar

That man over there says women need to be helped into carriages, and lifted over ditches, and to have the best place anywhere. Nobody ever helps me into carriages or over puddles, or gives me the best place ... and ain't I a woman? ... I have borne thirteen children and seen most of 'em sold into slavery, and when I cried out with my mother's grief, none but Jesus heard me—and ain't I a woman?

—Sojourner Truth, in her famous "Ain't I a Woman?" speech, delivered to quell male hecklers at a women's convention in Akron, Ohio

Campaigning Against Slavery: The Grimké Sisters

As white women from the South, Sarah and Angelina Grimké were unlikely standard bearers for the abolitionist movement. But they grew up despising the institution of slavery, and the uniqueness of their perspective made them highly influential members of the movement to eliminate it.

The Grimké sisters were born into a large and prominent Charleston family. The Grimkés had residences in town and in the country. Their country place, as many were, was a plantation. While there, the sisters saw the injustices of slavery on a daily basis.

Sarah, the older of the two by seven years, accompanied her father on a trip to Philadelphia in 1819. While there, she met other people with beliefs similar to hers, including some members of the Quaker church. When her father died two years later, she moved to Philadelphia and joined the Quaker community there in hopes of becoming a minister. Angelina, who shared Sarah's dim views of slavery, joined her there in 1829.

The sisters began their work as abolitionists in 1835 when Angelina wrote a letter to the editor of *The Liberator,* a prominent abolitionist newspaper. William Lloyd Garrison, the noted slavery fighter

A Woman's Place

Sarah and Angelina Grimké's strong feelings about slavery kept them from ever returning to the South after they left it.

who published the paper, wasted little time in running it. From then on, their names were inextricably linked to the abolitionist movement.

Because they had such a unique perspective on slavery, Sarah and Angelina soon became popular speakers at anti-slavery society meetings. They also became somewhat infamous after publishing several pamphlets on slavery, including "An Appeal to Christian Women of the South," published by the American Anti-Slavery Society. While its intended audience was white Southern women, very few of them saw it as postmasters in the South destroyed as many copies of the pamphlet as they could find.

Their printed message may have been thwarted, but the sisters had no trouble finding groups that would listen to them. Some people, however, felt it inappropriate for the two women to speak in public, which led to the sisters' censure by the Ministerial Association of Massachusetts in 1837. Now the Grimkés had another cause to fight for: women's rights. In letters published by *The Liberator,* Angelina both defended her right to speak publicly and called for expanded rights for women in general. Sarah wrote a pamphlet called "Letters on the Equality of the Sexes and the Condition of Women."

In 1838 Angelina wed Theodore Weld, a noted abolitionist minister. The audience at the wedding was mixed, which caused an uproar among many Philadelphians. Two days later, as Angelina was delivering a speech at an anti-slavery convention, an angry crowd gathered to express its disapproval. Riots later broke out, which both destroyed the building Angelina had lectured in as well as the neighboring Shelter for Colored Orphans.

Immensely saddened by the event and seeing the potential for similar demonstrations in the future, the sisters rarely addressed public audiences from then on. They both continued to speak to private groups, however, and they continued writing on both abolition and women's rights.

The following year, the Welds and Sarah Grimké retired from the public eye and moved to a farm on the Hudson River, where they worked the land and ran a school. The sisters remained connected to both causes that meant so much to them—in fact, Sarah and Angelina were among the women who put the Fifteenth Amendment to the test by trying to vote in the election of 1870.

Hear Me Roar

I ask no favors for my sex. All I ask of our brethren is that they take their feet off our necks and permit us to stand upright on the ground which God designed us to occupy.

—Sarah Grimké, in an 1837 letter to her sister

Organizing for Labor: Mary Harris "Mother" Jones

Called "Mother" by the coal miners and railroad workers for whom she ceaselessly lobbied, Mary Harris Jones devoted her entire life to organized labor and became one of its fiercest and most vocal proponents.

An immigrant from Ireland living in Memphis, Tennessee, Jones was 36 when the yellow fever swept through the city, killing her husband and her four young children. Heartbroken, she moved to Chicago and established a dressmaking business. Four years later, she lost everything in the Great Chicago Fire and had to start over again.

She didn't mind sewing for her wealthy customers, but what she did mind was seeing how well they lived when she knew that so many working-class people, like herself, were struggling to make ends meet. She began attending meetings of the Knights of Labor, and worked on behalf of organized labor—in particular, workers in the coal mines and on the railroads—for the rest of her life.

She lived the life of an itinerant, traveling around the country to organize workers and encourage them to stand up for their rights. She often had little more than her own clothing for a bed when she stopped to rest. Her passionate speeches helped raise the awareness of the conditions that these workers endured and helped set the stage for labor reform.

On one crusade, children from the textile mills of Pennsylvania, who had organized a strike in protest of their unsafe working conditions, marched more than 100 miles with her, talking to groups along the way and raising money for their efforts. Their goal was to talk to Teddy Roosevelt at his home in New York, but he refused to see them. In Colorado, Mother Jones led a group of miners' wives as they drove off workers who had taken their striking husbands' places in the mines.

Mother Jones' militant approach to labor reform landed her in jail more than once and earned her a fair share of negative press—at one point, she was called the most dangerous woman in America. But she never stopped working on behalf of the poor and the oppressed. When she died in 1930 at age 100, she was planning another campaign.

Exposing the Plight of the Mentally Ill: Dorothea Dix

Dorothea Dix used her experience of being brought up in an unstable home to galvanize her work on behalf of the mentally ill.

Dix's father, a physician, was emotionally unstable and had a drinking problem; her mother suffered migraines that often made it impossible for her to care for her children. When Dorothea was 12, her parents separated. She and her siblings were sent to live in Boston with relatives. Soon after, Dorothea decided that she wanted to be a teacher. Hardly much older than many of her students herself, she established her own school when she was 15 and ran it until she contracted tuberculosis in her late 30s. Dorothea was recuperating in 1841 when she visited a local jail to teach a Sunday school class. To her horror, she saw people who were clearly mentally ill locked up with criminals. Her experience there motivated her to launch a fuller investigation on how the mentally ill were treated in Massachusetts. She traveled to some 500 towns across the state over the course of the next several years, visited the various institutions where the mentally ill were housed, and recorded what she saw. She then presented her findings to the state legislature, which in 1843 passed a bill to provide more facilities and better accommodations for the insane.

Dix continued her work for the next several years, traveling across the United States and Canada and collecting statistics on as many of the mentally ill as she could find. She went to Europe in 1854 where she did the same. Over the course of her career, she founded or improved 32 hospitals for the mentally ill in the United States.

In recognition of her compassion and devotion to her cause, Dix was appointed superintendent of army nurses when the Civil War broke out in 1861. She directed their efforts throughout the four-year war, organized hospitals for the wounded, set up and staffed infirmaries, and worked to insure that adequate medical supplies were where they needed to be.

The Woman Who Launched a War: Harriet Beecher Stowe

She came from a family renowned for its high moral standards, its faith, its emphasis on education, and its crusades against social injustice. With a background like this, it's little wonder that Harriet Beecher Stowe would go on to help erase the leading social evil of her day. Harriet Beecher was the seventh of nine children born to the famous Congregational minister Lyman Beecher and his first wife, Roxana Foote. The family also included educator Catherine Beecher, one of the nineteenth centuries leading proponents of education for women and founder of two women's schools; and preacher Henry Ward Beecher, who became pastor of Brooklyn's Plymouth Church and a renowned leader of the abolitionist movement. Harriet was considered the genius of the family and was preoccupied by her studies more often than not. Small and quiet, she attended a girls school in the family's hometown of Litchfield, Connecticut, and then attended her sister Catherine's Hartford Female Seminary, where she later taught. When the family moved to Cincinnati in 1832, Harriet also taught at the school her sister established there, the Western Female Institute. She taught there until her 1834 marriage to Calvin Ellis Stowe, a professor of biblical literature. The two had seven children together.

She helped support her large family by writing. Her first book, published in 1833, was a geography text for children. She followed that work with a series of well-received stories and sketches of life in her native New England, winning a short story prize from *Western Monthly Magazine* for one of them. After the U.S. Congress passed the Fugitive Slave Act in September 1850, Stowe wrote her greatest work, *Uncle Tom's Cabin; or, Life Among the Lowly,* drawing from incidents she had observed while living in Cincinnati as well as contemporary accounts of slavery in newspapers and magazines. *Uncle Tom's Cabin* was serialized in *The National Era,* an anti-slavery weekly, from June 1851 to April 1852, where it captured a large audience. It was an immediate success as well when it was published in novel form in March 1852. As the biggest best-seller in nineteenth-century America—it broke all sales records with a half-million copies purchased by 1857—*Uncle Tom's Cabin* also inspired a number of unauthorized spin-off products, including plays, songs, toys, and china figurines, or "Tomitudes," based on the leading characters. It also netted its author some $10,000 in royalties, a vast sum for the day.

Harriet followed *Uncle Tom's Cabin* with another anti-slavery novel that wasn't as well received. Nothing was going to come close to the acclaim she had received with her first book—she even made a triumphant author's tour of Europe after its publication there—and she gave up trying. She spent her later years in Hartford, Connecticut, with her husband, and continued to write on topics other than slavery.

Hear Me Roar

So you're the little woman who wrote the book that started this great war.

—Abraham Lincoln, upon meeting Harriet Beecher Stowe

Sarah Winnemucca

The granddaughter of Truckee and daughter of Winnemucca, both Northern Paiute chiefs, Sarah Winnemucca worked for the return of her tribe's ancestral land. Although her efforts were in vain, she helped raise awareness of the plight of the American Indians and set the stage for Native American movements in the future.

As a young child, Sarah lived with her grandfather in the San Joaquin valley of California. When she returned to Nevada, she lived briefly with a white family, who gave her the name Sarah in place of Thocmetony (which means "shell flower"), her Paiute name. In 1860, she enrolled in a convent school in San Jose, California, but was forced to leave due to the objections of the parents of the white students there.

Sarah went back to her home in Nevada. However, her family was soon forced to relocate to Camp McDermitt in northeast Nevada. They had barely settled into their new home when they were moved again to the Malheur Reservation in Oregon. There, Sarah worked as a teacher at the Indian school and as an interpreter for the reservation agent. She also helped negotiate a peaceful settlement between her tribe and its enemies, the Bannocks, when war broke out between the two factions in 1876.

The Paiutes were relocated again in 1879, this time to the Yakima Reservation in Washington. Upset over the constant moves and how the Indian agents treated her people, Sarah launched a campaign for her people's rights. She lectured in San Francisco and then traveled to Washington, D.C., in 1880 to meet with President Rutherford B. Hayes and Secretary of the Interior Carl Shurz. She came away with a presidential order authorizing the Paiutes' return to the Malheur reservation. No money accompanied the order, however, and the Indian agent at Yakima Reservation refused to let them go.

After her 1881 marriage to L. H. Hopkins, an army officer, Sarah continued to campaign on her people's behalf and went on a year-long lecture tour from 1883 to 1884. She gave some three hundred speeches in all, usually garbed in authentic Indian ceremonial clothing, and gathered thousands of signatures on a petition calling for the U.S. government to make good on its earlier promise to return her people's land to them. In 1884 Congress passed a law that granted the land to her tribe, but it was stonewalled by the Secretary of the Interior, who wouldn't execute it.

After that failure, Sarah opened a school for Paiute children in her native Nevada. She taught there until she fell ill with consumption, which claimed her when she was just 47.

Carry Nation

Saloonkeepers quaked when they saw the tall, imposing Carry Nation in their doorway, and they had good reason to. Possibly the most famous advocate for *temperance,* she smashed dozens of saloons in her campaign to ban alcohol.

Carry's views on alcohol dated to her first marriage, which was to a doctor who turned out to be an alcoholic. Although she tried to reform him, he drank himself to death a few years after marrying Carry. Her second marriage was to David Nation, a lawyer and newspaper editor. (Some sources say he also was a minister.) Perhaps weary of her endless campaigning against the evils of alcoholic beverages, he divorced her in 1901 for desertion. The Nations moved several times, first to Texas and then to Medicine Lodge, Kansas. As David established his law practice, Carry involved herself in civic and religious activities, often working on behalf of the poor, for whom she had a special soft spot as many were victims of alcoholism—the social evil she most despised.

Words for Women

Temperance was the term used by nineteenth-century social reformers to describe the sober and self-restrained society they were trying to create.

By 1899 Carry was devoting most of her time to temperance issues. With several other members of the local Woman's Christian Temperance Union (WCTU), she closed seven illegal liquor outlets through nonviolent means. Her pacifist approach to doing away with liquor soon changed, however. Probably influenced by her frustration over trying to get the state of Kansas to enforce its anti-liquor laws, Carry had a dream in which she believed God told her to go to Kiowa, Kansas, about 20 miles from her home. There, she was to make a great public show of closing down a saloon. With the dream fresh in her mind, she headed to the Dodson Saloon, where, armed with a hatchet and bricks, she smashed everything inside, forcing the place to close. Her rabble-rousing made the news and earned her instant notoriety.

Nation was tall and powerful—she stood 6 feet tall and weighed close to 180 pounds. She also had a sharp tongue, which she rarely hesitated to use. During her crusade for temperance, she worked her way through the other saloons in town and then moved on to other towns in the state. By wielding the hatchet that God had told her to use, she managed to close dozens of saloons.

Nation took her message to other parts of the United States during a lecture tour in 1901. To promote her efforts (and pay for her travels), she sold miniature hatchets that said "Carry Nation—Joint Smasher." Her supporters also helped finance her tour and pay her court fines when she was arrested after smashing yet another saloon—she was arrested a total of 30 times in her life. At age 65, 9 years after she started touring the country, she collapsed on the stage. She died six months later.

Hear Me Roar

I felt invincible. My strength was that of a giant. God was certainly standing by me. I smashed five saloons with rocks before I ever took a hatchet.

—Carry Nation

Creating a New Model for Social Reform: Jane Addams

One of the foremost social reformers of the nineteenth century, Jane Addams inspired generations of women to take up causes they believed in. Born in Cedarville, Illinois, as the eighth of nine children, Jane was raised by her stepmother and older sister after her mother died when she was just a toddler. With her father's encouragement, she attended the Rockford Female Seminary from 1877 to 1881. After graduating from the seminary, she enrolled in medical school but was unable to complete her studies due to a problems related to a congenital spinal defect. She spent the next few years in and out of the hospital. When well enough, she traveled and studied in Europe for almost two years, then spent another two years

Words for Women

Settlement houses were neighborhood community centers, usually located in poor or immigrant neighborhoods, that offered free education and social programs to underprivileged women and men.

considering what her life's work should be. While on a second tour of Europe in 1888, Addams and her friend Ellen Gates Starr visited Toynbee Hall, a community center or *settlement house* in London's East End that offered social and educational programs to the community.

When they returned from Europe, Addams and Starr decided to open a similar establishment. In 1889 they leased a large home built by Charles Hull at the corner of Halsted and Polk Streets in Chicago. They named the place Hull House after its builder. Hull House would become the best-known settlement house in America. It offered kindergarten classes in the morning, clubs for older children in the afternoon, and a wide variety of courses for adults in the evening. At the height of its popularity, an estimated 2,000 people a week visited Hull House. Some came merely for the chance to share some coffee and talk to people from their own neighborhood. Others came to take advantage of programs that could help them escape the slums.

As Hull House's influence grew, Addams also used it as a center for social reform. Staff, volunteers, and residents alike worked together to improve housing, call for greater reforms in child labor laws, and lobby for changes to laws governing public welfare. Addams also began working for women's rights on the national level and became vice president of the national American Woman Suffrage Association in 1911.

Hull House supplied the values and strategies that allowed women to professionalize social work. Addams was an inspiration and example to women who worked in the Children's Bureau in the federal Department of Labor, as well as women who worked locally in voluntary organizations.

Going for the Vote

The women's suffrage movement in Australia was anchored by Louisa Lawson, whose interests in women's rights were fired after she was banned from meetings regarding a new school in the Outback. She left her husband and took her five children to Sydney where she supported herself by working as a seamstress. In her spare time, she founded a women's discussion group, The Dawn Club, in 1888, and published Australia's first feminist newspaper, *The Dawn*, from 1888 to 1905. Australia was the second country in the world to grant women the vote, doing so in 1902.

When World War I broke out, Addams, who had long aspired to rid the world of war, went to Europe with a group of women who were working for peace. When she came back to the United States, she was labeled unpatriotic due to her pacifist views—in fact, the Daughters of the American Revolution expelled her from membership. But the Nobel Peace Prize committee recognized her work by giving her the Nobel Peace Prize in 1931. She was the second woman to win it. (Bertha von Suttner, the former housekeeper of Nobel Prize founder Alfred Nobel, won it in 1905 for her pacifist work in Europe. Interestingly, she was also the one who suggested Nobel found a prize for peace.)

Unfortunately, Addams wasn't able to receive her prize in person. She had sustained a heart attack in 1926, from which she never fully recovered. On the day the Nobel Peace Prize was being awarded to her, she was admitted to a hospital in Baltimore. Due to her illness, she also never delivered a Nobel lecture as her physicians felt she wasn't well enough to travel abroad.

Addams died in 1935 after an operation revealed that she had cancer. Her funeral was held in the courtyard of Hull House.

Hear Me Roar

Let woman then go on—not asking favors, but claiming as a right the removal of all hindrances to her elevation in the scale of being—let her receive encouragement for the proper cultivation of all her powers, so that she may enter profitably into the active business of life ... Then in the marriage union, the independence of the husband and wife will be equal, their dependence mutual, and the obligations reciprocal.

—The last paragraph of Lucretia Mott's *Discourse on Woman*, delivered December 17, 1849

Lobbying for Women's Rights: Lucretia Mott

A leading abolitionist, Lucretia Mott got a good taste of what discrimination felt like when she was barred from participating in the 1840 World Anti-Slavery Conference—even though she had been chosen as a delegate—simply because she was a woman.

Elizabeth Cady Stanton, another delegate to the convention, was equally incensed when she, too, was denied a seat. When the two women met in the gallery where they were allowed to sit and observe, they compared their feelings about witnessing an event held to promote equal rights that denied the involvement of half of the human population.

Mott and Stanton continued their work on anti-slavery issues when they returned to the United States. But their experience in London opened their eyes to another equally worthy cause: women's rights. The time was ripe to elevate the plight of women to the same level as the other causes for which women were working. In the next decade, a women's rights movement developed that would affect the lives of women across the globe.

The Least You Need to Know

➤ Eradicating the evils of alcohol became the special focus of Carry Nation's reform efforts.

➤ Harriet Beecher Stowe's most famous work, *Uncle Tom's Cabin,* raised the public's awareness of the horrors of slavery with its intimate and emotional portrayal of the life of a slave family.

➤ Jane Addams based her plans for Hull House on the settlement houses she visited in London and influenced a generation of female reformers, helping to professionalize social work.

➤ Lucretia Mott used her disappointment over being denied participation at an anti-slavery convention to fuel her work on behalf of women's rights.

➤ Women found an outlet for their energies and talents working in reform movements.

Part 5

The Twentieth Century

The pace of civilization, which had accelerated into a fast trot during the latter quarter of the nineteenth century, turned into a mad gallop during the twentieth. Industrialization and urbanization transformed daily life for women and men. The world became both larger and smaller as technology opened new frontiers and erased global boundaries.

Ideas that were once the province of drawing boards and science fiction novels became realities—airplanes, submarines, radios, telephones, rocket ships. Computers learned to talk. Robots began replacing workers in factories. Men—and women—took to the sky and then slipped earth's bounds. Some of humankind's most crippling and deadly diseases were eradicated through the discovery of new drugs, medical procedures, and vaccines.

Once relegated to bystander status, women played a greater part in the events of the twentieth century than ever before. Getting the vote revolutionized virtually affected every aspect of a woman's life. What it meant to be a daughter, wife, or mother changed more during this century than at any other time in human history. So did a woman's ability to make her own choices and forge her own destiny.

Chapter 25

Twentieth Century Life

In This Chapter

➤ Marrying for love

➤ New contraptions

➤ The rise and fall of hemlines

➤ Becoming free spirits

Daughter, wife, mother—women have always been defined by their relationship to the men in their lives, and these definitions would remain in place during the twentieth century. But what it meant to be a daughter, a wife, or a mother would change more during this century than at any other time in human history.

Some of that change—a great deal, in fact—was driven by the nascent women's movement that began forming in the latter part of the nineteenth century. The efforts of the early suffragists and feminists would culminate in women finally gaining a public voice through the right to vote, in gaining greater control over their destiny through birth control and broader personal rights, in getting an education as good as the one men got, and in having careers open to them that were once forbidden.

The rest of it came about through the pistons and gears, the steam and smoke, the bits and bytes wrought by industry and invention.

Love and Marriage

By 1900 the Western world had shed its agrarian past and catapulted itself into the industrialized future.

The world of business and industry was moving forward, but the status of women remained mired firmly in the past and would stay there to a great extent until women gained the right to vote. As you'll read more about in later chapters, suffrage would unlock the door to many freedoms that had been denied to women for so long.

The strictures and mores of the Victorian era, so deeply imbedded in the minds and hearts of both women and men, remained in place at the turn of the century and continued to define the ideal woman as utterly devoted to her husband and family and dependent on her husband for most things.

Regardless of social status, women were expected to find a suitable mate and get married as quickly as they could once they reached the appropriate age so they wouldn't be burdens on their families. They were expected to fulfill their biological destiny to become wives and mothers. This expectation, in fact, wouldn't significantly diminish until the 1980s. Even when women began attending college in greater numbers, the belief was that they would graduate, maybe work a few years, and then settle down to a husband and family. The notion of having a career, either before marriage and family or concurrent with them, was alien then and would remain so for many years. In the first two thirds of the twentieth century, most American women moved from their parents' home directly into their husband's home, never having lived on their own.

Continuing a trend that had begun in the nineteenth century, the period between childhood and marriage expanded. More teenagers and young adults went to college rather than out to work, remaining dependent on their families longer. Courting became an art in the early twentieth century, giving young women and men the opportunity to get to know each other that they had often lacked in the past. Longer life spans made it possible for couples to delay marriage until they could afford homes of their own. Where in the

Hear Me Roar

We owe to women the charm and the beauty of life; for purity of thought and heart, for patient courage, for recklessly unselfish devotion, for the love that rests, strengthens and inspires, we look to women. These are the best things in life; in them men cannot compete with women.

—Dean Briggs, "Remarks," Smith College Quarter Centennial Anniversary *Proceedings*, 1900

A Woman's Place

The average life expectancy during the first decade of the twentieth century was 47.3 years for women and 46.3 for men. By 1997, they rose to 79.1 for women and 73.1 for men.

past newlyweds often remained in the house of one of their parents for a certain period of time after they wed (and sometimes forever), they now generally established their own home as quickly as possible, even if it was just a one-room flat.

As in the nineteenth century, women of the higher classes were expected to stay home and create the idyllic retreats for their husbands to retire to at the end of the day. Laboring-class women were still expected to work a full day outside the home and an equally full day inside it.

The early twentieth century is often referred to as the *Progressive Era*. It was yet another period of unrest and reform in the United States as the nation went through the upheavals and transformations that shape any young country.

America became the most industrialized country during this period, and the country's distinctive culture became a national product. For the first time, America influenced other cultures instead of the other way around. In the years to come, people would dance American dances, listen to American music, and wear American-style clothing.

Hear Me Roar

How are men and women to think about their maleness and femaleness in this twentieth century, in which so many of our old ideas must be made new?

—Anthropologist Margaret Mead

Words for Women

The **Progressive Era** (1890–1920) was characterized by various attempts by different coalitions of reformers to bring a measure of stability to American society. Progressives were concerned with social justice, like child labor laws; social control, like prohibition; and efficiency, reflected in health reforms such as meat inspection and sanitation issues. Many women were involved in groups that worked on these issues.

Creature Comforts

A large number of innovations, some of them developed over many years, revolutionized the industrial world during the twentieth century. They also transformed the household. Chores that once took hours could now be done in minutes. Days once filled with drudgery now had periods of time that could be filled in a variety of ways.

A Woman's Place

Household conveniences such as washing machines and other laborsaving appliances greatly expanded women's opportunities to pursue interests outside of the home and take on outside employment if they chose. Although household chores still comprised a large portion of housewives' days in the early twentieth century, their schedules were far less governed by what needed to be done at home than ever before. Women, however, continued to shoulder most of the responsibility for cleaning and cooking and would continue to do so for many years. Studies conducted in the 1970s and 1980s, for example, showed that women with paid jobs still had most of the responsibility for making sure their homes were clean and their families fed. Time spent working away from the home did not translate into fewer hours of housework, a situation that remains true in many households today.

In 1901 running water, the electric heater, and the electric motor came together to create the washing machine, a labor-saving device that had a profound impact on women's lives. If she didn't have servants, washing, drying, and ironing clothes could take up to one third of a woman's time. Electric washing machines combined many time-intensive tasks into one operation. Similar combinations brought forth kitchen sinks with hot and cold running water, toilets, bathtubs, and showers. By 1920 women could choose between vacuum cleaners and mechanical carpet sweepers, electric sewing machines or ones powered by foot treadle, and irons they heated in the fire or ones they could plug into the wall.

The growth of commercial canning companies and new refrigeration methods eliminated daily or even twice-daily trips to the grocer and market. Packaged breads and other bakery goods replaced weekly or even daily baking. Even routine cleaning tasks were simplified due to greater availability of pre-packaged soap and washing soda and such products as rubber, which was used to make easy-to-clean tiles for kitchen floors.

Neighborhood grocery stores had mostly disappeared by the 1950s and were replaced with giant supermarkets where women could buy shower curtains, a book, and dinner. The greatest change in twentieth-century foodways, however, was the advent of prepared meals that only needed to be heated. Frozen "TV dinners" relieved busy women from cooking every night and provided a selection of vegetables out of season. At the end of the century, supermarkets offered complete meals, such as rotisserie chicken and side dishes, and most restaurants provided take-out services. Twentieth-century working women were liberated from preparing three meals a day.

Department stores, which began to appear in the nineteenth century, flourished during the twentieth. Combined with smaller specialty shops, they created a new retail milieu where women could find a tremendous variety of items.

A Woman's Place

Unlike Henry Ford's Model T, which was cheap enough so virtually anyone could own one, many of the appliances introduced during the early twentieth century were so expensive that only the wealthy could afford them. At the same time, these devices also relaxed some of the rigidity between the classes. Technology eliminated the need to have dozens of servants, and wealthy women no longer had to command a full staff of domestics. The women who used to hold domestic jobs were freed from occupations that previously defined their social class.

Women in Europe

Similar changes were also improving the lives of European women. Improved sanitation systems made water safe to drink. Streets were paved and cleaned on a regular basis, which made cities and towns more pleasant to live in and houses easier to keep clean. Running water and flushing toilets were appearing in many homes, even those of the laboring class. Inventions such as pasteurization, which was developed in the mid-nineteenth century and came into wide use during the twentieth, both eliminated food-borne diseases and made canned or bottled milk available for the children of working mothers.

Life expectancy rates for women in Britain improved from a dismal 44 years in 1890 to almost 60 years in 1920. Similar improvements were seen in other European countries. Improvements in maternal mortality rates, through better nutrition and an understanding of sepsis and infections caused by bacteria, had a great deal to do with rising life spans, so did improvements in infant mortality and the shift to smaller families. Since their babies now had a far greater chance of surviving infancy, women could bear fewer children and still achieve the family sizes they wanted. Couples also decreased the number of children they had when it was no longer necessary to have large families to work in the fields.

Contraception was another factor affecting family size in Europe. Although it was rarely discussed, women were taking more control over their reproductive lives as they began to realize that they might enjoy greater freedom if they weren't tied down to large families. Such new devices as diaphragms and condoms were not widely available until the 1920s, so most contraceptive efforts involved such traditional methods as withdrawal or abstinence.

As in the United States, many women resorted to abortions—so many, in fact, that a number of European countries tried to ban them in order to maintain a steady or growing birth rate. As also was the case in the United States, the first birth control clinics in Europe were flooded with women seeking information and contraceptive devices.

Fashion Plate

The highly feminine styles of the Victorian era—tight shirtwaists, pompadour hairstyles, elaborate hats, and constrictive skirts—ruled the fashion world at the turn of the twentieth century. But such extreme styles would fade away as women's lives changed. For the first time, women were designing women's clothing—like many professions, men dominated fashion design until the twentieth century—and they revolutionized the fashion world by designing for comfort and style.

Comfort was a new term when it came to fashion, but women eagerly embraced styles that embodied it. Fabrics became lighter and colors brighter. During the day, women began wearing jackets over their skirts and blouses—a style favored by suffragists as well. At night, necklines plunged.

The new sport of motoring drove such fashions as tightly buttoned boots, caps with veils, goggles and dustcoats as protection against dust and mud. As more women took up sports, their wardrobes expanded to include clothing that allowed them the freedom to ride horses astride, play tennis, ride bicycles, swim, row, etc.

Hemlines remained at the ankles, as they had for many centuries, but not for long. They rose to mid-calf and even above during World War I when textile factories turned to making products needed in the war and fabric was in short supply. Hemlines dropped again during the Jazz Age, but they wouldn't reach the floor for anything other than formal wear until the 1960s, when designers introduced such styles as the granny skirt and the maxi dress.

The image of the New Woman, "lovely, expensive, and about 19," according to F. Scott Fitzgerald, became the symbol of the Roaring '20s. The Flapper was the free spirit of the Jazz Age. She was liberated or decadent, depending on your viewpoint—she smoked, danced the Charleston, frequented speakeasies, and cut her hair. She was epitomized by actress Clara Bow, the famous "It Girl" whose on-screen styles and behavior were much copied by young women in the 1920s.

A Woman's Place

Styles in men's and women's fashion were influenced by the same factors over the centuries and often mirrored each other. This began to change in the 1800s when a woman's wardrobe was seen as a reflection of her husband's wealth and status. A man's wardrobe became secondary to his wife's. By the 1900s, growing consumerism and the rise of popular culture helped fuel women's fashion trends that changed by the season. The basics of a man's wardrobe, on the other hand, changed only slightly from the turn of the century to today.

Now that women were spending less time washing clothes, they also wanted to spend less time washing their hair. Amid strong protests from men, women began replacing their "crowning glories" with shoulder-length and even shorter styles. As more women took jobs in factories and offices, shorter hair proved extremely practical, as long tresses were more likely to get caught in machinery.

The "bob," still popular today, became the symbol of the Jazz Age and women's new freedom. Fashion continued to reflect that freedom as well. Suffragists caught flack for wearing bloomers in the nineteenth century. So did the first women who wore pants in the twentieth. When such popular actresses as Lauren Bacall and Katherine Hepburn began sporting the mannish style, slacks slowly grew in acceptance as casual attire. In most public places, the prescribed apparel were skirts and dresses for both women and girls. In the early 1970s, schools began relaxing their dress codes to allow girls to wear certain types of pants but continued to encourage them to wear the more ladylike skirts or dresses. Pantsuits slowly gained acceptance in the workplace during this same period.

The invention of pantyhose in 1959 not only freed millions of women from garter belts and girdles, but it also let designers explore new fashions that decorum previously made impossible. Hemlines bounced around like crazy from the 1920s on, with lengths going up during wars as a way of conserving national resources and dropping afterward as a symbol of postwar prosperity.

In the 1960s hemlines went up to the knee, then to above the knee and way above the knee as the "mod" look ushered in a fashion revolution at the same time that the sexual revolution was gearing up. The philosophy was "anything goes," and everything did. Women were redefining the boundaries and rules in every area of their lives, and the clothing they wore reflected these changes.

Free to Be You and Me

Of all the changes that women experienced during the twentieth century, the one reflected by women's fashion is probably the most profound. For the first time in recorded history, women were no longer bound by a set of rules prescribed by men. They could now write their own rules.

As you'll read more about in the chapters to come, twentieth-century women worked within the boundaries of society's conventions and legalities to change the world around them and their status and roles within it. The vote gave them that freedom. Once they won it, they used that very basic right to gain more freedom when it came to who they wanted to be and how they wanted to live their lives.

The choices some women made at the end of the twentieth century included remaining single but having children with the help of a sperm donor, not changing their last names when they married (or hyphenating theirs to their husbands), and working from home (telecommuting) so that they were available to their children. Throughout the century, women stepped on the toes of society's conventions more often than not, but they were less concerned about doing so than ever before. Once they caught a glimpse of the possible, there was no turning back. They could choose to be married or not, have children or not, go to college or not, have a career or not. Instead of marrying a doctor or a lawyer, they became doctors and lawyers, as well as astronauts and firemen.

The Least You Need to Know

➤ Women's choices today may include marriage, children, and a career, but women are combining these elements in new patterns and shaping their lives to fit their needs and express their individuality.

➤ Better nutrition, advances in medicine, public hygiene programs, and the emphasis on smaller families contributed to longer life spans for twentieth-century women.

➤ Conveniences like washing machines, dishwashers, vacuums, and electric irons took much of the drudgery out of housekeeping.

➤ Comfort and freedom of movement became important influences on women's fashion during the twentieth century.

Chapter 26

The Women's Movement

In This Chapter

➤ Winning the right to vote

➤ The rise of the women's rights movement

➤ The fight for equal rights

➤ Women's rights today

During the nineteenth century, greater numbers of women than ever before made it very clear that they were fed up with the status quo. They took on the ills and evils of the society around them and fought for social reform. As they did, they realized that they wanted more control over their own lives, legal recognition of their basic human rights, and an active voice in what was happening around them.

The work these women did on behalf of others taught them a great deal about fighting for their own rights. Suffrage was the key, of course. Little change could take place if women were still denied the opportunity to voice their opinions at the polls. But the right to vote was just the beginning. During the twentieth century, it became one of many issues that the women's rights movement would fight for and win.

The Fight for Rights

As mentioned in Chapter 20, "The Fight for Rights," suffrage in America took a back seat to abolition efforts during the Civil War. After the war was over, women's rights failed to gain national attention as politicians addressed the status of freed slaves first. Suffragists split on this issue and formed two organizations that promoted different agendas with the same goal: getting the vote. Elizabeth Cady Stanton and Susan B. Anthony, who refused to subordinate suffrage issues, formed the National Woman Suffrage Association. More moderate suffragists formed the American Woman Suffrage Association.

The two groups merged in 1890 to form the National American Woman Suffrage Association (NAWSA), but Stanton and Anthony, who were elected the first and second presidents of the organization, found themselves at odds with their membership. The younger and newer members of NAWSA were on the conservative side and regarded suffrage as one of many important issues. Instead of a constitutional amendment, they supported a less aggressive state-by-state approach to getting the vote.

Hear Me Roar

Marriage, to women as to men, must be a luxury, not a necessity; an incident of life, not all of it. And the only possible way to accomplish this great change is to accord to women equal power in the making, shaping, and controlling of the circumstances of life.

—Susan B. Anthony

Going for the Vote

Because suffrage had taken second place to abolition, the United States lagged behind other countries in giving women the right to vote. By 1920, when the constitutional amendment granting this right was finally passed, women over 30 were already voting in the United Kingdom. Germany, Belgium, Denmark, Canada, Holland, and Sweden all also introduced women's suffrage after World War I. Women in France and Italy didn't gain suffrage until after World War II.

Anthony, who increasingly found herself in the minority when setting NAWSA's policies and agenda, stepped down as president in 1900. Carrie Chapman Catt, who took her place, supported the state-by-state approach favored by NAWSA membership. But this approach was going nowhere fast. Even Catt admitted that suffrage might not be achieved in her lifetime if NAWSA continued its state-based efforts.

A New Approach

Alice Paul, a NAWSA member and a veteran of the more militant English suffragette movement, was one of a growing number of women who were fed up with NAWSA's approach and believed it would be better to push for a constitutional amendment. She also felt that such an effort would need the president's support.

Under her leadership (and to the dismay of NAWSA's more conservative membership), NAWSA's Congressional Committee decided to send a strong message to incoming president Woodrow Wilson by organizing a huge suffrage parade on March 3, 1914, the day before Wilson would be sworn in as president. Paul recruited some 8,000 marchers representing every suffrage group in the country, and sent them down Pennsylvania Avenue accompanied by 26 floats, 10 bands, 6 chariots, and 5 cavalry units for crowd control.

The parade turned into a near riot when protestors moved on the marchers and police units did little to hold them back. A number of marchers were injured, but not seriously. More important, the group garnered a huge amount of attention. The media was out in full force, as was the city's population, which turned out in droves to watch the women march. When Wilson's presidential party arrived at Union Station, the crowd that would customarily have welcomed them was nowhere to be found. Everyone was watching the suffragists. It was a clear message to the soon-to-be president that he had an issue on his hands that he couldn't ignore.

After the parade, members of the Congressional Committee split off from NAWSA and was formed the National Woman's Party under Paul's leadership. At about the same time, Carrie Chapman Catt saw the writing on the wall for NAWSA's state-based suffrage effort and reversed its previous position. NAWSA, too, would lobby at the federal level for a constitutional amendment.

The Final Push

Although Paul's group had sent a strong message to Wilson, suffrage wasn't on the agenda he set for his administration. Nor did it appear on the list of emergency measures he agreed to work on during World War I. NAWSA decided it wouldn't push the issue and suspended its activities until after the war. The NWP, however, refused to let women's rights languish. The United States was fighting a war for democracy. What could be more democratic than giving women the vote? NWP members picketed the White House incessantly and embarrassed the heck out of Wilson's administration. Many protestors were arrested and jailed for their activities.

Wilson knew he couldn't ignore the issue much longer. The suffragists had done a great job of focusing attention on the issue and gathering the support they needed, and public sentiment was definitely heading their way. In 1918 Wilson put suffrage on his agenda and asked Congress to readdress the legislation that had passed in and out of committee for some 40 years since Susan B. Anthony first penned it.

A Woman's Place

Between 1878 when Anthony's amendment was first presented to Congress, and 1919, when it was passed, it was brought to a vote before the Senate or the House eight times. The last five of those votes took place between January 1918 and June 1919.

On May 21, 1919, the House of Representatives passed what had become known as the Susan B. Anthony Amendment by a vote of 304 to 89. The Senate passed it three weeks later. The amendment then went to the states for ratification. After nearly a century of struggle, women could vote for the first time in the presidential election of 1920.

The National American Woman Suffrage Association held its last meeting on March 24, 1919. Although the federal suffrage amendment hadn't passed final muster, all indications were that it would. With NAWSA's prime purpose achieved, it was time to set new goals, and Carrie Chapman Catt challenged NAWSA's membership to form a new organization with a broader agenda.

Although many members felt that such an organization wasn't necessary now that their right to vote was virtually assured, delegates to the convention agreed to form the League of Women Voters.

Suffrage Around the World

Suffrage became a key issue as well in the women's rights initiatives mounted in a number of countries around the world. By the 1950s, most of the reforms fought for by foreign feminists had been achieved. Of them, suffrage was the most widely successful (see the following table).

Where and When Women Got the Vote

Year	Country
1893	New Zealand
1902	Australia
1906	Finland
1913	Norway
1916	Denmark, Iceland
1917	Russia, the Netherlands
1918	Canada, Luxembourg
1919	Austria, Czechoslovakia, Germany, Poland, Sweden
1920	United States
1923	The Philippines
1928	Great Britain, Puerto Rico
1929	Ecuador
1930	South Africa
1931	Spain
1932	Brazil, Uruguay
1934	Turkey, Cuba
1941	Panama
1944	France
1945	Guatemala, Japan
1946	Italy, Mexico, Argentina
1947	Bolivia, China
1948	Belgium, South Korea, Israel
1949	Chile, India, Indonesia, Syria
1950	El Salvador
1954	Belize, Honduras
1956	Egypt, Greece, Nicaragua, Peru
1957	Tunisia
1958	Algeria, Mauritius
1961	The Bahamas, Cameroon
1962	Monaco
1963	Iran
1964	Libya, San Marino
1965	Afghanistan
1966	Barbados, Botswana
1968	Ireland

Where and When Women Got the Vote   (continued)

Year	Country
1970	Andorra
1971	Switzerland
1974	China
1977	Liechtenstein
1980	Cape Verde
1985	Bangladesh

In some countries, women campaigned long and hard for their right to vote only to win suffrage and lose it again. In Geneva, Switzerland, women lost the right to vote in 1914 because they didn't use it. In the years just prior to World War II, women in Germany, Poland, Greece, and Spain lost the voting rights they had earlier won when more conservative or fascist powers came into authority. In other countries, like Hungary, Portugal, and Belgium, the right to vote was only granted to certain women, those over 30, for example, or who had completed a certain level of education. Other rights were given and taken away as well. Russian women were given equal rights after the Bolshevik Revolution of 1917. When Lenin died in 1924, Stalin restored more traditional patriarchal values. He outlawed co-education, divorce, and abortion, which the USSR had been the first European country to legalize in 1920. German women, who had won equality after World War I, lost virtually all civil rights when the Nazis came to power in 1933.

Going for the Vote

One of the reforms called for by Chinese feminists was the elimination of foot binding. Practiced since the early ninth century, it rendered women helpless by subjecting their feet to tight stricture from an early age. China banned the practice in 1934.

In Britain, where the women's rights movement began, suffragettes (as they preferred to be called) chained themselves to buildings, blew up mailboxes, and invaded Parliament. By 1918 Englishwomen over age 30 had gained the right to vote and to run for election to the House of Commons. Women between the ages of 21 (the age at which men could vote) and 30 gained voting rights a decade later. They were originally thought to be too young and inexperienced to be given such rights.

Japanese women were banned from any kind of political activity, but this didn't stop the most fervent activists from organizing suffrage groups and other political organizations. The New Woman Society lobbied successfully for the repeal of the restrictive law and opened the door for other groups to form, but they met with strong opposition from the government, which established its own women's organizations that espoused party lines. When World War II ended, occupation forces pushed for liberalization of Japan's outdated laws. The new constitution gave women the right to vote, allowed them to participate in politics, increased their familial rights, and guaranteed them equal pay.

Women in Italy remained under the authority of their husbands until after World War II. Early efforts to gain the vote fractured the women's movement along the same lines as that in the United States. While many feminists united by joining the Socialist party, the issue of female suffrage remained secondary to eradicating capitalism. The fascist regime of Benito Mussolini further truncated suffrage efforts in Italy. After Mussolini, Italian feminists worked in the new republic to regain the freedoms they had lost.

Equal Rights

American women now could make their opinions known by going to the voting booth. But voting hadn't brought the equality it promised. They still faced discrimination and were far from being on equal political, social, or economic footing with men.

Equal rights was a divisive issue for the women's movement. The more liberal and aggressive feminist faction supported it, while the more conservative reformers preferred to work a more socially oriented agenda and form civic groups and associations to address such issues as birth control, labor rights, and education.

Both the League of Women Voters and the National Women's Party initially supported equal rights efforts, but the League abandoned its feminist agenda when it proved too politically volatile. The NWP became the movement's vanguard when Alice Paul drafted an Equal Rights Amendment for Congress to consider during its 1923 session.

The League of Women Voters had called it correctly when it dropped the ERA as a political hot potato. Congress was still a boy's club, and the men weren't about to give women further franchise. The amendment languished in Congress for nearly 50 years until the next wave of the women's movement brought it forward again in the early 1970s.

Hear Me Roar

Equality of rights under the law shall not be denied or abridged by the United States or by any state on account of sex.

—From the Equal Rights Amendment

The Body Politic

Giving women the right to choose if and when they wanted to become mothers also became part of the women's rights agenda after suffrage was passed. Another highly politicized issue, it drew fire from both secular and religious quarters. Strict legislation not only banned access to contraception, but it even denied women the right to read about it. With their ability to both learn about birth control and use it prohibited, women turned to more drastic measures. Abortion became the most common form of birth control. Because it, too, was illegal, it was almost never practiced under sanitary conditions. Many women performed abortions on themselves using knitting needles or wire hangers. Thousands died or became sterile as a result.

Margaret Sanger was the best known of the reproductive rights activists, but many others took up this issue as well. In 1936, their efforts resulted in a Supreme Court decision that declassified birth control information as obscene.

New birth control methods, including the 1960 introduction of the birth control pill, intensified the fight over women's reproductive rights. By 1965, married couples in all states could legally obtain contraceptives. Full access, however, wouldn't come until the 1970s.

The Second Wave

War—in this case World War II—had once again relegated women's issues to the back burner. In the early 1960s, they returned in full force. Women's rights activists had publicly voiced their anger over President John F. Kennedy's all-male cabinet, but they cheered when he established the Commission on the Status of Women in 1961 (see Chapter 28, "In the Workplace"), after Presidents Truman and Eisenhower had both refused to do so.

Kennedy wasn't a big supporter of women's rights, but he knew when to make a good political move. He wanted women's votes for the next election, and he saw the commission as an opportunity to gain female support.

Kennedy advanced women's rights again, albeit posthumously, when his civil rights agenda resulted in the passage of the 1964 Civil Rights Act. Title VII of the act prohibited employment discrimination on the basis of sex, race, religion, and national origin. For the first time, women's equal access to employment was legislated. The act also called for the establishment of the Equal Employment Opportunity Commission (EEOC) to enforce the legislation.

The Time Is NOW

The EEOC fielded 50,000 complaints regarding discrimination in the workplace in its first five years of operation. When it became clear that the commission was focusing on civil rights complaints and showing little interest in investigating those regarding sex discrimination, women went up in arms. Again, it was clear that they had to take matters into their own hands.

The National Organization of Women, or NOW, was established in Washington, D.C., on June 30, 1966, by women attending the Commission of the Status of Women's third annual convention.

Betty Friedan, the author of *The Feminine Mystique,* which had galvanized millions of women to expand their horizons beyond the home, served as the organization's first president.

NOW would serve as the catalyst for a number of other women's organizations reflecting the needs of specific audiences, such as minority groups, lesbians, welfare mothers, and working women. Thousands of young women on college campuses formed similar groups when their efforts to take an active role in anti-war and civil rights groups were thwarted by their male colleagues. Tired of being treated like second-class citizens by men who believed in freedom and equal rights for all—except women—female students organized "women's liberation" groups to voice their concerns about their status in these movements and in society as a whole.

A Second Shot at Equal Rights

The burgeoning women's movement not only gave women a stronger public voice and presence, but it also illustrated the fact that more women than ever before felt strongly about having the same privileges and responsibilities that men had. No longer divided over the question of equal rights, feminists again lobbied for the passage of the Equal Rights Amendment.

Congress debated the amendment and overwhelmingly passed it in 1972. It also placed a time limit on the ratification process, giving the states until 1978 to approve the measure.

Twenty states approved the amendment in the first six months of ratification. Eight more joined them by the end of the first year. But strong opposition to the amendment was surfacing, including the very vocal Phyllis Schlafly, whose STOP ERA organization argued that the Equal Rights Amendment would destroy the family and actually rob women of many of the rights they currently enjoyed.

By 1977, 35 states had ratified the amendment. Three more were needed. With just one year to go until the deadline, the amendment's supporters rallied one more time. More than 100,000 ERA supporters marched on Washington, D.C., in the summer of 1977. It was the largest gathering of women in support of one issue in the nation's history.

They succeeded in getting Congress to extend the ratification deadline to 1982. But conservative opposition remained strong, and the amendment failed to gain the support it needed to pass in the last few states.

The Education Act Amendments of 1972

Although the ERA failed to become law, other legislation passed during the early 1970s did give women far greater equality in education and sports.

Title IX of the Education Act Amendments of 1972 prohibited sex discrimination in any educational institution that received public funds. Equal access to higher education and professional schools was now the law. As quotas limiting women's enrollment in graduate schools were eliminated, the number of women pursuing careers in medicine, law, engineering, and other formerly male-dominated professions burgeoned.

Although the subject of heated debate, Title IX also gave girls and women equal access to athletic programs. By 1978, just six years after Title IX was passed, women's participation in intercollegiate sports increased by almost 600 percent. At the time of the act's passage, only 1 in 27 high school girls played sports. By 1990, one in three did.

Women's Rights Today

Unless you're of a certain age (over 50), it's sometimes difficult to put into perspective how much women's legal status has improved, how many more choices women have today and what role the move has played. While the reforms it created were revolutionary at the time, most people—women and men alike—now take them very much for granted.

It no longer comes as a surprise to be treated by a woman doctor or represented in court by a female attorney, although women in both professions were few and far between until the 1970s. Women think nothing of applying for and receiving credit in their own names. Before 1965, married women had to have their husbands' permission to do so. Single women were routinely turned down because they weren't married.

Until the passage of the Equal Pay Act of 1963 and the Civil Rights Act of 1964, employers segregated jobs according to sex, with women's jobs holding less status and paying far less than men's. It was the rare newspaper that didn't run sex- and race-segregated want ads. Although sex discrimination still exists in the workplace, women have far better access to the jobs they want and are paid considerably better for doing them.

Women have also benefited considerably when it comes to their personal rights. They have greater control over their sexuality and reproduction than ever

Hear Me Roar

Who knows what women can be when they are finally free to become themselves?

—Betty Friedan

before thanks to the decision in *Roe* v. *Wade* and continuing advancements in birth control methods. However, the conservative right continues to mount strong opposition against a woman's right to choose.

Sex crimes against women are handled differently now. Until the 1960s, wives could not charge their husbands with rape. Not only were women routinely dissuaded from bringing rape charges, but those who did also had to provide a witness to corroborate their testimony. A woman's past sexual history could be presented as evidence, and often was, to prove that she was promiscuous or had tempted her rapist. Today, rape shield laws prevent the introduction of such evidence.

A Woman's Place

In 1972, 26 percent of men and women said they would not support a woman running for president. By 1996, 95 percent of women and 92 percent of men said they would.

There are still battles to be fought, especially in developing countries and in the Middle East. Female genital mutilation, practiced in Africa, parts of Asia, and the Middle East, takes the lives of hundreds of thousands of girls and women every year and causes lifelong health problems for millions of others. Although such influential groups as the World Health Organization and others have condemned it, it is still widely practiced, often under the mistaken belief that it is a religious dictate.

Women throughout the world are at a disadvantage economically. This is especially true in countries that have experienced civil wars and social and economic upheaval. This also may be the result of poor education, the fact that they are single mothers supporting children, or that they do not have access to higher status jobs. In Afghanistan, girls are forbidden to go to school, although some brave women run illegal schools to educate girls. Women in some countries are willing to immigrate, leaving all that is familiar, in order to find a better life—more freedom and better economic opportunities. Some women, lured by the promise of good jobs and decent money, end up as prostitutes, held against their will. Others are forced into servitude, sometimes within a marriage. In the twenty-first century, some men are still trafficking in women.

The Least You Need to Know

➤ Two organizations, the conservative National American Woman Suffrage Association and the more liberal National Woman's Party, worked to make suffrage a reality in the United States.

➤ By the time women gained the right to vote in the United States, 15 foreign countries had already granted suffrage to its female citizens.

➤ Although the Equal Rights Amendment was never ratified, other laws expanded women's rights in education and the workplace.

➤ Women throughout the world have it much better than women 50 years ago, yet there's no room for complacency. Injustices and crimes against women still exist.

Leaders and Fighters

In This Chapter

➤ Reuniting North and South

➤ Preserving ancient legacies

➤ Improving the plight of millions

➤ England's "Iron Lady"

Ironically, while American women have had the right to vote since 1920, the highest office in the land has eluded them. It wasn't until 1984 that a major party chose a woman—Geraldine Ferraro—to run for vice president. In the 2000 presidential race, Elizabeth Dole made a good run at the Republican nomination but wasn't able to muster the support necessary to take on the front-runners. Nor was either of them willing to risk losing by adding her to their tickets.

It's a completely different situation in other countries, where the tradition of female leadership in monarchies often goes back for centuries. But even when it comes to elective office, the world has the United States soundly defeated. By 1970 three women held their countries' highest elective offices. Their numbers increased steadily during the last decades of the twentieth century. You'll meet some of them in this chapter.

Benazir Bhutto

Women were just beginning to emerge from their chattel status in Pakistan when Benazir Bhutto became the first woman to lead a Muslim country since the thirteenth century.

Bhutto rose to political power following the death of her father, Zulfikar Ali Bhutto, a wealthy and prominent politician who became prime minister of Pakistan in 1973 following a brutal civil war. In 1977 she returned from her studies at Oxford to witness a military coup led by General Muhammad Zia. Benazir's father was removed from office and imprisoned on trumped-up charges of conspiring to murder a colleague in his political party. He was executed in April 1979. Benazir, who was in jail for protesting Zia's government, didn't witness the death of her beloved father.

Over the next seven years, Benazir was arrested on numerous occasions and exiled more than once. After martial law ended in 1985, she was allowed to return to Pakistan for good in April 1986, and received a hero's welcome when she did. Soon after, she was elected co-chair, with her mother, of the People's Party. In that position, she demanded Zia's resignation and a new elected government, all in honor of her father.

Hear Me Roar

A ship in port is safe, but that is not what ships are built for.

—Benazir Bhutto

Bhutto honored her Muslim heritage by agreeing to an arranged marriage to businessman Asif Ali Zardari in 1987. A year later, Zia died in a somewhat mysterious plane crash. Bhutto, now a new mother, led her party to victory in the election that followed. As prime minister, she shared her authority with Ishaq Kahn, a former Zia lieutenant, who was elected as president by the opposition party.

Bhutto worked tirelessly to reunite the country, and Pakistan badly needed it. Years under Zia's control had nearly bankrupted the country. Ethnic tensions were high, thanks to the presence of millions of refugees who had fled from war-torn Afghanistan and battles between fundamentalist religious groups.

The shaky relationship between Bhutto and Kahn eroded several years after the election when he denounced her for being the daughter of a corrupt politician. Benazir's husband Zardari, whom she had appointed investment minister, was also facing similar charges, as were a number of his associates. The rumors were too much for Bhutto to overcome. She was deposed, and her party lost the next election to a military coalition.

Bhutto was able to overcome the past when she ran for re-election on an anti-corruption platform. She regained her seat as prime minister in 1993. But she lost the office again three years later amid new charges of corruption and mismanagement. In November 1996, Pakistan's president, Farooq Leghari, dismissed her from her office. In 1997, her attempt to return to politics went down in flames when she was soundly defeated in Pakistan's national election.

Corazon Aquino

Two and a half years after her husband's assassination in August 1983, Corazon Aquino became the leader of the Philippines, one of the world's most strife-filled countries. As president of the Republic of the Philippines from 1986 to 1992, she led her country during its difficult transition from dictatorship to democracy.

The sixth of eight children born to José and Demetria Cojuanco, Cory had a privileged upbringing. Her family was wealthy and politically connected—her father, whose family owned a sugar and rice empire, was a three-term congressman. Her mother, a pharmacist, was the daughter of a senator.

Cory was educated at private Catholic schools in the Philippines before traveling to the United States in 1946 to study at the College of Mount St. Vincent in New York. She graduated with a Bachelor of arts degree in French with a minor in mathematics. She then returned to the Philippines to study for a career as an attorney. She gave up her legal studies in 1956 when she married Benigno (Ninoy) Aquino.

Aquino, the leader of the opposition to the Marcos regime, was arrested in 1972 on charges of murder and subversion and was imprisoned for more than seven years. Cory helped him communicate with his followers throughout his imprisonment.

Aquino was given a brief respite from prison when he was allowed to have heart surgery in the United States in 1980. Cory went with him and the two spent the next three years in exile in Boston. When they returned to the Philippines in August 1983, Benigno Aquino was assassinated at Manila International Airport.

In 1985 Cory yielded to demands that she should run for president. Marcos supporters tried to sabotage the election, but Cory emerged as the true winner. As president, she reestablished the country's democratic institutions and brought about significant economic and social reforms. In 1986 *Time* magazine named her Woman of the Year in honor of her efforts to establish a democratic society in the Philippines. When her term of office expired in 1992, she presided over the peaceful and orderly transfer of power to the Philippines' new president, Fidel V. Ramos.

Aquino has received a number of awards and honorary degrees, including the 1996 J. William Fulbright Prize for International Understanding.

Leading Her Country to Peace: Nguyen Thi Binh

As the chief negotiator of the Paris peace accord that ended the Vietnam war, one thing was important to Nguyen Thi Binh above all else: She wanted the complete withdrawal of U.S. troops from South Vietnam. A cease-fire wasn't enough; they had to go. She got what she asked for.

Fiercely nationalistic, Binh fought against foreign infiltration of her country from an early age. The French were the infiltrators, and she took every opportunity to protest their occupation, leading to her arrest in 1951 for taking part in a public protest. She was imprisoned for three years, during which time she was periodically tortured with electric shock. When the 1954 Geneva peace accord was signed, which split the country into North and South regions (the north governed by the Communists, the south by the French), she was released. She then married and worked as a teacher.

When South Vietnam's President Ngo Dinh Diem refused to hold the national elections called for by the Geneva accord, Binh and her husband, Luu Van Nhon, joined the National Liberation Front of South Vietnam (also called the Viet Cong), which organized the bands of resistance fighters once scattered across the countryside into a massive, unified army. Binh, who chaired the NLF's Women's Liberation Association, recruited thousands of women to the NLF by promising them the same status and positions in the association that male members had. Binh was appointed minister of foreign affairs for the Provisional Revolutionary Government (PRG) of South Vietnam in 1969. When North Vietnam agreed to begin peace talks with the United States, Binh occupied a place at the table. She insisted on the complete withdrawal of U.S. troops, called for the formation of a coalition government and the eventual reunification of North and South Vietnam. Although she had to compromise on some of her demands, she won on the troop withdrawal.

In 1975 Binh was named minister of education after North and South Vietnam reunified as the Socialist Republic of Vietnam. She held the post for more than 10 years and was elected vice president of the country in 1992.

Wilma Mankiller

While the bulk of the electorate in the United States has refused to elect a woman to the highest offices, the Cherokee Nation showed no such prejudice in 1987 when they elected Wilma Mankiller the first woman to serve as chief of a major Native American tribe.

Mankiller became a vocal proponent of Indian civil and treaty rights after her entire family was abruptly relocated by the Bureau of Indian Affairs from their ancestral home on Mankiller Flats, Oklahoma, to one of the poorest areas of San Francisco. She returned to Oklahoma in 1977, where she established and managed a number of community renewal projects, including the establishment of utilities where none had previously existed and the rebuilding of crumbling homes.

Wilma entered politics in 1983 when Ross Swimmer, who was running for the office of principal chief, asked her to join his ticket as deputy chief. Although they were worlds apart when it came to their political beliefs, their common concern for their people united them and they won the election. When Swimmer was appointed director of the Bureau of Indian Affairs in 1985, Mankiller assumed his position in accordance with tribal law. Two years later, she was elected in her own right. She was reelected to a second full term in 1991 but decided not to seek another term in 1994.

While in office, Mankiller worked tirelessly to advance the Cherokee nation by establishing health care, educational, and employment programs for the Cherokee people that both honored their heritage and gave them the chance at living better lives. She developed a network of rural health care centers that have become a model for the country, a number of community development projects, the Institute of Cherokee Literacy, and the Cherokee Chamber of Commerce. Her efforts helped break the chain of poverty that has characterized most tribes during the twentieth century, decreased the Cherokee nation's dependence on the federal government, and restored the proud heritage of the Cherokee nation by preserving its culture and language.

Indira Gandhi

The daughter of the renowned political activists Jawaharlal and Kamala Nehru, Indira Gandhi dedicated herself to improving the quality of life in India.

Her parents' work to free India from British rule inspired Indira to follow in their footsteps at a young age. She was only 12 when she organized the Monkey Brigade, a group of children who helped carry clandestine communications between the leaders of the independence movement. Following her studies at Oxford, she returned to India where she resumed her involvement in politics especially in the independence movement.

In 1942, Indira married journalist Feroze Gandhi (no relation to Mahatma), with whom she had two sons. When Feroze was elected to Congress, Indira chose to live with her father, who needed her assistance as a hostess as her mother had died several years previously. In 1947, after India won its independence from Great Britain, Jawaharlal Nehru became the country's first prime minister.

Indira accompanied her father to many affairs of state, and it was clear that she was being groomed to succeed him in office. In 1959, she was elected president of the Indian National Congress party, the second-highest political position in the country. When Nehru died in 1964, Indira was elected to congress in his place and was named Minister of Information and Broadcasting by Lal Bahadur Shastri, her father's successor. When Shastri died in 1966, she became prime minister.

A Woman's Place

Indira Gandhi's aunt, Vijaya Lakshmi Pandit, also played a key role in her country's fight to remove itself from the British Empire. Pandit saw the inside of a jail more than once as the result of her continued protests against the British government. In recognition of her efforts, she was chosen to lead India's delegation to the United Nations in 1946. In 1953, she became the first woman to be elected president of the UN.

Although some hoped she would act as a shadow leader until the next elections could be held, Indira proved to be a shrewd and masterful head of state. She enhanced India's reputation on the world stage, as well as its power, and made the important step of improving its relations with the Soviet Union. She also led India to victory in its war with Pakistan in 1971.

During the 1971 elections, Indira ran on an anti-poverty platform that promised vast improvements in the lives of her people. A voluntary sterilization program to limit population growth was part of her plan, but it met with extreme resistance. People misconstrued the program as mandatory, and public criticism of her, which had begun with accusations of election law violations, swelled.

Thousands of people took to the streets in protest, making it necessary for Indira to declare a state of emergency. In all, more than 100,000 protestors were detained and held without trial. Other measures enacted to quell civil unrest included press censorship and the imprisonment of political opponents. None of this was good press for Indira or her party. In the 1977 elections, India's voters kicked both out of office.

Indira returned to politics two years later when the ruling Janata party proved weak and ineffective. After first running for Congress, she then won the election that restored her as prime minister. She continued to develop and implement reforms that she believed would improve the quality of life for her people, but her efforts weren't enough to effect the sweeping changes that India desperately needed. Nor could she stave off attacks on her leadership from opposing parties. During another state of emergency in 1984, called after protestors again took to the streets, Indira Gandhi was assassinated by the Sikhs in her security detail.

Aung San Suu Kyi

Aung San Suu Kyi would have liked to attend the Nobel Peace Prize ceremony in 1991. After all, she had won it. But there was a little snag holding her back—she was under house arrest for her political activities, had been for quite some time, and would be for years to come.

There is a powerful legacy behind this diminutive political activist who has fought on behalf of her country for most of her adult life. Her father, Aung San, led the movement that resulted in Burma's freedom from British rule. On the eve of the country's independence, he was assassinated. Suu Kyi was hardly three years old at the time. Although she knew her father when he died, she became intimately familiar with his work and philosophies through the books she read and the stories she was told of his valor.

Suu Kyi attended college in India, where she was inspired by Mahatma Gandhi's belief in nonviolent civil disobedience. She finished her education at Oxford, worked briefly as a research assistant at the University of London, and then went to New York where she spent three years on the staff of the United Nations secretariat. In 1971 she became engaged to Michael Aris, a British scholar whom she had met at Oxford. They married in 1972 and established their home in England.

In 1988 Suu Kyi received word that her mother had suffered a severe stroke. She left her husband and sons behind and immediately went to see her. Myanmar (formerly known as Burma) was in the throes of political upheaval caused by the oppressive military dictatorship that had been in power since 1962. Suu Kyi felt it was her job to do something about it.

In August 1988 she made what would become a legendary speech during a political rally at the foot of the Schwedagon pagoda of Rangoon. With a large picture of her father displayed behind her, she called for the government to cease using force against peaceful unarmed demonstrators and proposed the establishment of a People's Consultative Committee to help resolve the crisis. She spoke in fluent Burmese, which helped overcome the opposition she otherwise would have faced due to spending many years abroad and her marriage to a foreigner. Suu Kyi clearly was still devoted to her country and willing to do anything she could for it.

Words for Women

Aung San Suu Kyi's name translates as "a bright collection of strange victories."

Hear Me Roar

I could not, as my father's daughter, remain indifferent.

—Aung San Suu Kyi

With her speech, Suu Kyi became the leader of the National League for Democracy, the party that organized to oppose the country's military dictatorship. Her campaign to unseat the ruling powers, however, would last less than 11 months. Defying a ban against political gatherings of more than four people, she embarked on a speechmaking tour throughout the country and addressed more than one thousand meetings. She stressed the need for democracy and the need to accomplish it through nonviolent means.

Support for her beliefs grew, much to the dismay of the ruling powers. In April 1989 soldiers were sent to kill her, but she managed to escape. Three months later, she was placed on "restricted residence" and forbidden any contact with the outside world. She remains under house arrest to this day.

The National League for Democracy won the election in 1990, which effectively made Suu Kyi the leader of her country. But the military regime has refused to budge. Suu Kyi has been offered her freedom on numerous occasions with the stipulation that she never return to Myanmar, but she has refused to forsake her people and her country.

Margaret Thatcher

As Great Britain's first female prime minister, the "Iron Lady," as she was often called, gave her country's social and economic policies a much-needed overhaul. In the years after her 1979 election, she revamped England's social welfare system, broke powerful labor unions, and gave the private sector control over a number of state-owned industries. While she was often criticized for her inflexible approach to many of her reforms, she was the nation's longest-serving prime minister since 1827. During her time in that office, she was one of the most powerful world leaders.

Thatcher had established a successful tax practice as an attorney before her election to Parliament in 1959. Prime Minister Edward Heath made her the only women cabinet member in his administration when he named her education secretary in 1970. Thatcher succeeded Heath as the leader of the Conservative Party in 1974 and became prime minister when the Conservatives won the election four years later.

Hear Me Roar

Standing in the middle of the road is very dangerous; you get knocked down by traffic from both sides.

—Margaret Thatcher

Believing that England's woes were caused by a basic lack of conviction that resulted from too many years of socialistic politics, she set out to bolster both the country's economy and its spirit. She reduced public expenditures, slashed service to the poor, and promoted privatization of many industries that had long been controlled by the government, including British Telecom, British Gas, and British Airways. She established a free-enterprise economy and put in place controls against inflation. As often happens, things got worse before they got better. During her first two terms in office, unemployment tripled and the number of poor people increased, as did the bankruptcies caused by her efforts to curb inflation. The public's opinion of her dived as well. But England's 1982 victory in the Falkland Islands turned everything around.

By her third term, inflation had plummeted, income taxes had dropped, and the economy had bolstered through the sale of more than $50 billion of government assets.

Increasingly irritated by criticism of strict control over her cabinet and her country's economic agenda, Thatcher resigned as prime minister in November 1990. She wasn't about to change. Nor did she feel she had to.

For her service to her country, Thatcher was awarded the Order of Merit by Queen Elizabeth II in 1990. Since resigning as Prime Minster, Thatcher has written two volumes of memoirs, *The Downing Street Years* and *The Path to Power*.

Golda Meir

A fierce *Zionist*, Golda Meir was one of the architects of modern Israel and spent her life insuring that it would remain in place for generations to come.

Born Golda Mabovitch, Meir moved with her family to Milwaukee, Wisconsin from Russia, where attacks against Jewish homes and families formed her earliest memories.

While studying to be a teacher, Golda became active in the developing Zionist movement. When she married her husband, Morris Meyerson, it was on the condition that the couple would immigrate to Palestine, which they did in 1921. They lived on a kibbutz for two years until Morris' health failed, after which they resettled in Jerusalem. Golda took in washing to make ends meet. She also began working in the labor movement and the World Zionist Movement and earned a great amount of respect for her work in each.

In 1928 Golda was named secretary of the Women's Labor Council, which was part of Palestine's Jewish government. When the state of Israel was established on May 14, 1948, she was one of 25 people who signed the Proclamation of Independence. Soon after, she was named minister of labor

A Woman's Place

Thatcher's agenda for revitalizing her country, which included economic reforms, an emphasis on individual responsibility, and rousing patriotism became known as "Thatcherism."

Words for Women

A **Zionist** is a person who supported the principles of Zionism, which reestablished and now supports the Jewish national state.

in the country's first cabinet under its new prime minister, David Ben-Gurion. She served in this position for seven years and was named as foreign minister in 1956.

The years she spent in politics took their toll on Meir, and she retired from government in 1968. Although she meant to stay out of the public arena, she reentered it the following year when the Labor Party asked her to serve out the remainder of Prime Minister Levi Eshkol's term following his death. At the end of the term, she ran for and was elected prime minister in her own right.

Meir was obsessed with Israel's security during her years as prime minister. Although she often said she would meet the Arab leaders anytime and at any place, and did enter into peace negotiations with them, she was criticized for not being willing to compromise on key issues, including Israel's occupation of such areas as the Gaza Strip, East Jerusalem, the West Bank, and the Golan Heights. Long-simmering resentment between Arabs and Jews flared in October 1973 when Egypt attacked Israel across the Suez Canal and Syria attacked the Golan Heights during the Jewish High Holy Days. Israel's armies successfully protected the small country but lost many troops in the process. The fact that the attack took place during one of the most important times of the year for the Jewish people wasn't an excuse for Israel's relative lack of preparedness. After all, war can happen at any time.

Meir took responsibility for not having Israel in better combat condition. She stepped down from her position as prime minister soon after.

A Woman's Place

After the establishment of the state of Israel, many Jews took Hebrew names to reflect their new status as Israelis. David Ben-Gurion suggested that Golda change her last name to Meir, which means "to illuminate."

The Least You Need to Know

➤ While women haven't reached the highest office in the United States, top spots in other countries haven't eluded them.

➤ Although she successfully revitalized Britain's sagging economy, Margaret Thatcher fought opposition to her efforts throughout most of her time as prime minister.

➤ Aung San Suu Kyi, prevented from receiving in person the Nobel Peace Prize that she won in 1991, continues to practice nonviolent civil disobedience by remaining under house arrest in Myanmar.

➤ Indira Gandhi placed her political career and her responsibilities to her father ahead of her marriage.

Chapter 28

In the Workplace

In This Chapter

➤ The rise of women workers

➤ Building a common voice

➤ Changes during the 1960s, 1970s, and 1980s

➤ The workplace today

When we think about all the different arenas in which women work today, it's sometimes hard to believe that it was only a century ago when most professions weren't open to them. In the early twentieth century, it was the rare woman who practiced law or medicine. And if she did, she wasn't accorded anywhere near the same status or pay as her male counterparts commanded.

The revolution that took place in the workplace for women in the twentieth century was truly remarkable, especially when we consider how things were at the beginning of the century. Victorian sensibilities still dictated that home was the be all and end all for women. Both men and women subscribed to this philosophy, which makes it easier to understand the mixed emotions that gripped many women when they did enter the workforce.

It also helps explain, but not justify, why it's been so difficult for women to attain equal status in the labor force. After all, it's pretty tough to convince an employer that you're serious about a job when the expectation is that you'll quit the moment you get married or have children. Because of this, women entering the work force were generally slotted into the least-skilled, lowest-paying jobs.

While there still isn't true equality in the workplace, the gap between the sexes is far narrower now than it has ever been. In this area, women have (pardon us, but you had to see it somewhere in this book) come a long way, baby!

Arise, Women Workers!

As was the case in the nineteenth century, few women worked outside of the home at the beginning of the twentieth. Those who did were generally young and single, and it was expected that they would work to support themselves until they got married. It also was expected that they would quit working when they tied the knot. In some cases, like the teaching profession, retirement was mandatory upon marriage. Most women of color, immigrants, and working-class women did not have the choice to stay home after marriage, however. Due to their lower economic status, they knew they'd be working after they married whether they wanted to or not.

In the United States, suffrage work and other social reform issues brought together women of all colors and classes. Their work in these areas convinced them that similar efforts might help revolutionize the workplace as well. The union movement, which began in the nineteenth century, gained momentum in the twentieth. The issues women workers were concerned with, unfortunately, were much the same that had plagued them in the 1800s—poor or unsafe work conditions, long hours, low pay.

Hear Me Roar

Among poor people, there's not any question about women being strong—even stronger than men—they work in the fields right along with the men. When your survival is at stake, you don't have those questions about yourself like middle-class women do.

—Dolores Huerta, co-founder of the United Farm Workers

Because unions run by men often downplayed or even overlooked the concerns of women members, women began organizing on their own. In 1900 coat makers in New York established the International Ladies' Garment Workers' Union. They started with about 2,000 members located in four cities—New York, Baltimore, Newark, and Philadelphia.

Four years later, membership had doubled and spread to 27 cities. In 1909 this group staged a massive strike that is often referred to as the Uprising of 20,000 (or 30,000, depending on the source).

Three years later, labor leader Elizabeth Gurley Flynn organized a similar protest in Lawrence, Massachusetts. This event, sometimes referred to as the Bread and Roses Strike, turned violent, with workers smashing sewing machines and otherwise damaging the insides of factories. One woman lost her life while fighting with police. Public sentiment was high for the workers, and the mill owners ended up meeting most of the strikers' demands.

A Woman's Place

Statistics show that one in five women worked outside of the home during the early twentieth century. Most worked as domestics. Factory work was also popular, with many young women working in various aspects of textile production. Some middle-class women, continuing a pattern started in the nineteenth century, were writers, allowing them to earn money and stay at home. A small number of middle-class women worked at various clerical jobs. Women entered the clerical workforce during the Civil War when bureaus in Washington needed many hands to keep and copy records. Clerical work was considered a male occupation, but that soon changed. By 1960, 96 percent of all clerical workers—clerks, typists, and what have you—were women.

Flynn, who had a strong socialist bent (she was also a prominent member of the Industrial Workers of the World), organized another strike in Paterson, New Jersey, in 1913. Mill owners there had attempted to increase the workload of silk weavers and dyers without giving them more pay. This protest, however, didn't do much good. By the end of the summer the mill workers were back at their loom and dye vats without one concession from their employers.

In 1903 Mary Kenney O'Sullivan and Leonora O'Reilly organized the National Women's Trade Union League after they attended an AFL (American Federation of Labor) meeting and realized that union leaders there had relegated women to secondary status. The NWTUL welcomed both women in the work force as well as middle- and upper-class women sympathetic to the cause as members. With the motto "The Eight Hour Day; a Living Wage; to Guard the Home," the NWTUL worked for women's suffrage, full unionization, equal pay for equal work, the eight-hour work day, and mandatory minimum wages.

By 1911 the NWTUL had organized chapters in 11 cities. After the tragic Triangle Shirtwaist Fire in 1911, which killed 146 young women factory workers in New York, it helped investigate the conditions that caused the fire and pushed for laws requiring companies to establish and follow minimum safety precautions.

A Woman's Place

The small number of women working in professional and white-collar jobs in the early 1900s found a common voice in the National Federation of Business and Professional Women's Clubs (BPWC), founded by Lena Madeson Phillips in 1919. The BPWC advocated the right of married women to remain in the workforce, which was virtually unheard of at the time. In 1930 Phillips also helped establish the International Federation for Business and Professional Women, which today has membership of more than a quarter million women in over 100 countries around the world.

In Europe the protection laws passed during the nineteenth century that sought to make working conditions better for women (and preserve their roles as mothers and homemakers) were augmented by new legislation at the beginning of the twentieth century. Supported by women union members, regulations prohibiting women from working underground first passed in England during the 1800s and were adopted by all European countries by 1914. Other protective legislation brought about shorter work hours, allowed women to take time off for a few weeks after childbirth, and prohibited their working at night.

Women had joined unions in Europe in great numbers during the 1800s and continued to do so at the beginning of the 1900s. In Germany more than 200,000 women were union members by 1912. France had close to 100,000, and England has close to a half million.

While these numbers sound impressive, they actually represent a tiny fraction—less than 10 percent—of the women in Europe's labor force. Union membership wasn't open to most of them, so they remained outside the fold. If they could leave the labor force, they did. The standard of living was on the rise, both in the United States and Europe, enabling increasing numbers of women to quit working if they chose to, even if only while they were raising their children.

Many of the women left in the workforce eschewed agricultural, factory, and domestic jobs for new white-collar positions in stores and offices. Women on both sides of the Atlantic began taking jobs as clerks, typists, and telephone operators, much to the delight of their employers who could save a few bucks by hiring them instead of men. By the mid-1930s, an estimated 30 percent of all European women holding jobs outside of the home worked in this sector of the economy.

At the same time that working-class women were finding new jobs, more middle-class women began attending college. These were the women who invented the female professions of nursing, teaching, and social work, which for many years were thought to be the only professions appropriate for women as they were "natural" extensions of a women's domestic nature.

Only Misses Need Apply

Married women had the toughest time of all when they tried to enter the work force. In the United States, married women who sought work during the Depression stepped into a hostile environment more often than not. Even if their husbands were unemployed, they were often accused of taking jobs that should go to men. Although the spheres of work were so separate in most businesses and industries that women rarely competed directly with men for the same jobs, a number of cities and states passed laws that either limited or prohibited hiring married women. So did many school boards.

The same was true in countries like England, which also suffered a depression throughout most of the 1920s. Women who married were almost virtually assured of losing their jobs when they did and had little hope of regaining them should they want to return to work. Laws were even passed to dissuade them from the thought—in 1922, for example, legislation was enacted that automatically excluded married women from unemployment benefits unless they could prove that losing their jobs would be a hardship.

World War II signaled the end of the Depression and the beginning of an economic boom. It also gave more married women in the United States and Europe the chance to go to work. Workers were in such short supply that business owners often had no choice but to hire women regardless of their marital status.

Going for the Vote

During World War II women in the Soviet Union virtually took over agricultural production when men were called to the battlefields. Soviet women also held the majority of industrial jobs by the end of the war. They even were drafted as soldiers. Although they were never formally called to battle, some did carry arms and fight at certain times. Most who were drafted provided support services for male troops, including operating radios, sending code, and transporting male soldiers. Others worked on farms or in factories.

In the United States, six million women who had never worked outside the home before entered the labor force during this period—and got bounced right back out of it at the end of the war. Most didn't want to go—they liked the feelings of self-worth and independence they were beginning to develop—but they didn't have much of a choice when the men returned from the battlefield and wanted their jobs back.

In the United States the economy continued to expand after the war, providing new wealth and more jobs for both sexes. Fewer young women were seeking jobs—they were more likely to go straight from school to marriage, and their husbands were now often earning enough so they could make homemaking a full-time career. In contrast, married women in their 30s and 40s now had time on their hands as their children were in school and the new labor-saving devices were making housework a breeze. These women—middle-class, married, educated—comprised the majority of the women who went to work outside the home in the 1960s and 1970s.

As they did, they found that many jobs once off-limits to them were now more accessible. While many jobs were still in the service sector, not all were. Anything approaching a top-level management position was still few and far between, but middle-level jobs were within reach. Jobs were also plentiful in the traditional women's professions of nursing and teaching, thanks to the post-war baby boom.

A Woman's Place

Women are still stuck in middle management, according to recent statistics from the Feminist Research Center. In 1968 15 percent of all managers were women. If they had been able to work their way up the corporate ladder, there should be more female senior executives. However, in the early 1990s women comprised only slightly more than 3 percent of senior executives at Fortune 500 companies, and the number hasn't risen appreciably since then. At the current rate of increase, it would take until the year 2466 for women to reach equality in executive suites.

Such was not the case in Europe, where the war had devastated cities and populations. It would be the early 1960s before the European economy regained its footing. When it did, the standard of living rose substantially, but the labor market for women remained largely the same. Women were still paid less than men working similar jobs, and their access to higher-paid jobs was limited. Traditional work roles remained in place, with most women taking jobs in the service sector or in factories.

Equal Pay for Equal Work

Although their numbers were steadily increasing, the women who entered the workforce in the United States during the early 1960s encountered a fair amount of resentment for doing so. They also had to put up with extreme pay inequities—to the point where the difference between what they were being paid and what men in similar positions could get was beyond demeaning. These were some of the concerns that prompted Esther Peterson, the director of the Department of Labor's Women's Bureau and a former labor leader, to ask President Kennedy to appoint a Commission on the Status of Women.

Going for the Vote

In Japan, the number of women in the labor force increased substantially following World War II, fueled by the growth in employment opportunities in the service sector and in higher educational levels. At first, many women worked in family businesses. Today, that number has decreased while more Japanese women pursue positions outside of the family. According to recent estimates, Japanese women now comprise 40 percent of the country's labor market—down from almost 50 percent in 1995. Traditionally, Japanese women have worked until they had children, stayed at home until the children were in school, and then returned to work. More than one third of Japanese women now say they don't feel they should have to stop working after getting married or having children. The majority of Japanese men still want their wives to stay at home while their children are young.

The commission, headed by Eleanor Roosevelt, was charged with reassessing women's place in the economy, the family, and the legal system. What it came up with was hardly shocking to the women in the workforce—it documented unequal pay, persistent and pervasive employment discrimination, legal inequalities, and the lack of needed services such as childcare. But it made them want to do something about it. As they had before, women—many of them in management positions with some clout—banded together and established similar commissions in most states. These groups could, and did, exert political pressure. Policies were changed as a result.

After the commission made its report, the president ordered the civil service to hire people for career positions without regard to sex. Congress passed the Equal Pay Act in 1963 outlawing differences in pay between men and women for the same work. In

1964, Title VII of the Civil Rights Act was enacted to prohibit discrimination in employment on the basis of race, religion, national origin, and sex.

Treating women equally in the workforce in all areas was now legislated. However, many companies continued discriminatory practices, and the government was making little effort to enforce its own laws. Again, women took matters into their own hands. NOW, which you read about in Chapter 26, "The Women's Movement," addressed Title VII's lack of enforcement, among other issues.

In 1974 clerical workers in Boston and Chicago created new organizations to help them build community in the workplace. In Chicago, a group called Women Employed protested in support of a secretary named Iris Rivera who had been fired for refusing to make coffee by conducting a sit-in at her former employer. The protest received national coverage, and Rivera got her job back. Similar protests were staged against discriminatory employers in Boston by both Women Employed and another group, 9 to 5.

Women in labor unions felt similarly isolated by the traditional union structure and created their own organization called the Coalition of Labor Union Women (CLUW). It not only helped bring these women together; it forced the labor movement to recognize women as an important part of its constituency.

The New Workforce

By the early 1970s the workplace had changed dramatically. There were now more women in almost all professions, including such highly male-dominated fields as medicine and law. The Equal Employment Opportunity Commission (EEOC) was investigating and enforcing Title VII infractions more aggressively. Women still faced discrimination, but of a much more subtle nature. For the most part, if they wanted to advance in their careers, they had to stay employed. If they took time off to have a family, or even expressed the desire to do so, they often found themselves on the "mommy track," which placed them in dead-end jobs with little chance for advancement. Many women put off marriage and childrearing because of this.

A Woman's Place

According to a study by Donaldson, Lufkin, and Jenrette, the Wall Street securities firm, the number of families with one wage earner grew at a rate of 1.8 percent a year between 1990 and 1995, reversing the trend from the 1980s when the number of dual income families rose.

More than half of all adult women worked outside the home by the 1980s. The traditional family structure—man at work, woman at home, man's income supports everyone—was long gone. Instead, most couples worked. The dual career or two-job family became the norm, and remains so to this day, although more families, tired of the balancing act between job and family, are returning to the lifestyle of the 1950s where one parent worked and the other stayed home.

A Business of My Own

There weren't many women business owners at the beginning of the twentieth century—that trend wouldn't begin in earnest until the 1980s. Women who did start their own businesses in the early 1900s tended to stick with feminine pursuits—cosmetics, clothing, and the like. Some of the more famous were ...

➤ Sarah Breedlove, also known as Madame C. J. Walker, who invented a popular line of grooming products for black women, including one that straightened and added shine to their hair. By 1910 she had factories in Denver, Indianapolis, and Pittsburgh. She also opened beauty schools to give black women the chance at jobs other than domestic service. The first African-American woman to become a millionaire, her firm was the largest black-owned company of the time.

➤ Florence Nightingale Graham, better known as Elizabeth Arden, who started a chain of beauty salons in New York in 1910 and developed a well-known line of cosmetics that remain one of the top sellers today.

➤ Gabrielle "Coco" Chanel, who started a millinery shop in 1913 and revolutionized the fashion world shortly thereafter with simple but elegant designs that women embraced for their ease of wear.

➤ Helena Rubinstein, who opened beauty salons in England and Paris in 1914 after making a small fortune selling creams to soothe the parched skins of Australian women. In addition to her legendary face creams—the formulas for which were based on herbal recipes she obtained from an Hungarian friend of her family—she also pioneered the use of colored face powder and foundation. She also was the first to use silk in cosmetics formulation.

➤ Elsa Schiaparelli, who began designing clothing after World War I. Previously a film scriptwriter and translator, she first gained notice for her line of modernistically decorated sweaters. She then developed a sportswear line for women looking for clothing with comfort and style. Schiaparelli is credited for originating the idea of separates and the evening dress with a matching jacket.

As more women began hitting the glass ceiling in the private sector during the 1980s and 1990s, they left to do their own thing. According to the National Foundation for Women Business Owners, an estimated 9.1 women owned their own businesses in the United States in 1999, employing more than 27.5 million people and generating more than $3.6 trillion in sales.

The Workforce Today

While the workforce continues to favor men, women have a stronger position in it than ever before. Of the nearly 65 million jobs created between 1964 and 1997, 40 million were for women. In 1997, women made up 46.2 percent of the total U.S.

labor force, holding 49 percent of managerial and professional specialty occupations. An estimated 95 percent of the highest ranks in corporate America are still held by men, but the numbers of companies with at least one female corporate officer have increased dramatically.

Women have gained greater opportunities to work in the profession of their choice, but they haven't made the same gains in what they get paid. Women's salaries continue to fall short of what men are paid, although this gap has narrowed in recent years as well. Still, at the management level, white women earned 74 cents for every dollar a man made in 1998. Women of color fell even shorter—African-American women were paid 58 cents, Hispanic women earned 48 cents, and Asians/other earned 67 cents.

The Least You Need to Know

➤ Women came together in unions and other organizations to revolutionize the workplace.

➤ Legislation passed during the 1960s helped remove much of the discrimination women experienced in the workplace.

➤ While some women started and operated their own businesses in the early twentieth century, it would be another 70 years or so before large numbers of women quit working for others and became entrepreneurs.

➤ Salaries paid to women and men remain unequal, with women earning an average of 61 cents for every dollar a man makes.

Chapter 29

Oooooh...

Leveling the Playing Field

In This Chapter

➤ Taking to the skies

➤ Breaking sex and race barriers

➤ Proving that women can be athletic and feminine

➤ Reaching the mountaintop

After years of oppression and of hearing they weren't made of the right stuff, women proved that they had what it took to be successful in many arenas during the twentieth century. They seized on their newfound freedoms and ventured forward as athletes, as explorers, as businesswomen, forging new ground and setting new standards as they did.

The accomplishments of the women profiled in this chapter set precedents and opened the doors for many others who followed.

Up, Up in the Air

Men may have wished that they could keep air flight to themselves, but women proved to be as excited about the chance to slip earthly bounds as the guys were. Flying fever hit both sides of the Atlantic. A Madame de Laroche received her pilot's certificate in 1910, just six years after the historic flight at Kitty Hawk. Hilda Hewlett, a British woman, received her pilot's license in 1911 as did Harriet Quimby, the first American woman to qualify as a pilot. By the First World War, 11 women had been granted pilot's licenses; many more were flying without them. Women and men both flew as barnstormers and in air shows during the 1920s.

Women took to the air in great numbers during World War II thanks to the efforts of another pioneering female pilot—Jackie Cochran—who created the Women's Air Service Pilots (WASPs) along with Air Corps General "Hap" Arnold after she was refused permission to organize a corps of female pilots as a branch of the U.S. military.

The WASPs were in action for three years during World War II and flew the same aircraft as male pilots. Although they didn't fly in combat, they did assist military flight operations in many other areas by flying training missions, breaking in new aircraft, towing targets for target practice, and testing out planes with mechanical problems.

As good as they were, and for all the contributions they made to the war effort, the WASPs never were recognized as a military organization. Men didn't want to compete against women for crucial post-war flying jobs, so when Cochran petitioned the male-dominated U.S. Congress for such recognition, her request was denied. The WASPs were disbanded in December 1944.

A Woman's Place

Since it wasn't a military organization, women who wanted to join the WASPs had to cover many of their own expenses, including their licenses, instruction, and, in the beginning, their uniforms. They had no military rank or insurance, which meant that the families of the women who died in action were responsible for their funeral expenses.

A Woman's Place

Jackie Cochran was one of many female pilots who delighted in setting and breaking records. In 1953, she became the first woman to break the sound barrier. She followed that feat in 1964 by becoming the fastest woman pilot of the time, flying at a speed of 1,429 miles per hour.

In Love with the Sky: Amelia Earhart

As one of America's foremost aviators of either sex, Amelia Earhart set an unprecedented number of aviation records. Although it wasn't her goal, she also captured the heart and imagination of a country and inspired a generation of women to follow in her footsteps.

Earhart was hooked on flying when she went to an air show in California in 1922. She took lessons from Neta Snook, one of the first women aviators, and bought her own plane, which she used to set her first record as the first woman to fly to an altitude of 14,000 feet in the air.

Amelia gained fame in 1928 as the first woman to cross the Atlantic in a plane, a flight arranged by George Putnam, a publisher and promoter who later became her husband. Even though she landed to great public acclaim and was dubbed "Lady Lindy," she was uncomfortable with the adulation being heaped upon her as she was only allowed to keep the logbook for the flight. In 1932, she crossed the Atlantic on her own, piloting a Lockheed Vega from Newfoundland to Ireland. In doing so, she became the first woman to complete a solo flight across the Atlantic, justifying her celebrity status in her own mind. She followed that accomplishment by becoming the first pilot to fly solo from Honolulu to the American mainland in 1935. She made the first nonstop flight from Mexico City to Newark, New Jersey, that same year.

In 1937, at age 39, Earhart set out on an around-the-world flight in her twin-engine Lockheed Electra, which she had received as special advisor in aeronautics at Purdue University. On June 1, accompanied by navigator Fred Noonan, she took off from Miami, Florida. One month later, as they neared tiny Howland Island in the South Pacific, radio contact with the plane became faint and then disappeared altogether. The last messages Earhart and Noonan sent indicated that they were having trouble locating the island. No trace was ever found of them or their plane.

Less is known about Earhart's support of commercial aviation. She was a co-founder of Boston and Maine Airways, one of the first commercial airlines, and worked at one time as a sales rep for a commercial airport.

A Woman's Place

Earhart was also a founding member and first president of the Ninety-Nines, an association of women pilots she helped organize in the late 1920s. The group took its name from the number of its charter members. Other founding members of the association included Jacqueline (Jackie) Cochran, who supervised hundreds of women pilots in the Women's Air Service during World War II; and Olive Anne Beech, who owned and operated Beech Aircraft for a number of years.

Going Where No Woman Had Gone Before

Almost no record exists of the fact that 25 women were chosen as candidates for America's space program. Thirteen of them passed the rigorous physical and mental tests required of all potential astronauts. While they proved to be the equal of the male candidates and were shown to be superior to them in several areas, they were banned from further participation in the nascent space program. It would be almost another 20 years before the first American woman astronaut went into space.

That privilege was given to Sally Ride, who was a member of the *Challenger* shuttle crew in 1983. However, she was beat to the punch some 20 years earlier by the Soviet government, which launched cosmonaut Valentina Tereshkova into space in 1963.

A Woman's Place

Janet Guthrie, who would go on to fame in 1977 as the first woman to drive in the Indianapolis 500, was one of the women selected as a NASA astronaut candidate.

Tereshkova was one of five women who entered the cosmonaut program in 1962 at Star City, the Soviet Union's space exploration center. An expert parachutist, she received the same training as her male colleagues and won the only slot open to a woman.

On June 16, 1963, she rode a one-person capsule called *Vostok 6* into space and the history books, becoming the first woman to orbit the earth. The United States, which was trailing in its battle with the Soviets over the race to space, derided the mission as a publicity stunt from the beginning. Perhaps it was, but the Soviets made their point. Tereshkova stayed in space for 3 days and orbited the earth 48 times, longer than all the U.S. *Mercury* astronauts combined. She proved that women were clearly as capable as men were to explore the last frontier.

As the first American woman in space, Ride spent six days in orbit around the earth. Since her mission, a number of shuttle teams have included at least one woman member, including Mae Jemison, who was selected in 1987 as the first African-American woman astronaut. A physician who had served as a Peace Corps medical officer in Africa, she spent eight days as part of the *Endeavor* crew in 1992.

A Woman's Place

Two of the women candidates for the space program, Jerrie Cobb and Jane Hart, organized a congressional hearing on NASA's ban on women in space. In 1962, John Glenn and Alan Shepherd appeared before a subcommittee and testified that women weren't qualified to go to space as they couldn't meet the jet-test requirements. What they didn't say was that women weren't allowed to participate in the training that would qualify them for the test. The subcommittee let stand NASA's no-female rule.

Women in Sports

Thought too weak and fragile to participate in sports during the nineteenth century, women executed their newfound freedoms in many areas by taking to athletic fields, arenas, rinks, and pools by storm in the twentieth. At first, many women participated in sports thought to be appropriate for their more delicate natures—croquet, badminton, and the like. But before long they felt no compunction to do so and they pushed the envelope in many athletic endeavors.

Eleanora Sears, the daughter of a shipping and real estate tycoon, pursued a wide variety of sports in the early part of the century. Born with a daredevil streak, she couldn't say no when she was dared to do something new. She was one of the first women to race a car or fly a plane. Among her many endeavors were speedboat racing, sailing, polo (she played on an all-male team, which was unheard of at the time), and skating. She also competed in squash and tennis and trained and rode show horses. In 1910, the press proclaimed her as the top all-around athlete in America. Another early athlete equally as daring was Gertrude Ederle, who became the sixth person and first woman to swim the English Channel in 1926.

Opening the Doors of Competition

Playing sports was one thing. Competing at them was another. When it came to competitive athletics, women athletes often found themselves having to strike a balance between their abilities and their femininity. Women who were too good in their sports could suffer attacks on their identities and reputations, even if they were competing against other women.

One of the earliest competitive female athletes did manage to balance talent and femininity even though she was better than many male athletes at the time. Mildred "Babe" Didrikson showed up the boys when she played sandlot baseball and the men when she played golf. But they couldn't ignore her brilliance as an athlete. Over the course of her career, Didrikson won titles in basketball, track, and golf, and was named Woman Athlete of the Year six times in a row by the Associated Press.

There was seemingly nothing this gifted athlete couldn't do. After showing her stuff on baseball sandlots and basketball courts, she turned to track and field, which she also dominated. In the Amateur Athletic Union Championships of 1932, she won five gold medals, tied in one event, and placed second in another. In the Los Angeles Olympics that followed, she won a gold medal and set a new world record in the javelin toss, a gold in the 80-meter hurdles, and a silver in the high jump.

Called Babe by her fans after another legendary athlete of the time—Babe Ruth—Didrikson developed a passion for golf after playing a round with a group of sportswriters during the Olympics. She went on to win the U.S. Women's Amateur Tournament in 1946 and an unprecedented seventeen amateur tournaments in a row afterward. She was also the first American to win the British Ladies Amateur Tournament.

At the time, professional tournaments for women golfers were few and far between, which hampered Didrikson's competitive nature. In 1949, she helped found the Ladies Professional Golf Association to give women more opportunities to compete in professional golf. Over time, the LPGA became the premiere organizer of women's golf tournaments in the United States. Didrikson herself won 31 of its tournaments, including the U.S. Women's Open in 1949 and 1950. She was the LPGA's top money winner in 1949, 1950, and 1951.

Didrikson was in the middle of another winning streak when she was diagnosed with colon cancer in 1952. After surgery, she recovered sufficiently to again win the Open in 1954. Unfortunately, the cancer reappeared in 1955. Didrickson died a year later.

Breaking Race Barriers

Women of color found it particularly difficult to compete in athletic events for many years. Althea Gibson helped break racial barriers in tennis by becoming one of the top players in the late 1940s and early 1950s. After growing up playing stickball in Harlem, she learned tennis thanks to several individuals who recognized her talent and gave her the opportunity to learn the sport.

At first she was only allowed to play against black players, but her talent finally earned her membership in the all-white United States Ladies Tennis Association. Still, she was restricted to playing matches on indoor courts. After intense lobbying by several leading players of the day, she was finally permitted to compete outdoors and made her first appearance at the U.S. National Championship at Forest Hills in 1950. A year later, she became the first African American of either sex to compete at Wimbledon. In 1957, she became the first black player to win Wimbledon and the U.S. Nationals. She repeated her wins in both venues the following year. She also helped widen the African-American audience for tennis by playing exhibition matches during the half-times at Harlem Globetrotters games.

Going for the Vote

Manon Rheaume, a Canadian, was the first woman to play in the National Hockey League. In 1993, she started as a goalie in a preseason game for the Tampa Bay Lightening. She also played for the minor league Las Vegas Thunder during the 1994–1995 season.

The legendary track star Wilma Rudolph also didn't let her race, or an earlier handicap, hold her back from becoming one of the top stars of the 1960 Olympics. She was the first American woman—and the first African-American woman—to win three gold medals in track and field in a single Olympiad.

After recovering from a series of childhood illnesses that had left her without the use of her left leg, Rudolph went on to a stellar career in high-school track. She qualified as a member of the U.S. track and field team for the 1956 Olympics and helped her team win a bronze medal. She competed again in 1960 in

Rome, where the French press dubbed her "La Gazelle" for her wins in the 100- and 200-meter dash. She tied the world record in the 100-meter and set a new one in the 200. She also anchored her 400-meter relay team and brought them from behind to the victory.

Wilma retired from amateur athletics after the 1960 Olympics. But she never strayed far from the athletic arena. While working as a schoolteacher and raising a family of four, she found time to coach aspiring athletes. She also helped open and run several inner-city sports clinics, and in 1981 she established the Wilma Rudolph Foundation to promote amateur athletics. She died from a malignant brain tumor in 1994 at age 54.

Other women who broke barriers in sports during the twentieth century include ...

➤ Lucy Harris, who made history as the first woman to be drafted by an NBA team, picked by the New Orleans Jazz in 1977. She never played for them but did play in the Women's Professional Basketball League for the Houston Angels.

➤ Nancy Lieberman, who became the first woman player in men's professional basketball, signing with the U.S. Basketball League in 1986. In 1987 she joined the Washington Generals, the team that tours with the Harlem Globetrotters.

➤ Kathy Kusner, who became the first woman to obtain a jockey license in 1968 after her initial application, made the previous year in Maryland, was turned down. She won her first race but had problems keeping her weight down, which led to a short career.

➤ Martina Navratilova, the first openly gay tennis professional, whose sheer brilliance on the court and sheer class off of it helped her rise above the attacks and slurs made about her sexual preference.

➤ Billie Jean King, who showed that women tennis players could be as good as men when she beat Bobby Riggs in straight sets in a highly promoted battle of the sexes in the Houston Astrodome in 1973.

The efforts of these women and the many others who exercised their talent as athletes have legitimized the world of female athletic competition. They also helped put to rest the belief that working up a sweat makes a woman less feminine.

Exploring the Earth

The precedent for women's exploration was set in the earliest days of Christianity as both women and men worked as missionaries to spread the new religion to far-flung populations. Women also took to the fields during the eighteenth and nineteenth centuries as part of their studies and research in such sciences as botany and astronomy. But the number of women who wandered the earth in search of new experiences and knowledge increased significantly in the twentieth century. Some

A Woman's Place

Fanny Bullock Workman was an advocate for women's suffrage and even took a "Votes for Women" banner on one of her trips to the Himalayas.

accompanied their husbands on scientific trips. Others went purely for adventure and the chance to try something new.

In the early 1900s Fanny Bullock Workman accompanied her husband on seven mapping and photography expeditions through the northwest Himalayas. Together they made the first descent of the country's Kalberg glacier.

Alexandra David-Neel, a Frenchwoman, became the first white woman to visit the forbidden city of Lhasa in Tibet. A student of Oriental philosophy and religions, she went to India in 1910 to conduct Oriental research for the French Ministry of Education. In 1913 she began making short and secret trips to neighboring Tibet—virtually unheard of at the time as much of Tibet was off-limits to foreigners. She also visited Japan, Burma, Korea, and China.

Other noted female explorers during the twentieth century include the following:

➤ Gertrude Benham, a British woman who spent more than 30 years walking the world and visiting virtually every part of the British Empire. She climbed more than 300 peaks of 10,000 feet or higher and was the first woman to climb Mount Kilimanjaro, which she accomplished in 1909. She also walked across Africa and South America. She traveled alone, only using porters when absolutely necessary.

➤ Annie Smith Peck, who climbed Peru's Mount Coropuna in 1911 at age 61. Peck was also the first woman to climb Mexico's Mount Orizaba. Like Fanny Bullock Workman, Peck was a suffragist. When she reached the summit of Mount Coropuna, she unfurled a banner that read "Votes for Women."

➤ Myrtle Simpson, another British woman, attempted to reach the North Pole in 1969. Her team of three failed in their attempt, but she did become the first woman to walk across the North Polar ice cap.

➤ Anthropologist Margaret Mead, whose desire to study human behavior in cultures far away from Western society led her to such countries as Samoa, New Guinea, and Bali.

➤ Junko Thaei, who became the first woman to conquer Mount Everest in 1975. As part of a group of 15 Japanese women intent on climbing the world's tallest mountain, she was the only member of the group to reach the summit.

One of the best-known female explorers of recent years is Ann Bancroft, who became the first woman to reach the North Pole as part of the 1986 Steger Expedition.

Bancroft followed that accomplishment by heading south—to Antarctica, the coldest, driest, and windiest place on the planet. She and her three teammates—all women—spent 67 days trekking across the bitter landscape and reached the South Pole on January 14, 1993. That accomplishment made Bancroft the first woman to trek to both poles.

She returned to Antarctica again in 2001 with Liv Arnesen, a Norwegian, determined to be the first women to ski and sail across Antarctica. They took nothing more than their skis, two sleds, and enough food and equipment to sustain them through the 100-day, 2,400-mile excursion, which they completed on February 11, 2001. Thanks to the power of the Internet, they were able to inspire generations of future explorers with to-the-minute news of their trek on their Web site.

Hear Me Roar

... I feel empowered from the strength of women like your-selves ... who go forward eagerly, breaking barriers, stereotypes, stigmas.

—Feedback from a visitor to www.yourexpedition.com, the Bancroft/Arneson exploration Web site

Breaking Hollywood's Sound Barrier

By the time Hollywood became a mecca for film production, women had become well-respected ac-tresses on the stage. But they had to fight for equi-table treatment in the new world of the movies. The studios were owned by men and controlled by men. Men raised the money for films, directed them, lit them, and often costumed and made up the actors and actresses who appeared in them. Women worked behind the scenes in a variety of jobs. They would remain there for a number of years.

Mary Pickford, one of America's first film stars, was willing to allow her studio to portray her as an in-nocent victim, but off the screen she used her fame to lobby for equal treatment to that enjoyed by male stars. She insisted on, and received, pay equal to Charlie Chaplin's. She also controlled her film projects by directing them herself. The studio con-tinued to hire male directors for her films, and they received the credit for it, but Pickford called the shots from behind the camera.

Although her efforts made her powerful and wealthy—she was the first actor of either sex to become a millionaire—Pickford maintained a low

Hear Me Roar

If a man wants to get it right, he's looked up to and respected. If a woman wants to get it right, she's difficult or impossible. If he acts, produces, and directs, he's called multitalented. If she does the same thing, she's called vain and egotistical.

—Barbra Streisand

profile in all her work off-camera, including the formation of United Artists, a studio she founded with D. W. Griffith, Chaplin, Douglas Fairbanks (her second husband), and businessman William S. Hart. She feared that it would destroy her onscreen persona if people caught wind of her business acumen.

A Woman's Place

The legendary television comedienne Lucille Ball was no slouch when it came to business off the screen. There was no funny business in how she ran Desilu Studios, the production house she founded with husband Desi Arnaz. In addition to *I Love Lucy*, which Ball and Arnaz debuted in 1951, Desilu produced 18 shows, including *Star Trek*, *Mission Impossible*, and *The Untouchables*. When the two divorced in 1960, Ball bought Arnaz out and became the first woman to head a major Hollywood production company. She sold Desilu to Gulf and Western in 1967 for $17 million.

Barbra Streisand was nowhere near as discrete when she wrote, directed, produced, and starred in the 1981 movie *Yentl*. The incomparable diva oversaw the entire project, and the press gladly reported every minor detail of what she did and how she did it. *Yentl* met with moderate success. People's impressions of it seemed to vary depending on how they felt about Streisand's daring to wield so much power. Her second project, *The Prince of Tides*, was much more successful, although she was overlooked for a directing nomination that many felt would have been hers if she had been a man.

Women play a far greater role in the film industry now than ever before. Although a woman still hasn't won an Oscar for best director, there is no doubt that the day will come.

The Least You Need to Know

➤ Although they made a substantial contribution to the war effort, the World War II WASPs never gained status as a military institution.

➤ Martina Navratilova, the first admitted lesbian tennis star, helped remove prejudice regarding sexual preference in that sport and others.

➤ Ann Bancroft is the first woman to conquer both the North and South Poles.

➤ Even though she was known as a ditzy redhead onscreen, Lucille Ball's business savvy off of it built one of the most successful television studios in Hollywood.

Notorious Women of the Twentieth Century

After looking at women's history from virtually every angle and perspective, it seems fitting that we end by profiling a group of women who have had, in one way or an-other, a great deal to do with writing its most recent chapters.

Frankly, deciding who to include here was a difficult task. Not only is the twentieth century full of amazing women, but we also know more about them than ever before. And we know a lot more about why they pursued a particular course of action.

It's an amazing legacy when you think about it. Future generations won't have to guess at the motivation behind a woman's decision to run for Congress or litigate a civil rights matter in court. They can get the scoop, so to speak, straight from the horse's mouth, thanks to the body of knowledge that now exists that women have created. Never again will the history of women be reflected through the filters of male perspective.

In choosing the women profiled in this chapter, we've had to stick to celebrities by necessity, as we know the most about them. But we also know that for every woman who has captured the spotlight there are many, many more who are equally as qualified, equally as remarkable, and who could have been there just as easily.

Margaret Sanger

Margaret Sanger took on the medical community and the federal government in her crusade to give women control over their reproductive rights. It was a hard-fought battle, but she emerged victorious in the end.

Sanger grew up in a large Irish-Catholic family and saw firsthand the toll that large families can take on women. Her mother was pregnant 18 times in 30 years and gave birth to 11 living children. Worn out and suffering from tuberculosis, she died when she was just 49.

The needs of such a large family left little money for education, but Margaret's siblings made it possible for her to attend Claverack College in New York from 1896 to 1899. She had to leave before she could graduate because her funds ran out, but she was later able to get the training she needed to be a nurse.

While attending nursing school, she met and married William Sanger, an artist and architect. The couple moved to Westchester, where they had three children. But Sanger wasn't comfortable with the easy life of a housewife. When a fire destroyed the Sangers' home, she took the disaster as an opportunity to put her nursing skills to use in an area she felt passionately about. The family moved to New York City, where Sanger worked with poor families on Manhattan's Lower East Side as a public health nurse. Her marriage, however, didn't survive the shift in her life's focus. The two divorced in 1920. Sanger married millionaire J. Noah Slee, who financed many of her efforts, two years later.

In her work as a public health nurse, Sanger routinely saw women living in squalid conditions made no better by the fact that they kept on having babies. Unfortunately, women living during the early twentieth century had few options open to them if they wanted to control the size of their families. Birth control devices like diaphragms and douches were available at the time, but they were priced beyond the means of most women. Worse yet, they were illegal. The Comstock Law of 1873 had criminalized even sending contraceptive information through the mail.

Abortion, also illegal, was the primary method of contraception. Women usually performed the procedure on themselves. Many died as a result.

Sanger wanted to get birth control information into women's hands but lacked a public forum in which to do so. She found a Socialist newspaper willing to carry a series of articles, which she called "What Every Girl Should Know." The articles contained only rudimentary reproduction information but were deemed obscene under the terms of the Comstock Law. Undaunted, Sanger decided to challenge the law and hopefully overturn it. In 1914, she founded a newspaper called *Woman Rebel* that dealt with feminist issues and sex education, although it gave no specific advice on birth control. In defiance of Comstock, she sent it by mail to her subscribers. She was arrested, but decided to leave the country rather than stand trial. Margaret spent a year in Europe researching family planning in other countries. When she returned to the United States, the case against her was dropped.

Sanger and her sister, Ethel Byrne, opened the first birth control clinic in America in 1916. Although they were only able to keep it open for 10 days before they were arrested, once again for violating the Comstock Law, more than 500 people passed through the doors of the clinic during that period, proving Sanger's belief that women wanted to know more about controlling their reproductive systems.

She spent the rest of her life working for the legalization of birth control, organizing the American Birth Control League (now the Planned Parenthood Federation of America), and planning the first world population conference in Geneva, Switzerland.

Sanger's efforts paid off handsomely. By 1932 there were more than 80 birth control clinics in the United States. Four years later, the Comstock Law was reinterpreted to allow mailing information about contraception when a United States Federal Court ruled that information about birth control was not obscene. And in 1937 the American Medical Association recommended that medical schools teach contraception and that birth control methods be researched.

Sanger retired from active involvement in Planned Parenthood in 1938, but she continued to give speeches on birth control. In 1966, just six years after the first birth control pills were released, she died of heart failure in an Arizona nursing home.

Hear Me Roar

No woman can call herself free who does not own and control her body. No woman can call herself free until she can choose consciously whether she will or will not be a mother.

—Margaret Sanger

Eleanor Roosevelt

It's hard not to use the word legendary in describing Eleanor Roosevelt. There had never been a First Lady like her before she came to the White House; nor has there been one like her since she left it. Her integrity, her sense of social justice, and her force of will, coupled with the unusual

Hear Me Roar

You must do the things you think you cannot do.

—Eleanor Roosevelt, *You Learn by Living*, 1960

circumstances created by her husband's disability, made her the first First Lady to have a broad public agenda. Her decision to range far beyond the traditional role of official hostess and occasional spokesperson ascribed to presidential wives set the precedent for future First Ladies to have more freedom in defining their own roles.

Born into the affluent and politically connected Roosevelt family, Anna Eleanor Roosevelt was the daughter of Elliot Roosevelt and Anna Hall Roosevelt. Her early life was far from happy. Elliot, whom Eleanor adored, was an alcoholic who gave little thought to his family responsibilities. Anna, Eleanor's mother, was a legendary beauty who didn't quite know what to make of her shy and gawky daughter. She nicknamed Eleanor "Granny," which undermined the young girl's already shaky self-confidence. The loss of both her parents and her younger brother by the time she was 10 robbed Eleanor of her sense of security as well. She and her older brother were sent to live with their Grandmother Hall, a stern woman who was ill prepared to rear two young children.

Only when Eleanor attended boarding school as a teenager at Allenswood, a girls' finishing school in England, did she come to terms with her unusual looks and repair her bruised psyche. Thanks to the nurturing she received from Marie Souvestre, the school's headmistress, Eleanor also discovered her other talents, of which there were many. She had a keen intellect and a true love of knowledge. Her tall, slender body made her a natural athlete, and she delighted in sports of all types. Horseback riding, a particular favorite, remained a long-time passion.

A Woman's Place

Affordable housing was a lifelong crusade for Eleanor Roosevelt. Since she knew what it felt like to not have a home of her own, she deeply identified with those who dreamed of having them. During FDR's first term in the White House, Eleanor worked on the creation of a model community for the poor in West Virginia. Called Arthurdale, it opened in June 1934. Eleanor supported the community during its early years by raising funds for it and donating most of her own earned income. But Arthurdale was the focus of public attack from its beginning by conservatives who feared the spread of communism and saw the New Deal as a communist plot. To them, the planned community of Arthurdale was the epitome of a communistic project. Arthurdale never became everything Eleanor wanted it to be—public sentiment against it was too strong for that to happen. But it was far from a failure, as many historians have judged it.

Eleanor returned to New York at age 17. Instead of becoming a socialite and making her debut, as was expected of women of her class and social status, she, instead, decided to work toward social reform. She taught dancing and literature at a settlement house and visited needy children living in slums. By the time she married her fifth cousin, Franklin Delano Roosevelt, in 1905, Eleanor knew firsthand how the poor lived. She would continue to pursue the social issues important to her for the rest of her life. She was a tireless advocate for the poor and the disadvantaged and gave many disenfranchised groups their first voice in the White House.

Roosevelt, whose bout with polio in 1921 limited his ability to move about freely, depended on Eleanor to be his eyes and ears in places where he couldn't go. As First Lady, she performed her official duties in addition to maintaining a full agenda of her own and serving her husband's interests. She was the first First Lady to extensively use the media for communicating with the public. She held press conferences, some of them open to women only, wrote a daily syndicated newspaper column, and gave lectures and radio broadcasts. She traveled across the country on her husband's behalf. She also lobbied him on issues on which they didn't agree.

A Woman's Place

Because Franklin Delano Roosevelt held four successive terms as president, Eleanor Roosevelt served as First Lady longer than any other woman in U.S. history. It's a distinction she will hold forever thanks to the constitutional amendment passed after Roosevelt's term in office that placed term limits on the highest office in the land.

After FDR's death in 1945, Eleanor returned to a cottage at his Hyde Park estate where she lived quietly for about a year before returning to public life. When she returned, it was to a full agenda. After she lobbied President Harry S. Truman on civil rights and foreign policy, he made her a delegate to the United Nations. In 1946 she was named to the chair of the UN's Commission on Human Rights.

In 1961 Eleanor heeded the call from another president and chaired John F. Kennedy's Commission on the Status of Women. It was her last official public position. She died of tuberculosis in 1962. She was 78 years old.

Evita, Evita, Evita!

An icon, a legend, a cult figure long before Andrew Lloyd Webber brought her story to the stage and Madonna portrayed her on screen, Eva Perón combined a canny sense for social climbing with the common touch to become the most beloved woman in Argentine history.

Maria Eva Duarte began her life as the poorest of the poor in a tiny rural Argentine town. Her impoverished upbringing fired her desire to become something other than what her heritage guaranteed her.

As a tall, pretty teenager, Eva decided to pursue an acting career after being cast in a small part in a school play. She was just 14 when she went to Buenos Aires to seek her fortune as an actress.

Eva's inexperience, coupled with a voice hobbled by a strong provincial accent, kept her away from starring roles at first. But she kept at it, and she soon started to get occasional roles in movies and radio, in large part thanks to the relationships with influential Argentineans she had also developed. She eventually landed a starring role on a popular weekly radio serial.

It was during her run on the radio series that she met Colonel Juan Domingo Perón, the government's labor minister. Like Eva, he came from the lower classes, which gave them a common bond that transcended the large gap in their ages—at 48, he was twice Eva's age. Eva liked the fact that Perón was advancing bills that were favorable to the poor as part of his agenda to replace the existing government with one more closely aligned with *fascist* beliefs. He liked the fact that she was pretty, smart, and politically savvy. They married in 1945.

Words for Women

Fascism is a system of government characterized by rigid one-party dictatorship and forcible suppression of the opposition.

A Woman's Place

In her earliest acting days, Eva patterned her style after famous American actresses. One of her favorites, clearly apparent in the hairstyles she affected, was Dorothy Lamour.

The Peróns became the toast of Argentina. When not wowing high society, they spent a great amount of time visiting working-class neighborhoods and urged the people to support a government that would give them decent working conditions and better wages. Juan was aiming for the presidency, and Eva did everything she could to get him there, including wrangling a spot as president of the radio actors union, where she could use her influence to control what was said about her husband and herself on the airwaves.

Evita's efforts on behalf of her husband were derailed in October 1945 when embarrassing details from Perón's earlier days were exposed. Accused of repressing the masses rather than uplifting them, Perón was dismissed from his party and sent to prison. But Eva rallied the masses. The unions organized a countrywide strike, after which Perón was released. When freed, he spoke eloquently about his wife and her heroic efforts on his behalf. His remarks elevated Eva to near saintly status and fueled what would become a cult-like following.

Eva functioned as an unofficial minister of health and labor in her husband's government. Through her charitable organization, the Eva Perón Foundation, she provided funds for schools, hospitals, orphanages, and homes for unmarried mothers and the elderly. She also skimmed a fair amount off the top for her husband and herself, depositing the money in a Swiss bank account.

Eva also became a champion of women's rights, arguing for equal pay, the right to vote (which was granted in 1947), and equal treatment in the courts. As her star rose along with Perón, she became a prominent figure in international politics. Heady with success, she made a bid at the vice presidency. Some accounts have her husband vetoing her effort to run for office. Others chalk it up to opposition from the military.

Her failure to capture elected office resulted in her physical and emotional collapse. Already ill with uterine cancer, Eva lived barely long enough to see her husband elected to a second term.

Betty Friedan

With her simple yet elegant prose, Betty Friedan exposed to the world the growing dissatisfaction that characterized the lives of middle-class American women in her landmark book, *The Feminine Mystique*.

Born Betty Goldstein in Peoria, Illinois, Friedan followed the prescribed path for women in post-war America: school, career, marriage, home, babies. It sounds dull, and it was dull. Even though Friedan continued her writing career after her marriage to Carl Friedan, an advertising executive, and while raising three children, the life of a housewife bored her to distraction, and she had the sense that she wasn't alone. No one wanted to talk about the obvious. But Betty did.

At her 15-year college reunion with her Smith classmates, Betty handed her friends a questionnaire to fill out. Their responses confirmed her suspicions. Women felt unfulfilled and stuck, and they didn't know what to do about it. Betty knew she had the makings for a book in her hands, but she needed to do more research to insure the legitimacy of the conclusions she was heading toward. She pitched the idea to a book publisher and received the funds she needed to proceed.

A Woman's Place

Eva Perón helped her husband in a bid for elected office even after her death. After a fall from power in 1955, Perón laid low until the late 1960s. His supporters used Eva's likeness to bolster their candidate's prospects in a 1973 presidential election, which he won handily thanks to those who still worshipped "Saint" Evita.

Hear Me Roar

The problem lay buried, unspoken, for many years in the minds of American women. It was a strange stirring, a sense of dissatisfaction, a yearning that women suffered in the middle of the twentieth century in the United States.

—Betty Friedan, *The Feminine Mystique*

The result of Friedan's inquiry was *The Feminine Mystique,* which contended that the prevailing idea of middle-class women finding fulfillment through domesticity was, for the most part, folly. Sure, some women led happy lives as housewives. But for many others, being relegated to chief cook and bottle washer was the next best thing to a lobotomy.

The Feminine Mystique touched a nerve in millions of women who felt worthless because they couldn't use their talent and education outside of the home. It became an instant best-seller and made Friedan the vanguard of the new women's movement in the United States.

Betty used her new-found celebrity status to help found the National Organization for Women (NOW) and served as its first president. Since its establishment, NOW's goal has been to "take action" to bring about equality for all women. But Betty soon took issue with both NOW and the women's movement as a whole, which she believed was bending to the influence of a few highly vocal, and highly radical, feminists.

She attacked the trend toward radical feminism in two later books, *It Changed My Life,* published in 1976, and in 1981's *The Second Stage,* in which she argued against playing sexual politics and railed against the women's movement's growing focus on racism, poverty, and lesbian rights, fearing that the approach would alienate more mainstream feminists. Perhaps it did, but many women also found a voice that the women's movement had lacked before.

NOW eventually grew to encompass more than a half million members and 550 chapters in all 50 states and the District of Columbia. Its agenda continues to focus on many of the special interests that Friedan decried, which probably explains why the organization downplays her role in it. Visit NOW's Web site and you'll see only passing mention of its first president.

Hear Me Roar

Women have gotten where we are today mainly through individual women telling the truth.

—Gloria Steinem

Gloria Steinem

Like Betty Friedan, Gloria Steinem is also considered one of the vanguards of the modern women's movement. Her vision and passion have done much to improve the lives of millions of women and have inspired many people to take a critical look at the world around them and change what they didn't like about it.

Steinem had a tough childhood. Her mother was often severely depressed and incapable of taking care of her. In fact, the roles between them were reversed more often than not, especially when her parents divorced.

Gloria attended Smith College, where she majored in government and discovered her love for activism. She also discovered that activism ran in her family. Her mother had been a suffragette who helped women win the right to vote. She had also been a successful newspaperwoman in Toledo, where Steinem grew up. The elder Steinem had given up her career to marry and have children. Soon after, she began suffering the severe bouts of depression that Gloria knew so well.

Because she saw a link between her mother's sacrifice and her illness, Gloria decided to stay far away from the same combination. When she became pregnant during her junior year in college, she went overseas and had an abortion. She then went to India on a study fellowship.

In 1959 Gloria returned to the United States to pursue a journalism job, only to find that very few women were being hired for such work. She eventually landed a job at a now-defunct magazine called *Help!* and did a number of freelance articles for such publications as *Esquire, Glamour,* and *Show.* In one of her more notorious pieces, she went undercover as a Playboy bunny.

In 1968 Steinem was assigned to cover George McGovern's presidential campaign. Her stories led to a position at *New York* magazine, which had just started publishing. There, she could sink her teeth into the meaty issue of the day, which happened to be abortion rights. She soon turned her full attention to the feminist movement.

In 1972, Gloria co-founded *Ms. Magazine,* the first publication for and by women. Since then, she has founded several organizations, including the Ms. Foundation, the National Women's Political Caucus, and the Coalition of Labor Union Women. She also wrote several best-sellers, including *Revolution from Within: A Book of Self-Esteem, Outrageous Acts and Everyday Rebellions,* a collection of her magazine stories and columns. Her latest book, *Moving Beyond Words/Age, Rage, Sex, Power Money, Muscles: Breaking the Boundaries of Gender,* was published in 1995.

Hear Me Roar

Though I've worked for many years to make marriage more equal, I never expected to take advantage of it myself. I'm happy, surprised, and one day will write about it, but for now, I hope this proves what feminists have always said—that feminism is about the ability to choose what's right at each time of our lives.

—Gloria Steinem, from the press release announcing her marriage to David Bale

In September 2000 the woman who said she'd never get married and who dismissed marriage as an institution that destroys relationships tied the knot with entrepreneur David Bale. The event took place at the Oklahoma home of Wilma Mankiller, the former chief of the Cherokee Nation and a long-time friend of Steinem's.

Sex and the Single Girl

Could women have it all—a successful career, a fulfilling marriage, and a satisfying love life? They could and they would if they followed the advice proffered by Helen Gurley Brown's *Cosmopolitan* magazine.

During the 1960s Brown single-handedly changed the tone and complexion of women's magazines. Up to that point, they had largely focused on the domestic sciences—darning socks, fixing perfect meals, and such. *Cosmopolitan* told women how they could excel at work, beguile men, establish their own credit, dress for success, and have a great sex life.

Much of the information the magazine contained, especially in the beginning, came from Brown's own experiences as a single working girl. She started as a secretary at 18 after 1 year of college and used her talent as a writer to work her way up the corporate ladder in the world of advertising. By age 36, long after most women had quit working to get married and have babies, she joined the Los Angeles ad firm of Kenyan and Eckhardt as an account executive and became the West Coast's highest-paid woman in the field.

A year later, she married film producer David Brown, who encouraged her to write a book based on her experiences. *Sex and the Single Girl* debuted to great acclaim in 1962. Gurley penned it as a comprehensive guide to dating, work, beauty, and finance. She told women they didn't have to be exceptionally beautiful, smart, or wealthy to be successful, but they did have to use what they had to their best advantage. By April 1963, 150,000 copies of *Sex* had been sold. It was also turned into a movie.

The Browns had planned on extending the *Sex* franchise by launching a magazine aimed at the 18- to 24-year-old single career woman. They sold the idea to the Hearst Corporation in 1965, which planned to use it to revive *Cosmopolitan,* its aging magazine. Brown was named editor-in-chief.

Maggie Kuhn

A mighty mite of a woman who was still going strong well into her eighties, Maggie Kuhn refused to allow her age to stop her. Nor did she believe that age should be a hindrance to anyone else. When she was forced to retire at age 65 from a job she loved and excelled at, she didn't just take to her rocker. Instead, she got together with five friends and started the Consultation of Older and Younger Adults for Social

Change, the precursor to the Gray Panthers, an organization that works to end age discrimination and other forms of injustice.

Kuhn began her life as an activist when she organized a chapter of the League of Women Voters at Case Western Reserve University, where she earned her college degree. After she graduated, she worked for the YWCA, heading the Professional Department of Business Girls at its facility in the Germantown area of Philadelphia. She later said that she valued the Y's philosophy of the ability of groups to empower the individual and change society.

At the beginning of World War II, Maggie took a job as a program coordinator and editor for the YWCA's USO program. After the war, she worked for the General Alliance for Unitarian and Other Liberal Christian Women in Boston, Massachusetts. In 1950, in order to be closer to her ailing parents, she moved to Philadelphia and took a job as assistant secretary of the Social Education and Action Department at the Presbyterian Church's national headquarters.

Maggie was a passionate advocate for desegregation, affordable housing, nuclear disarmament, and national health care throughout her career. At the time she and her friends founded the Gray Panthers, the elderly were a forgotten population. The Panthers promoted the belief that age discrimination was as serious a social evil as any other form of discrimination, and they lobbied for nursing home reform, universal access to health care, better treatment by health care workers, and the continuation of Social Security. In large part due to their efforts, Congress passed the Age Discrimination in Employment act in 1978, which raised the mandatory retirement age to 70 from 65.

Kuhn had the energy of someone half her age and spent the remainder of her life traveling around the United States on behalf of the rights of the elderly. She promoted intergenerational housing, one of her pet passions, by sharing her home with a group of people of different ages. She also wrote three books: *Get Out There and Do Something About Injustice, Maggie Kuhn on Ageing;* and her autobiography, *No Stone Unturned.*

Maggie Kuhn never married, nor did she ever try to hide her many affairs, including a 15-year affair with a married minister and a liaison with a man 50 years her junior. She died in her sleep in 1995 three months before her ninetieth birthday.

The fact that a woman like Maggie Kuhn felt no compunction to apologize for how she chose to live her life speaks volumes about what women today are all about. While it's impossible to predict the exact road that lies ahead, it's clearly been paved by the experiences of the centuries of women who have come before them, and it's that collective experience that will guide them in the years to come.

Hear Me Roar

When you least expect it, someone may actually listen to what you have to say. Well-aimed slingshots can topple giants.

—Maggie Kuhn

If the past is any indication of the future, women will continue to work for the causes that are important to them. They'll make new scientific discoveries and push the boundaries of many envelopes. They'll lead countries and shape public opinion. They'll fly to the stars and write songs about them. They will continue to manifest their destinies and shape the world around them. They'll live the lives they want to live, and, like dear Maggie, find little reason to explain why.

The Least You Need to Know

➤ Aware of the toll constant pregnancies took on women, Margaret Sanger campaigned for the dissemination of birth control information for all women.

➤ Betty Friedan's *The Feminine Mystique* exposed the unhappiness middle-class women felt over living less-than-fulfilling lives.

➤ Helen Gurley Brown's *Cosmopolitan* magazine helped women define their images during the women's liberation years.

➤ Believing that age truly was a matter of mind, Maggie Kuhn devoted her "retirement" years to battling the increasing marginalization of the elderly.

Glossary

anarchic   Refers to the complete absence of government and law created by anarchy.

Anglo-Saxon   The term Anglo-Saxon describes the people of two Germanic groups—the Angles and the Saxons—who lived in England before the Norman Conquest in 1066.

Aragon   Located in the northeastern region of Spain, Aragon was a separate kingdom during medieval times.

banns   Announcements of a couple's intention to marry. They were posted and generally announced in church on three successive Sundays.

Benedictines   Members of the monastic order founded in the fifth century based on the teaching of Saint Benedict.

bulls   Official edicts or decrees issued by popes.

bye industries   The equivalent of part-time jobs for women in the Middle Ages.

Calvinism   The religious system founded by the French Protestant reformer John Calvin (1509–1564). It emphasizes the doctrines of predestination and salvation solely by God's grace.

canon   A clergy person on the staff of a cathedral.

Castile   A former kingdom of central Spain.

charivari   The noisy and raucous charivari was a fourteenth-century invention designed as a mock celebration to express displeasure when a widow remarried, usually staged by her children on her wedding night.

The Comstock Law   Named after Anthony Comstock, its chief proponent and a New York morals crusader of the late nineteenth century, this federal law passed in 1873 prohibited sending obscene material through the United States mail.

concubines   Women who lived with men they weren't legally married to, often as one of several or many women of the same status. Even though they had no marital status or rights, their children were generally regarded as legitimate.

Crusades   Military expeditions launched by the Christian Church during the eleventh, twelfth, and thirteenth centuries, with the goal of recovering the Holy Land from the Moslems.

dauphin   A title used from 1349 to 1830 by the oldest sons of French kings. It was originally given as a proper name in noble families living in the province of Dauphine.

***droit de seigneur* (the lord's right)**   Established by King Ewen III of Scotland, it gave kings or lords the right to deflower the brides of retainers and serfs.

dropsy   An abnormal accumulation of fluid in body cavities or tissues.

The Enlightenment   An eighteenth-century intellectual movement in Western Europe that emphasized reason and science in philosophy and in the study of human culture and the natural world.

entail   A law that limits property inheritance to a specific line of heirs so that it can never be legally transferred outside of the family.

fascism   A system of government characterized by rigid one-party dictatorship and forcible suppression of the opposition.

femmes soles   Literally, "women alone," this medieval legal term described women who conducted their affairs independent from their husbands or other male family members.

feudalism   The economic, political, and social organization of medieval Europe in which land (fief) was granted to knights in return for loyal military service to their lord. Serfs worked the land and provided food to their lord's manor in exchange for protection from other feudal lords.

guilds   Joined together people who worked in the same trade or craft for mutual economic, social, and religious benefit. They were the first formal organizations to protect the interests of skilled workers.

gynaeceum   A place in which women worked and lived.

hetaerae   The hetaerae were Greek courtesans of the highest-class. The term comes from the word *heter,* meaning "companion."

Huguenots   French citizens who practiced the Protestant faith.

Industrial Revolution   Commonly refers to the period during the 1700s and 1800s when large manufacturing establishments, powered by coal or steam, began to mass-produce products and the resultant social changes that occurred during this period.

matrilineal   Tracing descent and kinship through the mother's side of the family.

matrilocal   Societies where households are established and led by women.

oath-helpers   Witnesses in early courts. They also collected evidence for presentation to the court.

Paleolithic Venuses   Prehistoric figurines, usually fashioned of clay, stone, or ivory, that represent the female form in an exaggerated manner.

paraclete   From the Greek word *parakletos,* meaning "advocate or intercessor," the term paraclete is sometimes used in the Christian church in reference to the Holy Spirit.

paranormal   Refers to events or phenomena that can't be explained or understood in scientific terms.

patriarchy   Describes families or tribes led by the eldest male or father.

polygamy   Having two or more partners at the same time, or having plural marriages.

precieuses   Early modern salonieres who rose above their sexual desires and rejected physical love. They believed that their chastity reflected higher moral standards and gave them power over others. It also gave them the freedom to assume roles other than that of courtesan or wife.

primogeniture   The legal right of the first-born male to inherit.

Progressive Era (1890–1920)   In the United States, this period was characterized by the attempts by different coalitions of reformers to bring a measure of stability to American society. Progressives were concerned with social justice, like child labor laws, social control, like prohibition, and efficiency, reflected in health reforms such as meat inspection and sanitation issues. Many women were involved in organizations that worked on these issues.

The Reformation   This sixteenth-century religious movement, aimed at reforming the Roman Catholic Church, resulted in the formation of Protestanism.

regent   A man or woman who rules in place of a minor child.

settlement houses   Neighborhood community centers, usually located in poor or immigrant neighborhoods, that offered free education and social programs to underprivileged women and men during the nineteenth and early twentieth centuries.

stomachers   Padded undergarments that resembled duck breasts, popular during the Renaissance.

suffrage   From the Latin *suffragium,* meaning "vote."

suriname   A Dutch protectorate on the coast of South America.

temperance   The term used by nineteenth-century social reformers to describe the sober and self-restrained society they were trying to create.

troubadours   Poets and minstrels who lived in Provence, France, Catalonia, Spain, and northern Italy in the eleventh, twelfth, and thirteenth centuries.

The Victorian Era   Named after Queen Victoria, who ruled England and its global empire from 1837 to 1901, it was characterized by middle-class values of respectability that were often expressed as prudery and bigotry. It was an age of relative peace and prosperity for Europe.

Zionist   A person who supported the principles of Zionism, which reestablished and now supports the Jewish national state.

Resources

Barber, Elizabeth Wayland. *Women's Work: The First 20,000 Years*. New York: W. W. Norton & Co., 1994.

Bell, Rudolph. *Holy Anorexia*. Chicago: The University of Chicago Press, 1985.

Bennet, Judith. *Ale, Beer and Brewers in England: Women's Work in a Changing World, 1300–1600*. New York: Oxford University Press, 1996.

Bridenthal, Renate, Claudi Koonz, Sarah Stuard, eds. *Becoming Visible: Women in European History, Second Edition*. Boston: Houghton Mifflin, 1987.

Bynum, Caroline Walker. *Holy Feast and Holy Fast: The Religious Significance of Food in Medieval Women*. Berkley: University of California Press, 1987.

Clinton, Catherine. *The Other Civil War: American Women in the Nineteenth Century*. New York: Hill and Wang, 1984.

Cott, Nancy. *The Bonds of Womanhood: "Women's Sphere" in New England, 1780–1835*. Cambridge: University Press, 1977.

Cowan, Ruth. *More Work for Mother: The Ironies of Household Technology from the Open Hearth to the Microwave*. New York: Basic Books, 1983.

Duby, Georges. *The Knight, the Lady and the Priest: Making a Modern Marriage in Medieval France*. New York: Pantheon Books, 1983.

Evans, Sara. *Born for Liberty*. New York: The Free Press, 1989.

Fox-Genovese, Elizabeth. *Within the Plantation Household: Black and White Women of the Old South*. Chapel Hill: University of North Carolina Press, 1988.

Fraser, Antonia. *The Warrior Queens*. New York: Vintage Books, 1988.

Hufton, Olwen. *The Prospect Before Her: A History of Women in Western Europe 1500–1800*. New York: Alfred A. Knopf, 1996.

Jones, Jacqueline. *Labor of Love, Labor of Sorrow: Black Women, Work and the Family from Slavery to Present*. New York: Basic Books, 1985.

Kaplan, Marion, ed. *The Marriage Bargain: Women and Dowries in European History*. New York: Hawthorne Press, 1985.

Karlsen, Carol. *The Devil in the Shape of a Woman: Witchcraft in Colonial New England*. New York: Norton, 1987.

Kessler-Harris, Alice. *Out to Work: A History of Wage-Earning Women in the United States*. New York: Oxford University Press, 1982.

Leavitt, Judith Walzer. *Brought to Bed: Childbearing in America, 1750–1950*. New York: Oxford University Press, 1986.

Miles, Rosalind. *The Women's History of the World*. Topsfield: Salem House Publishers, 1989.

Pomeroy, Sarah. *Goddesses, Whores, Wives and Slaves: Women in Classical Antiquity*. New York: Schoken, 1975.

Rose, Mary Beth. *Women in the Middle Ages and the Renaissance*. Syracuse: Syracuse University Press, 1986.

Ryan, Mary. *Womanhood in America from Colonial Times to the Present*. New York: Viewpoints, 1975.

Smith, Bonnie. *Changing Lives: Women in European History Since 1700*. Lexington: D.C. Heath & Co., 1989.

Ulrich, Laurel Thatcher. *Goodwives: Images and Realities in the Lives of Women in Northern New England 1650–1750*. New York: Alfred A. Knopf, 1990.

Welter, Barbara. "The Cult of True Womanhood, 1830–1960." *American Quarterly* 16 (1996): 151–174.

Women of the Ages

Hatshepsut   years of reign: ca. 1486–1468 B.C.E.

Nefertiti   thirteenth century B.C.E.

Semiramis   ca. ninth century B.C.E.

Helen of Troy   ancient Greece

Sappho   ca. 610–640 B.C.E.

Aspasia   ca. 400 B.C.E. (420 B.C.E. in some sources)

Cleopatra   69–30 B.C.E. (31 B.C.E. in some sources)

Boadicea   ca. 25–62 C.E.

Phung Thi Chinh   ca. 40 C.E.

Trung Nhi   died 42 C.E.

Trung Trac   died 42 C.E.

Pan Chao   ca. 45–115 C.E.

Mary the Jewess   ca. 50 C.E.

Galla Placida   ca. 288–450 C.E.

Hypatia   ca. 365–416 C.E. (370–415 in some sources)

Empress Theodora   ca. 497–548 C.E.

Empress Wu Chao (Fu Hao)   625–705 C.E.

Queen Bathilde   ca. 630–680 C.E.

Murasaki Shikibu   ca. 978–1030 C.E.

Anna Comnena   1083–1148

Hildegard of Bingen   1098–1174

Heloise   1101–1164 (1163 in some sources)

Eleanor of Aquitaine   1122–1204

Tamara of Georgia   died 1212

Blanche of Castile   1188–1252

Christine de Pizan   ca. 1365–ca. 1403

Margery Kempe   1373–1438

Queen Jadwiga   1374–1399

Joan of Arc   1412–1431

Queen Isabella I (Isabella of Castile)   1451–1504

Lucretia Borgia   1480–1519

La Malinche   ca. 1500–ca. 1527

Anne Boleyn   1507–1536

Mary Tudor   1516–1558

Catherine de Medici   1519–1589

Jeanne d'Albret   1528–1572

Queen Elizabeth I   1533–1603

Mary, Queen of Scots   1542–1587

Louise Bourgeois   1563–1643

Molly Frith   1589 (1584 in some sources)–1663

Artemisia Gentileschi   1593–ca. 1652

Anne Bradstreet   1612–1672

Christina of Sweden   1626–1689

Aphra Behn   1640–1689

Sor Juana Ines de la Cruz   1651–1695

Emilie du Châtelet   1706–1749

Madame de Pompadour   1721–1764

Catherine the Great   1729–1796

Marie Antoinette   1755–1793

Mary Wollstonecraft   1759–1797

Deborah Sampson   1760–1827

Emma Willard   1787–1870

Sarah Grimké   1792–1873

Lucretia Mott   1793–1880

Sojourner Truth   ca. 1797–1883

Dorothea Dix   1802–1887

Angelina Grimké   1805–1879

Harriet Beecher Stowe   1811–1896

Elizabeth Cady Stanton   1815–1902

Maria Mitchell   1818–1889

Queen Victoria   1819–1901

Florence Nightingale   1820–1910

Susan B. Anthony   1820–1906

Elizabeth Blackwell   1821–1910

Antoinette Brown Blackwell   1825–1921

Mary Harris "Mother" Jones   1830–1930

Lakshmi Bai   ca. 1830–1858

Belva Lockwood   1830–1917

Empress Tz'u-hsi (The Dowager Empress)   1835–1908

Queen Liliuokalani   1838–1917

Victoria Woodhull   1838–1927

Ellen Richards   1842–1911

Sarah Winnemucca   ca. 1844–1891

Carry Nation   1846–1930

Queen Min   1851–1895

Tatyu Betul   1853(?)–1918

Jane Addams   1860–1935

Manya Sklodowska (Marie Curie)   1867–1934

Nellie Bly   1867–1922

Margaret Sanger   1883–1966

Eleanor Roosevelt   1884–1962

Amelia Earhart   1897–1937

Golda Meir   1898–1978

Maggie Kuhn   1905–1995

Mildred "Babe" Didrickson   1911–1956

Indira Gandhi   1917–1984

Eva Perón   1919–1952

Betty Friedan   1921–

Helen Gurley Brown   1922–

Margaret Thatcher   1925–

Althea Gibson   1927–

Nguyen Thi Binh   1927–

Corazon Aquino   1933–

Gloria Steinem   1934–

Valentina Tereshkova   1937–

Wilma Rudolph   1940–1994

Billie Jean King   1943–

Aung San Suu Kyi   1945–

Wilma Mankiller   1945–

Benazir Bhutto   1953–

Women Geographically

Argentina:

➤ Eva Perón

Byzantium:

➤ Empress Theodora
➤ Anna Comnena

China:

➤ Empress Tz'u-hsi (The Dowager Empress)
➤ Empress Wu Chao (Fu Hao)
➤ Pan Chao

Egypt:

➤ Mary the Jewess
➤ Hypatia
➤ Hatshepsut
➤ Cleopatra
➤ Semiramis
➤ Pheretima

England:

- ➤ Boadicea
- ➤ Aphra Behn
- ➤ Anne Boleyn
- ➤ Elizabeth I
- ➤ Molly Frith
- ➤ Margery Kempe
- ➤ Mary Stuart
- ➤ Queen Victoria
- ➤ Mary Tudor
- ➤ Mary Wollstonecraft
- ➤ Gertrude Benham
- ➤ Myrtle Simpson
- ➤ Fanny Burney
- ➤ Lady Godiva
- ➤ Florence Nightingale

Ethiopia:

- ➤ Tatyu Betul

France:

- ➤ Christine de Pizan
- ➤ Joan of Arc
- ➤ Heloise
- ➤ Emilie du Châtelet
- ➤ Madame de Pompadour
- ➤ Louise Bourgeois
- ➤ Marie Antoinette
- ➤ Alexandra David-Neel
- ➤ Marie de Gournay
- ➤ The Marquise de Rambouillet
- ➤ Jeanne Dumee
- ➤ Jeanne d'Albret

Germany:

- ➤ Hildegard of Bingen
- ➤ Maria Sibylla Merian
- ➤ Maria Kirch

Greece:

- ➤ Aspasia
- ➤ Sappho
- ➤ Helen of Troy
- ➤ Holland
- ➤ Judith Leyster

India:

- ➤ Lakshmi Bai
- ➤ Indira Gandhi

Italy:

- ➤ Christine de Pizan
- ➤ Artemisia Gentileschi
- ➤ Catherine de Medici
- ➤ Lucretia Borgia
- ➤ Elena Cornaro Piscopia
- ➤ Maria Agnesi

Judea:

- ➤ Athaliah

Korea:

- ➤ Queen Min

Mexico:

- ➤ Sor Juana Ines de la Cruz
- ➤ La Malinche

Myanmar:

➤ Aung San Suu Kyi

Norway:

➤ Liv Arnesen

Pakistan:

➤ Benazir Bhutto

Philippines:

➤ Corazon Aquino

Poland:

➤ Manya Sklodowska (Marie Curie)

➤ Elisabetha Hevelius

Roman Empire:

➤ Acca Laurentia

➤ Zenobia

➤ Messalina the Elder

➤ Agrippina II

➤ Galla Placida

➤ Pulcheria

Russia:

➤ Catherine the Great

Scotland:

➤ Mary, Queen of Scots (Mary Stuart)

Spain:

➤ Queen Blanche

Sweden:

➤ Christina of Sweden

United States:

➤ Jane Addams

➤ Lucille Ball

➤ Ann Bancroft

➤ Antoinette Brown Blackwell

➤ Elizabeth Blackwell

➤ Nelly Bly

➤ Anne Bradstreet

➤ Jackie Cochran

➤ Mildred "Babe" Didrikson

➤ Dorothea Dix

➤ Amelia Earhart

➤ Christine Franklin

➤ Betty Friedan

➤ Althea Gibson

➤ Sarah and Angelina Grimké

➤ Mary Harris "Mother" Jones

➤ Billie Jean King

➤ Maggie Kuhn

➤ Queen Liliuokalani

➤ Belva Lockwood

➤ Margaret Mead

➤ Maria Mitchell

➤ Lucretia Mott

➤ Carry Nation

➤ Mary Pickford

➤ Eliza Lucas Pinckney

➤ Harriet Quimby

➤ Ellen Richards

➤ Eleanor Roosevelt

➤ Wilma Rudolph

➤ Eleanora Sears

➤ Elizabeth Cady Stanton

- Harriet Beecher Stowe
- Gloria Steinem
- Barbra Streisand
- Sojourner Truth
- Sarah Winnemucca
- Mary Whitney
- Emma Willard
- Victoria Woodhull
- Fanny Bullock Workman

USSR:

- Valentina Tereshkova

Vietnam:

- Trung Trac
- Trung Nhi
- Phung Thi Chinh
- Trien Au
- Nguyen Thi Binh

Index

345

F

H

M

357

359

X–Y–Z